Wireshark Esse

Dive into the capabilities of Wireshark with *Wireshark Essentials*, a concise guide focused on utilizing packet analysis for network security and troubleshooting. This book is ideal for IT professionals, network administrators, and cybersecurity enthusiasts. It details how to use Wireshark's filtering features to effectively monitor and secure networks. Each chapter includes practical scenarios and MCQs to reinforce concepts, making this an essential resource for anyone looking to enhance their network diagnostic skills. Whether you're a beginner or a seasoned expert, *Wireshark Essentials* provides the tools needed to master network analysis in real-world situations.

Wireshark Essentials

Simplifying Network Security and Troubleshooting

Arun Soni, CEH, DES
Certified Ethical Hacker (EC-Council)
Digital Evidence Specialist
(Asian School of Cyber Laws, Pune, India)

CRC Press is an imprint of the
Taylor & Francis Group, an **informa** business

Designed cover image: Shutterstock Image ID 2563879485

First edition published 2026

by CRC Press
2385 NW Executive Center Drive, Suite 320, Boca Raton FL 33431

and by CRC Press
4 Park Square, Milton Park, Abingdon, Oxon, OX14 4RN

CRC Press is an imprint of Taylor & Francis Group, LLC

ISBN: 978-1-032-85812-8 (hbk)
ISBN: 978-1-032-88709-8 (pbk)
ISBN: 978-1-003-53926-1 (ebk)

DOI: 10.1201/9781003539261

Typeset in Sabon
by Deanta Global Publishing Services, Chennai, India

Contents

Preface

Welcome to *Wireshark Essentials: Simplifying Network Security and Troubleshooting*, a comprehensive guide designed to empower readers with the skills to master network analysis using Wireshark. This book is tailored for individuals eager to deepen their understanding of network security and troubleshooting through the powerful lens of Wireshark, the world's foremost network protocol analyzer.

The core of network analysis and cybersecurity revolves around efficiently handling and interpreting data packets. Wireshark's most celebrated feature—its ability to filter and analyze packets—forms the backbone of this guide. The emphasis on forming filters is crucial, as it is the primary tool users employ to sift through vast data streams, pinpoint issues, and secure networks against malicious activities.

Throughout this book, we delve into the practical applications of Wireshark, with a special focus on crafting effective filters that serve both security and troubleshooting purposes. Each chapter is structured to build your skills progressively, starting from basic concepts and moving toward complex scenarios. We explore a variety of real-life situations where Wireshark's tools are applied to detect, diagnose, and resolve network problems and security threats.

To enhance your learning experience, each chapter includes multiple-choice questions (MCQs) that challenge your understanding and application of the material discussed. These quizzes are designed to test your knowledge, reinforce critical concepts, and encourage practical application.

Additionally, a detailed glossary is provided to help you become familiar with the terminology and jargon associated with network analysis. This resource supports your learning by offering quick references and clarifications, ensuring terms and concepts become second nature as you progress through the book.

Whether you are a student, an IT professional, or a cybersecurity enthusiast, *Wireshark Essentials: Simplifying Network Security and Troubleshooting* offers the tools and insights needed to elevate your networking skills. By the end of this book, you will be equipped to use Wireshark effectively to analyze and secure networks, making you a valuable asset in your professional field.

Thank you for choosing this book as your guide into the world of network analysis with Wireshark. Let's embark on this journey together, with each page bringing you closer to becoming a proficient and knowledgeable user of this essential tool.

Happy reading and analyzing!

Author biography

Arun Soni is an internationally acclaimed author and cybersecurity expert from Chandigarh (India). He has authored 182 books covering various subjects, including IT, AI, and Cybersecurity. His books are widely read in India and abroad by millions of students.

He is a Certified Ethical Hacker (CEH) from the EC Council (US), a Digital Evidence Specialist (DES) from the Asian School of Cyber Laws in Pune, and a Cybersecurity Consultant. He is a cybersecurity trainer who also works to spread awareness by conducting webinars/seminars and workshops in schools, colleges, and corporations.

He has been honoured with the prestigious "Distinguished Author Award" by the Federation of Educational Publishers in India (FEPI).

His name appears in the Limca Book of Records for writing the most computer books at 37. He also holds many other national and international records.

Since February 2024, he has been associated with India's topmost National Stock Exchange Academy (NSE Academy) as a content writer, creating cybersecurity modules for the worldwide market.

He is also a former Director of the YMCA, Computer Center, Chandigarh (India).

For his contribution to computer education and Cybersecurity, he has been admired and covered by many major news portals, magazines, and newspapers such as *The Tribune, The Indian Express, Times of India, Dainik Bhaskar, Yahoo News, The Economic Times, Business Standard, ANI News, The Print, Zee 5, Daily Hunt, England News portal, France Network Times, Kuwait Times, UAE Times, Vancouver Herald*, and many others. He also appeared as an expert commentator on several nationwide TV channels and FM radio.

Chapter 1

Cybersecurity foundations and Wireshark

INTRODUCTION

This chapter introduces the foundational concepts of cybersecurity, focusing on understanding common threats, particularly in network environments, and the role of tools like Wireshark in monitoring and securing networks. For beginners, this chapter guides you and equips you with the basic knowledge required to navigate the complex landscape of network security.

WHY CYBERSECURITY?

In today's digital world, cybersecurity is paramount for several compelling reasons. Here's a detailed exploration of why protecting digital assets, networks, and data is more critical than ever (Figure 1.1):

Figure 1.1 Icon of a shield with a padlock and checkmark, surrounded by circuit-like lines, symbolizing cybersecurity.

DOI: 10.1201/9781003539261-1

Increasing cyber threats

The sophistication of attacks: Cyberattacks have become increasingly sophisticated, with hackers using advanced techniques such as ransomware, phishing, and zero-day exploits to breach security defenses. These attacks can bypass traditional security measures, making it essential to have robust defenses.

Volume of attacks: The sheer number of cyberattacks has surged. According to various reports, cyber incidents are becoming more frequent, affecting millions of systems worldwide. This escalation underscores the need for vigilant and proactive cybersecurity measures.

Expansion of digital infrastructure

IoT and connected devices: The proliferation of Internet of Things (IoT) devices has expanded the attack surface. These devices, often with limited security features, can be exploited to gain access to larger networks (Figure 1.2).

Figure 1.2 IoT diagram with a central "IOT" circle connected to security, Wi-Fi, home, and innovation icons.

Cloud computing: The widespread adoption of cloud services has introduced new security challenges. While cloud computing offers scalability and flexibility, it also requires new security strategies to protect data and applications hosted on the cloud.

Critical infrastructure protection

Impact on essential services: Many critical infrastructures, such as power grids, water supplies, and healthcare systems, increasingly rely on digital technologies. A successful cyberattack on these systems can have devastating consequences, affecting public safety and national security.

Economic impact: Cyberattacks targeting critical infrastructure can lead to significant economic losses. For instance, ransomware attacks can cripple businesses, halt operations, and cause substantial financial damage.

Data breaches and privacy concerns

Sensitive data exposure: Data breaches have become commonplace with digitizing personal and business information. These breaches expose sensitive data, such as personal identification information (PII), financial details, and intellectual property, leading to identity theft, fraud, and financial losses.

Regulatory compliance: Various regulations, such as GDPR (General Data Protection Regulation) in Europe and CCPA (California Consumer Privacy Act) in the US, impose strict requirements on data protection. Non-compliance can result in hefty fines and reputational damage.

Increased digital dependency

Remote work and connectivity: The COVID-19 pandemic has accelerated the shift toward remote work, increasing reliance on digital communication tools and networks. This shift has expanded the attack surface, making securing remote access and communications crucial.

Digital transformation: Businesses are increasingly adopting digital transformation strategies, integrating advanced technologies like AI, machine learning, and blockchain. While these technologies offer significant benefits, they also introduce new security vulnerabilities that must be managed effectively.

Global cybercrime economy

Organized cybercrime: Cybercrime has evolved into a global, profitable industry. Cybercriminals operate with high levels of organization and efficiency, often using ransomware-as-a-service (RaaS) and other criminal services to conduct attacks.

Motivations and rewards: The motivations behind cyberattacks range from financial gain to political motives and personal vendettas. The potential rewards for cybercriminals, including monetary gain and disruption, make these activities highly attractive.

Challenges in security practices

Skills shortage: The cybersecurity field faces a significant skills gap, with a shortage of qualified professionals to defend against complex threats. This gap challenges organizations to maintain adequate security defenses.

Evolving threat landscape: The threat landscape is constantly evolving, with new vulnerabilities and attack vectors emerging regularly. Staying ahead of threats requires continuous monitoring, threat intelligence, and the adaptation of security strategies.

SOME COMMON CYBER THREATS WITH EXAMPLES

The digital world is full of cyber threats. Those are uncountable. Although this book is about network-specific attacks, everything is directly or indirectly part of a more extensive network. Moreover, the purpose of each attack is to infiltrate the network. So, it is essential to know about common cyberattacks too. Here, we mention the most common cyber threats that cause the maximum damage in the cyber world, with one example for each.

Below are some significant cyber threats, each detailed with a description, example, and a notable recent case study to illustrate the real-world implications and challenges of managing these threats:

Phishing attacks

Description: Phishing involves tricking individuals into revealing sensitive information by mimicking legitimate entities in digital communications.

Example: An attacker sends an email posing as a popular service, requesting the recipient to reset their password via a provided link that leads to a fraudulent website.

Case study: In 2021, a sophisticated phishing campaign targeted 10,000 Microsoft email users, pretending to offer bonuses to lure victims into revealing their credentials (Figure 1.3).

Figure 1.3 Illustration of a phishing attack with a laptop, hook, fake login screens, warning signs, and binary code.

Ransomware

Description: Ransomware is malicious software that encrypts the victim's data, with attackers demanding a ransom to restore access.

Example: Malware encrypts all data on a victim's computer, and a ransom note demands payment in Bitcoin for the decryption key.

Case study: The 2021 Colonial Pipeline attack in the USA, where attackers locked up the billing systems, causing fuel supply disruptions across the East Coast until a ransom was paid (Figure 1.4).

Figure 1.4 Ransomware attack image with a locked padlock, "ENCRYPTED FILES" text, warning signs, and binary code.

SQL injection

Description: This attack exploits vulnerabilities in data-driven applications to execute malicious SQL code, affecting database integrity (Figure 1.5).

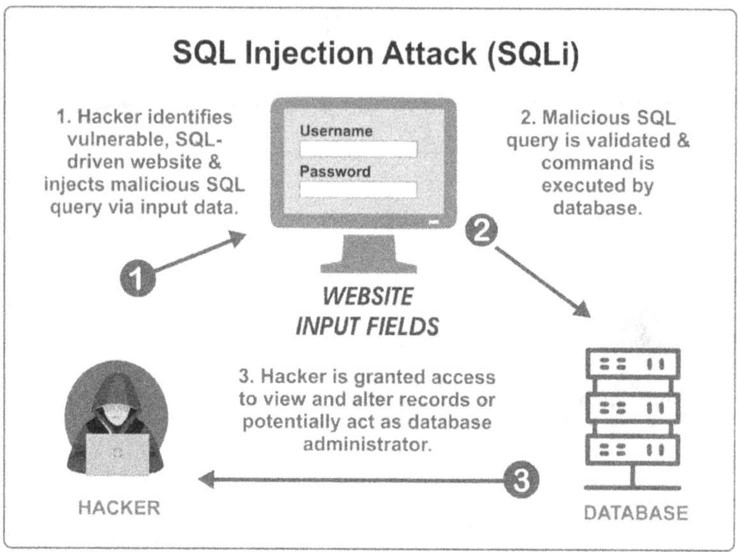

Figure 1.5 SQL Injection diagram showing a hacker injecting a malicious SQL query to access or alter database records.

Example: An attacker enters malicious SQL commands into a website's search box, tricking the server into executing unintended commands that manipulate the database.

Case study: In 2019, a major SQL injection attack affected 500,000 San Diego Unified School District students, leaking sensitive data, including social security numbers.

Cross-site scripting (XSS)

Description: XSS attacks inject malicious scripts into web pages viewed by other users, affecting user interactions with web applications (Figure 1.6).

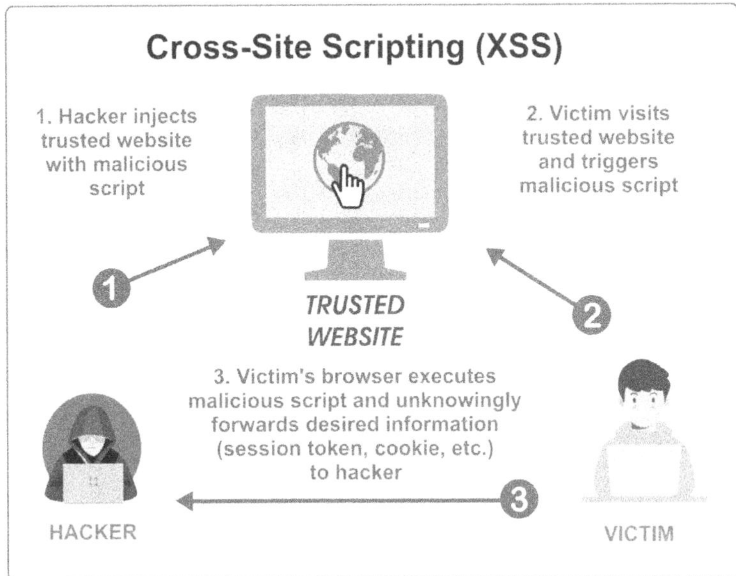

Figure 1.6 XSS attack diagram where a hacker injects a script into a trusted website to steal sensitive data.

Example: An attacker embeds malicious JavaScript into a comment on a blog. When other users view the comment, the script executes, potentially stealing cookies or session tokens.

Case study: In 2017, XSS vulnerabilities in eBay allowed attackers to inject malicious scripts that could steal users' credentials.

Denial-of-service (DoS)/distributed denial-of-service (DDoS)

Description: These attacks make a resource (such as a website or service) unavailable, overwhelming it with a flood of requests (Figure 1.7).

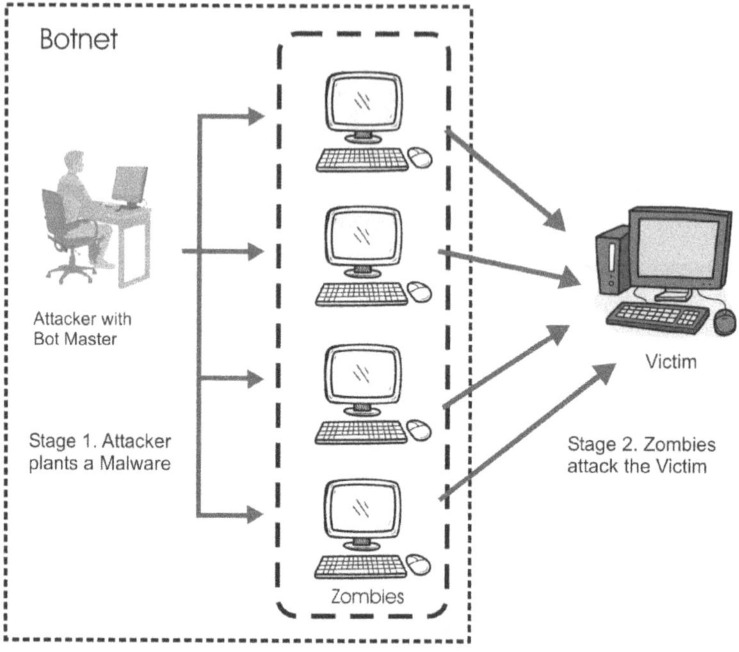

Figure 1.7 Botnet attack diagram showing an attacker planting malware to create a network of zombie computers.

Example: Multiple compromised computers bombard a bank's website with traffic, making it temporarily inaccessible to legitimate users.

Case study: In 2020, Amazon Web Services experienced a severe DDoS attack that disrupted operations for hours.

Man-in-the-middle (MitM) attack

Description: This attack involves intercepting and potentially altering the communication between two parties without their knowledge (Figure 1.8).

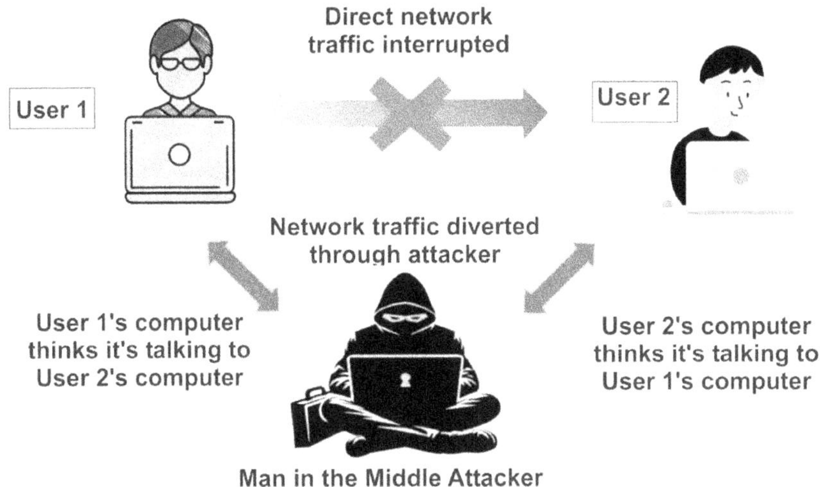

Figure 1.8 MitM attack diagram where an attacker intercepts network traffic between two users.

Example: During an unsecured Wi-Fi session, an attacker intercepts communications between a user's device and the network to steal sensitive data.

Case study: In 2019, a MitM attack on cryptocurrency exchange GateHub resulted in the loss of nearly $10 million worth of Ripple (XRP).

Malware

Description: Malware refers to any software intentionally designed to cause damage to a computer, server, or network.

Example: A user downloads a seemingly benign application, which secretly contains malware that begins to corrupt files and systems.

Case study: The WannaCry ransomware attack in 2017 affected over 200,000 computers across 150 countries encrypting data and demanding Bitcoin payments.

Advanced persistent threats (APTs)

Description: APTs are prolonged, targeted attacks where attackers infiltrate a network to steal data over a long period without detection (Figure 1.9).

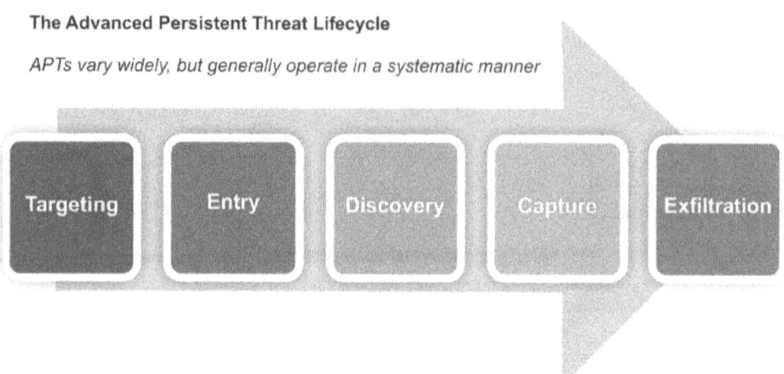

Figure 1.9 APT lifecycle flowchart with five stages: targeting, entry, discovery, capture, and exfiltration.

Example: Attackers gain a foothold in a government network and remain undetected for months, systematically stealing classified data.

Case study: The 2015 US Office of Personnel Management (OPM) breach, where hackers associated with the Chinese government stole sensitive data about millions of federal employees, is a notable example of an Advanced Persistent Threat (APT) attack.

Cryptojacking

Description: Cryptojacking involves secretly using someone else's computing resources to mine cryptocurrency.

Example: A user visits a website that secretly runs crypto mining scripts in the background, using the visitor's computing power without their knowledge.

Case study: In 2018, thousands of websites, including several government sites in the UK, were compromised to run Coinhive, a script that mined Monero cryptocurrency.

Zero-day exploit

Description: This type of exploit targets unknown, unpatched vulnerabilities in software or hardware.

Example: Hackers discover a vulnerability in a popular operating system that developers have not yet detected and use it to launch attacks on users before a patch is available.

Case study: The Stuxnet worm discovered in 2010 exploited several zero-day vulnerabilities in Windows to target Iranian nuclear facilities

Deepfake phishing

Description: Deepfake phishing involves using AI-generated audio and video clips that mimic real people, typically high-profile individuals, to trick victims into believing they are interacting with a trusted person.

Example: An employee receives a video message purportedly from the CEO, created using deepfake technology, asking for immediate transfer of funds or sensitive information.

Case study: In 2020, a bank manager in the UAE received a phone call from what seemed to be his boss's voice, engineered using AI, instructing him to transfer a large sum of money urgently, leading to significant financial loss.

AI-powered attacks

Description: These attacks use artificial intelligence to automate tasks usually performed by hackers, such as cracking passwords or finding vulnerabilities, making the attacks faster and more efficient.

Example: An AI system is trained to perform rapid password guessing against a database of leaked credentials, adapting its approach based on responses from the attacked system to improve its chances of success.

Case study: In 2021, AI-powered bots were used to attack e-commerce sites during high-traffic periods like Black Friday, exploiting vulnerabilities at a speed and precision that overwhelmed traditional security defenses.

Fileless malware

Description: Fileless malware resides only in memory and does not write any part of its activity to the hard drive, making it extremely difficult to detect with traditional antivirus solutions that monitor file changes.

Example: Malware is injected into the RAM through a legitimate-looking email attachment or link. Once opened, it exploits vulnerabilities to execute malicious actions while remaining resident in memory, leaving minimal traces.

Case study: The Astaroth trojan, active since 2020, uses fileless execution techniques to steal sensitive information and credentials by leveraging legitimate system tools to remain undetected.

Cloud jacking

Description: Cloud jacking involves the exploitation of security weaknesses in cloud computing environments to infiltrate and hijack accounts or services.

Example: Cybercriminals exploit misconfigured AWS S3 buckets to gain unauthorized access and extract large volumes of sensitive corporate data.

Case study: In 2019, a significant media service had its cloud storage misconfigured, leading to unauthorized access and exposure of hundreds of business documents and confidential agreements.

Note: An AWS S3 Bucket is a storage resource in Amazon Simple Storage Service (S3), a cloud-based object storage service provided by Amazon Web Services (AWS). S3 buckets are designed for storing and retrieving any amount of data from anywhere on the web, offering scalability, high durability, and accessibility.

5G-based attacks

Description: With the rollout of 5G technology, new vulnerabilities inherent to the architecture are being exploited by attackers to conduct surveillance, intercept data, or launch targeted attacks that leverage increased connectivity and speed.

Example: Attackers exploit vulnerabilities in the initial handshake protocols between 5G devices and networks to intercept data or deploy malware at high transmission speeds.

Case study: As 5G technology is still in its rollout phase, specific cases are under investigation or undisclosed. However, simulated testing environments have already demonstrated vulnerabilities that could be exploited in denial-of-service or man-in-the-middle attacks on 5G networks.

NETWORK-SPECIFIC ATTACKS

Here are five network-specific attacks, each with a detailed description, examples, and recent relevant case studies to demonstrate the scale and impact of these threats:

SYN flood attack

Description: A SYN flood attack is a form of Denial-of-Service (DoS) attack where the attacker sends a rapid succession of SYN requests to a target's system to consume enough server resources to make the system unresponsive to legitimate traffic (Figure 1.10).

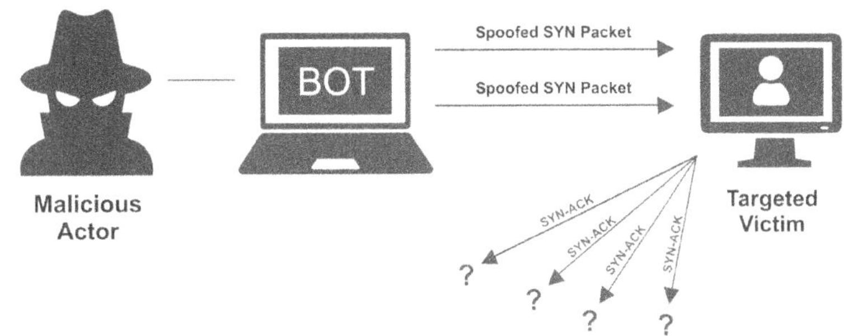

Figure 1.10 SYN flood attack diagram showing a bot sending spoofed SYN packets to overload a victim's system.

Example: An attacker sends a server's repeated SYN packets using fake IP addresses. Each request causes the server to initiate a handshake and wait for the final ACK, which never arrives, eventually overloading the server.

Case study: In 2020, an online retailer's e-commerce platform was temporarily offline due to a massive SYN flood attack during the Black Friday sales, resulting in substantial financial losses.

Smurf attack

Description: A Smurf attack is a distributed network attack where large numbers of Internet Control Message Protocol (ICMP) packets with the intended victim's spoofed source IP are broadcast to a computer network using an IP broadcast address.

Example: The attacker sends ICMP requests to the network's broadcast address from a spoofed IP address (the victim's). Each device on the network responds to the request, overwhelming the victim with traffic.

Case study: A European bank suffered a Smurf attack in 2019, which resulted in intermittent downtime over several hours, affecting online banking services and customer transactions.

Note: ICMP (Internet Control Message Protocol) is a network-layer protocol used primarily for diagnostic and error-reporting purposes within IP networks. Unlike TCP or UDP, ICMP is not used to exchange data between systems but to facilitate communication about the health and status of the network.

ARP poisoning

Description: Address Resolution Protocol (ARP) poisoning is a technique used to attack an Ethernet network by altering the ARP cache with a false MAC to IP address mapping. This results in sending data meant for one machine to another, leading to data interception or session hijacking (see Table 1.1).

Table 1.1 ARP table

IP address	*MAC address*	*Interface*
192.168.1.1	00:1A:2B:3C:4D:5E	Ethernet 0
192.168.1.2	00:1A:2B:3C:4D:5F	Ethernet 1
192.168.1.3	00:1A:2B:3C:4D:60	Wi-Fi 0

Example: An attacker sends ARP responses linking their MAC address to the IP address of the company's server. Network traffic intended for the server is mistakenly sent to the attacker instead.

Case study: In 2021, an ARP poisoning attack targeted a corporate network, allowing attackers to intercept and modify confidential communications between employees, including login credentials.

DNS amplification attack

Description: A DNS amplification attack is a Distributed Denial-of-Service (DDoS) attack that exploits publicly accessible domain name system (DNS) servers to overwhelm a target with DNS response traffic.

Example: The attacker sends a small query to a DNS server with the source address spoofed to the victim's address. The DNS server then sends an extensive reply to the victim's IP address, exponentially multiplying the traffic directed at the victim.

Case study: In 2018, a major DNS amplification attack targeted several US-based financial institutions, disrupting consumer and corporate banking services for several days.

IP spoofing

Description: IP spoofing involves an attacker disguising themselves as another user by falsifying data to gain an illegitimate advantage, such as impersonating another system to launch attacks on the network.

Example: An attacker sends packets from a spoofed IP address that appears to be part of the internal network, bypassing IP-based security measures to exploit vulnerabilities within the network.

Case study: In 2020, an IP spoofing attack was used to access restricted areas of a government agency's digital infrastructure, facilitating a data breach that exposed sensitive data related to national security.

Each of these attacks exploits specific network vulnerabilities and requires tailored security strategies to mitigate. Awareness and understanding of these methods are crucial for defending against sophisticated network intrusions.

ABOUT WIRESHARK

Wireshark is a powerful, open-source network protocol analyzer widely used in the networking and cybersecurity industries to troubleshoot network problems, analyze network traffic, and gather data for forensic and informational purposes. It captures network packets—the small chunks of data the network sends and receives—and makes them available for review.

Key features of Wireshark

Packet capture: Wireshark can capture packets live from many types of networks, including Ethernet, Bluetooth, Wireless (IEEE.802.11), and even PPP connections.

Detailed analysis: It can display the precise details in each packet, decoded from raw binary to human-readable form. This includes protocol-level information.

Filters: Users can apply filters only to view the data relevant to their specific issue or analysis. Filters can be based on almost any network packet detail, such as IP addresses, protocols, and packet types.

Color coding: Wireshark uses color coding to help users identify the types of traffic at a glance. For example, it might color HTTP traffic green and TCP traffic blue.

Graphical tools: It offers graphical tools for analyzing trends in network traffic, such as IO graphs, TCP stream graphs, and protocol hierarchy statistics.

Export and import: Users can export their findings in various formats or import packet data captured using other tools for analysis in Wireshark.

SIGNIFICANCE OF WIRESHARK IN NETWORK ANALYSIS AND CYBERSECURITY PRACTICES

Wireshark is a powerful tool in network analysis and cybersecurity due to its comprehensive capabilities for capturing and analyzing network traffic (Figure 1.11).

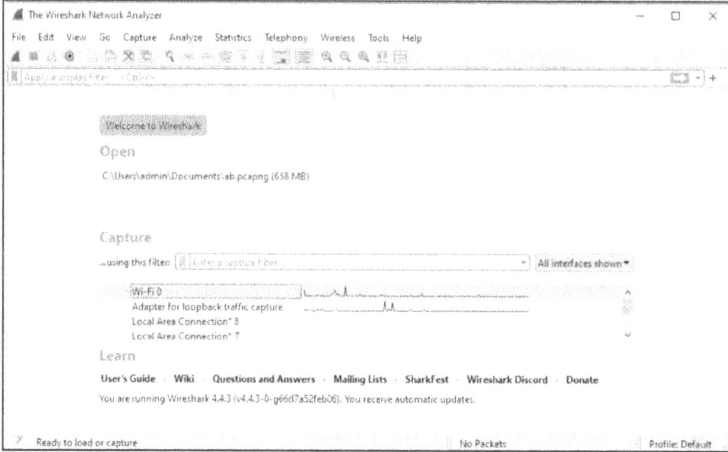

Figure 1.11 Wireshark interface showing the welcome screen, menu options, available network interfaces, and capture readiness status.

Here's an outline of its significance in network analysis and Cybersecurity practices:

Diagnosing network problems

Scenario: A network administrator notices slow network speeds in an office.

Using Wireshark: The administrator captures traffic and filters using protocols such as TCP or HTTP. They find an unusually high number of retransmission packets, indicating packet loss and suggesting issues with the network's physical layer or a congested link.

Identifying malicious activity

Scenario: There's suspicion that a device on the network has been compromised.

Using Wireshark: By capturing traffic to and from the suspicious device, the administrator might discover unexpected communications with known malicious IP addresses or unusual data exfiltration activities. For example, they might see a continuous data stream sent to an external IP, which isn't part of the company's standard communication patterns.

Monitoring network usage and compliance

Scenario: A company has a policy against peer-to-peer file sharing, which can sap bandwidth and pose security risks.

Using Wireshark: The IT department can monitor network traffic and use filters to detect P2P protocols. If traffic is detected, the source can be traced back to specific devices, and the users can be reprimanded or blocked.

Optimizing application performance

Scenario: A web application is experiencing intermittent delays affecting user experience.

Using Wireshark: The network team uses Wireshark to capture the traffic between the web server and clients. By analyzing the time sequences and filtering by HTTP/HTTPS protocols, they identify slow responses to specific queries, indicating inefficient backend processing or database queries.

Validating network security configurations

Scenario: A security team must ensure no legitimate traffic is accidentally blocked after updating firewall rules.

Using Wireshark: They set up Wireshark to monitor network traffic that hits the firewall. By checking the dropped or rejected traffic, the team verifies the effectiveness of the new rules and adjusts them to optimize both security and accessibility.

Training and education in real time

Scenario: During a cybersecurity training session, trainees must understand network packet structures and protocol behaviors.

Using Wireshark: The trainer uses Wireshark to capture live traffic, demonstrating the flow of TCP and UDP packets across the network, the effects of security protocols like TLS, and how data encapsulation works in different networking layers.

Quality of service (QoS) monitoring

Scenario: A network administrator must ensure critical business applications receive priority bandwidth over less critical traffic.

Using Wireshark: By analyzing the differentiated services code point (DSCP) values in the IP headers of captured packets, the administrator can verify that QoS policies correctly classify and prioritize traffic according to the organization's policies.

Detection of network anomalies

Scenario: An IT department observes unusual spikes in network activity during off-hours, which could indicate unauthorized access or malfunctioning equipment.

Using Wireshark: The department uses Wireshark to capture and analyze traffic during these periods. By examining the protocols and traffic volumes, they can pinpoint the source of the activity, whether it's an internal system malfunction or an external security threat, such as a botnet attack.

Ensuring data encryption compliance

Scenario: A company must comply with industry standards requiring encryption of sensitive data in transit.

Using Wireshark: Network administrators use Wireshark to inspect the encryption protocols, such as TLS/SSL, during data transmission. They verify that only strong encryption standards are used, ensuring compliance with regulatory requirements and safeguarding against data breaches.

Forensics and investigation

Scenario: After a security breach, investigators must understand how the attackers gained access.

Using Wireshark: By analyzing the captured packets from the attack, investigators can piece together the attacker's actions, such as exploiting a zero-day vulnerability in an application or using a phishing email to install malware.

CONCLUSION

Wireshark's ability to dissect network traffic in such granular detail makes it invaluable for anyone responsible for a network's operation or security, from system administrators to security professionals. Its comprehensive set of tools enables deep dives into traffic patterns, helping diagnose problems, ensure network optimizations, comply with policies, and secure the network against threats.

MULTIPLE CHOICE QUESTIONS (MCQs)

1. What is the primary role of Wireshark in network security?
   A) To increase the speed of the network
   B) To monitor and analyze network traffic

C) To serve as a firewall
D) To increase bandwidth usage

Answer: B)

2. Which cyber threat involves tricking individuals into revealing sensitive information through digital communications?
   A) Ransomware
   B) Phishing Attacks
   C) SQL Injection
   D) Cryptojacking

Answer: B)

3. What kind of cyberattack is described as exploiting security weaknesses in cloud computing environments to hijack accounts or services?
   A) Advanced Persistent Threats
   B) Denial-of-Service
   C) Cloud Jacking
   D) Zero-Day Exploit

Answer: C)

4. What type of attack is characterized by malicious software that encrypts the victim's data and demands a ransom to restore access?
   A) Malware
   B) Ransomware
   C) Man-in-the-Middle Attack
   D) Distributed Denial-of-Service

Answer: B)

5. During which scenario would a network administrator use Wireshark to verify that Quality of Service (QoS) policies correctly prioritize traffic?
   A) To ensure that critical business applications receive priority bandwidth over less critical traffic
   B) To monitor compliance with a company's no peer-to-peer file-sharing policy
   C) To check for unauthorized access during off-hours
   D) To validate the encryption of data in transit

Answer: A)

GLOSSARY

1. **Advanced Persistent Threat (APT)**: A sophisticated, prolonged cyberattack in which an intruder gains access to a network and remains undetected for an extended period.

2. **Botnet:** A network of private computers infected with malicious software and controlled as a group without the owners' knowledge, typically used to send spam or launch attacks.
3. **Cryptojacking:** The unauthorized use of someone else's computer resources to mine cryptocurrency.
4. **DDoS Attack (Distributed Denial-of-Service):** An attack that renders a computer or network incapable of providing regular services by overwhelming it with excessive traffic from multiple sources.
5. **Encryption:** The process of encoding messages or information so only authorized parties can access it.
6. **Firewall:** A network security system that monitors and controls incoming and outgoing network traffic based on predetermined security rules.
7. **ICMP (Internet Control Message Protocol):** is a network layer protocol used primarily for diagnostic and error reporting in IP networks. It facilitates communication between devices by sending messages about network issues or the status of a connection.
8. **Malware:** Software designed to interfere with a computer's normal functioning or to collect sensitive information from users without their knowledge.
9. **Phishing:** A cyber technique involving fraudulent attempts to obtain sensitive information by disguising oneself as a trustworthy entity via electronic communications.
10. **Ransomware:** Malware that locks or encrypts data, holding it hostage until a ransom is paid.
11. **Rootkit:** A malicious software designed to remotely access or control a computer without being detected by users or security programs.
12. **Social Engineering:** The use of deception to manipulate individuals into divulging confidential or personal information that may be used for fraud.
13. **SQL Injection:** A code injection technique that might destroy your database. It is one of the most common web hacking techniques.
14. **SSL/TLS (Secure Sockets Layer/Transport Layer Security):** Protocols for establishing authenticated and encrypted links between networked computers.
15. **Vulnerability:** A weakness in a system or its design that a threat actor, such as a hacker, could exploit
16. **Zero-Day Attack:** An attack that exploits a previously unknown vulnerability in a computer application or program that developers have had zero days to address and patch.

Chapter 2

Networking concepts and the OSI model

INTRODUCTION

Understanding the OSI (Open Systems Interconnection) model is essential for anyone working with networks as it provides a standardized framework for data communication between systems. By dividing communication into seven distinct layers, the OSI model simplifies the troubleshooting process, allowing issues to be isolated and addressed efficiently, whether they involve physical connections (Layer 1), IP configurations (Layer 3), or applications (Layer 7). It facilitates a clear understanding of how protocols operate and interact, enabling better design and scalability of networks. Additionally, the OSI model enhances security awareness by identifying vulnerabilities at specific layers and supports integrating emerging technologies like IoT and 5G. By serving as a universal language for networking professionals, it promotes effective communication, robust network design, and adaptability in an ever-evolving technological landscape.

INTRODUCTION TO NETWORKING

Networking involves exchanging data among various devices like computers, routers, and switches over a shared or dedicated medium. Networks enable functionalities ranging from simple communication like emails to complex data transfers across the globe.

Types of networks

Local area network (LAN): A network confined to a small geographic area, like an office building.

Wide area network (WAN): Covers a broad area, connecting geographically dispersed LANs.

DOI: 10.1201/9781003539261-2

Metropolitan area network (*MAN*): Larger than a LAN but smaller than a WAN, such as a city.

Personal area network (*PAN*): Small networks, typically within a user's reach, like Bluetooth and USB connections.

ABOUT DATA PACKETS

Data packets are the basic units of communication over a digital network. When data—such as an email, a webpage, or a video—is sent over the Internet, it is broken down into smaller, manageable pieces known as packets. These packets contain the actual data being sent (the payload) and important control information that ensures the data reaches its intended destination correctly.

COMPONENTS OF A DATA PACKET

Here's a breakdown of what typically makes up a data packet

1. *Header*: This part of the packet contains essential routing and delivery information, including:
   - Source and destination IP addresses (tells where the packet is coming from and where it is supposed to go).
   - Sequence numbers (helps in rearranging the packets in the correct order when they arrive at their destination, as packets can arrive out of order).
   - Protocol type (indicates the type of protocol that the packet should conform to, such as TCP or UDP).
2. *Payload*: This is the actual data carried by the packet. It can be a portion of an email text, a web page segment, or a video or audio file slice.
3. *Trailer* (sometimes called a footer): Contains additional data required for error checking and other purposes. It often includes a checksum, which the receiving device uses to ensure data integrity. If the data is corrupted in transit, the checksum does not match, signaling an error that needs to be addressed (Figure 2.1).

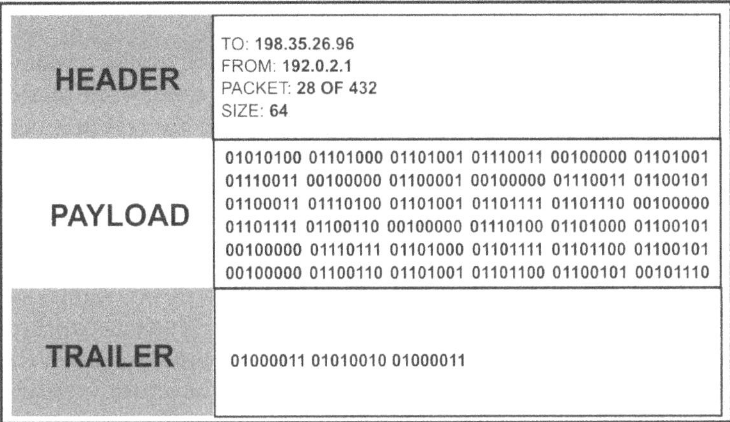

HEADER
TO: 198.35.26.96
FROM: 192.0.2.1
PACKET: 28 OF 432
SIZE: 64
PAYLOAD
01010100 01101000 01101001 01110011 00100000 01101001
01110011 00100000 01100001 00100000 01110011 01100101
01100011 01110100 01101001 01101111 01101110 00100000
01101111 01100110 00100000 01110100 01101000 01100101
00100000 01110111 01101000 01101111 01101100 01100101
00100000 01100110 01101001 01101100 01100101 00101110
TRAILER
01000011 01010010 01000011

Figure 2.1 A network packet structure with Header, Payload, and Trailer sections, showing binary data.

HOW DATA PACKETS WORK

When you send data to a network, here's what happens:

1. The data is segmented into packets.
2. Each packet is independently routed through the network, taking the most efficient path available at that moment.
3. Packets may arrive out of order or might even get lost in transit. Error-checking mechanisms are used to detect problems and request retransmission if necessary.
4. At the destination, the packets are reassembled into their original order based on the sequence numbers, reconstructing the original data.

Data packets are crucial for efficient, reliable, and secure data transmission across computer networks. Their design allows high-speed data transfer that can adapt to varying network conditions, optimize bandwidth, and effectively manage network congestion. Moreover, understanding the structure and function of data packets, including the roles of headers and trailers, is fundamental in fields like network engineering, cybersecurity, and information technology.

Note: Packets are routed through a network based on their headers, which include IP addresses that determine their path from the source to the destination. Routers and switches use this information to make forwarding decisions, directing the packets across various network segments.

THE OSI MODEL

The OSI (Open Systems Interconnection) model is crucial for understanding networking because it provides a standardized framework that defines the different processes and activities involved in a functioning network. The model is conceptual and used primarily for teaching and understanding how different network protocols interact. Understanding the OSI model helps network professionals design, understand, and troubleshoot network architectures more effectively.

The OSI (Open Systems Interconnection) Model is a theoretical framework describing how data should be transmitted between any network points. Developed by the International Organization for Standardization (ISO) in the late 1970s, the OSI Model is a seven-layer architecture specifying the communications requirements between two computing endpoints. Each layer serves a specific function and communicates with the layers directly above and below to help partition the communication process into smaller, more manageable parts (Figure 2.2).

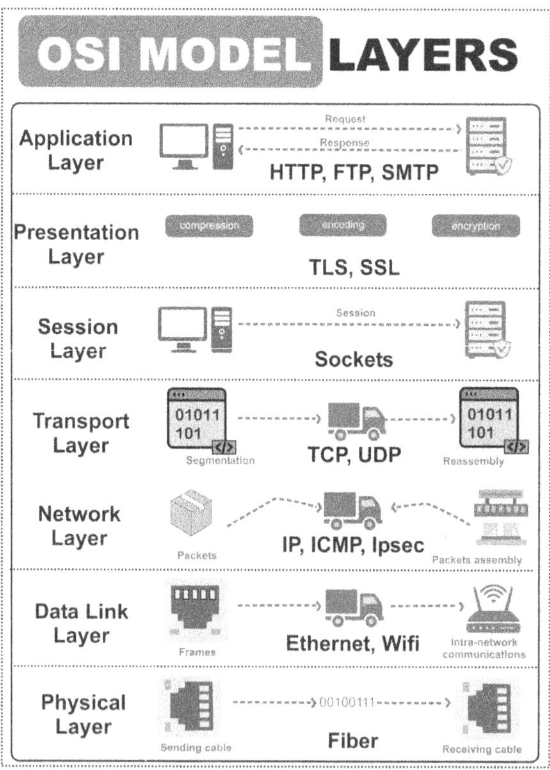

Figure 2.2 OSI Model Layers diagram illustrating seven layers, their functions, and associated protocols.

DETAILED DESCRIPTION OF THE OSI MODEL

Here is the detailed layer-wise description of the OSI model. Remember, the OSI model forms the foundation of everything in networks.

Physical layer (Layer 1)

Function: This is the lowest layer of the OSI model. It deals with the physical connection between devices, including voltage levels, timing of voltage changes, physical data rates, maximum transmission distances, and physical connectors. This layer is responsible for the raw, unstructured transmission of data.

Components: It contains cables (coax, fiber, twisted pair), hubs, repeaters, network adapters, and other hardware that handle electrical and physical connections.

Data link layer (Layer 2)

Function: This layer establishes and maintains links between nodes on the same network. It provides error detection and correction to ensure frames (data units for the Data Link layer) are not corrupted or lost, and controls the data flow, ensuring that data transmission is reliable.

Components: Bridges and switches.

- Sublayers:
    1. *Media access control* (*MAC*): Controls how devices uniquely identified by MAC addresses on the network gain access to the data and permission to transmit it.
    2. *Logical link control* (*LLC*): Manages device communication over a single network link.

Network layer (Layer 3)

Function: This layer manages device addressing, identifies devices independently of their physical network connections, and determines the best way to move data across a network. This includes routing packets from source to destination across multiple hops in different networks.

Components: Routers.

Key protocols: IP (Internet Protocol), ICMP (Internet Control Message Protocol).

Transport layer (Layer 4)

Function: The transport layer manages data packets' delivery and error checking. It ensures complete data transfer and provides connection-oriented communication, reliability, flow control, and multiplexing services.

Key protocols: TCP (Transmission Control Protocol), UDP (User Datagram Protocol).

Session layer (Layer 5)

Function: This layer establishes, manages, and terminates connections (sessions) between applications. It is responsible for setting up, coordinating, and terminating conversations, exchanges, and dialogues between the applications at each end.

Services: It authenticates and reconnects after a disconnection.

Presentation layer (Layer 6)

Function: It is often called the syntax layer. It converts incoming and outgoing data from one presentation format to another. For example, it ensures that data from a text file sent from a Windows machine is readable on a Mac, which uses different encoding methods.

Services: It does data encryption, compression, and data translation between different formats.

Application layer (Layer 7)

Function: This is the top layer of the OSI model, directly interfacing with end users. It provides services directly to user applications. It is responsible for network services such as file transfers, email, and other distributed information services.

Key protocols and services: HTTP (Hypertext Transfer Protocol), FTP (File Transfer Protocol), SMTP (Simple Mail Transfer Protocol), DNS (Domain Name System).

DATA FLOW IN AN OSI MODEL

To effectively utilize network analysis tools like Wireshark, it's essential to have a fundamental understanding of how data travels through a network. This journey is elegantly structured by the OSI (Open Systems Interconnection) Model, which breaks down the complex networking process into seven manageable layers. Each layer has a distinct role, ensuring that data packets move seamlessly from one point to another. In this chapter, we explore these layers in detail, demonstrating how an email travels from creation to receipt, thereby setting the stage for deeper insights into network behavior and troubleshooting.

Here's a step-by-step breakdown of how data flows through the OSI model:

Transferring information from one device to another travels through 7 layers of the OSI model. First, data travels down through 7 layers from the sender's end and then climbs back 7 layers on the receiver's end (Figure 2.3).

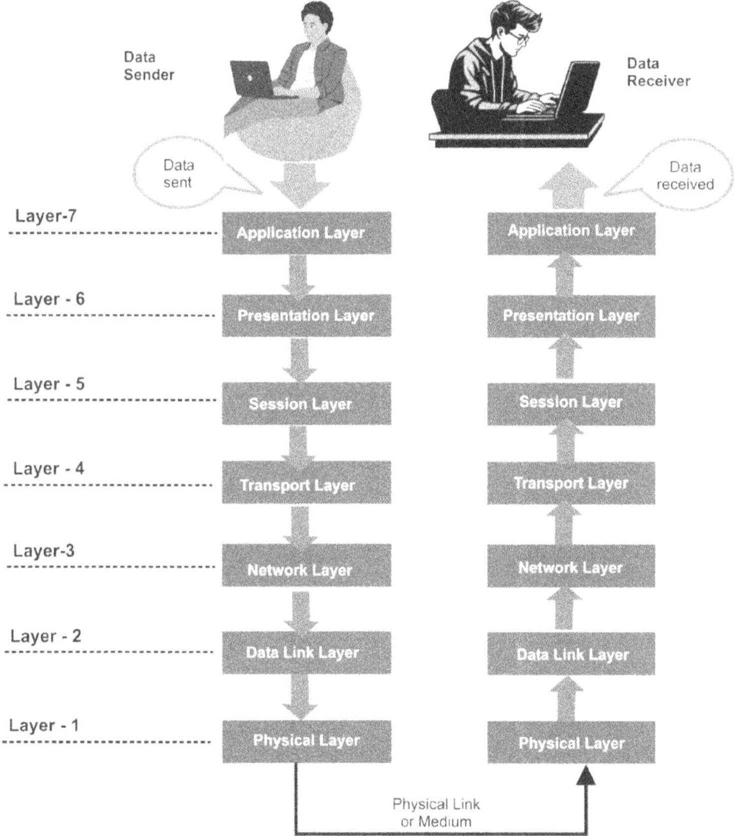

Figure 2.3 OSI Model data flow diagram showing sender-receiver communication across all seven layers.

Data flows through the OSI model in a step-by-step process:

1. *Application layer*: This is where applications generate the data to be sent.

2. *Presentation layer*: Data undergoes formatting and encryption to prepare for transmission at this level.
3. *Session layer*: This layer establishes and maintains connections between network devices.
4. *Transport layer*: Data is segmented into smaller pieces to ensure reliable delivery.
5. *Network layer*: These segments are packaged into packets and routed to the correct destination.
6. *Data link layer*: Packets are framed with necessary headers and trailers for network transit.
7. *Physical layer*: Finally, frames are converted into bits and physically transmitted over the medium, such as copper wires, fiber optics, or wireless.

Each layer adds specific information to ensure the data reaches its destination correctly, and these steps are reversed upon arrival.

DATA FLOW EXAMPLE: SENDING AN EMAIL

In this example, we explore how an email moves through the different layers of the OSI model from the moment it is sent until it is received. The process starts at the Application Layer, where the email is created and ends back at the Application Layer of the recipient's device. This journey illustrates the flow and the transformation of data as it passes through each layer, ensuring accurate and efficient communication over a network.

Step 1: Creation of the email

Application layer (Layer 7): The email is composed and initiated by the user in an application that functions at the Application Layer.

Step 2: Data formatting and encryption

Presentation layer (Layer 6): The email data is formatted (e.g., character encoding, data compression) and possibly encrypted to prepare it for secure transmission over the network.

Step 3: Session management

Session layer (Layer 5): A session is established between the sending and receiving devices to manage email data exchange. This includes opening, maintaining, and terminating the connection.

Step 4: Data transport setup

Transport layer (Layer 4): The email data is divided into smaller segments; transport protocols like TCP are used to set up a reliable connection, ensuring all segments reach their destination correctly.

Step 5: Network routing

Network layer (Layer 3): Segments are then packaged into packets, and logical addressing (such as IP addresses) determines the best route these packets take across the network.

Step 6: Data framing

Data link layer (Layer 2): Packets are framed, adding the hardware addresses of the sender and receiver, error detection, and other necessary information for the physical transmission.

Step 7: Physical transmission

Physical layer (Layer 1): The frames are converted into electrical, optical, or radio signals and transmitted over the physical network medium (like Ethernet cables or Wi-Fi).

Step 8: Arrival and processing at destination

Physical layer (Layer 1): Signals are received by the physical interface of the recipient's device.

Data link layer (Layer 2): The incoming data is processed back into packets, checking for errors and extracting hardware addresses.

Network layer (Layer 3): Packets are routed internally within the network to reach the final destination software.

Transport layer (Layer 4): Segments are reassembled into the complete data message, ensuring all parts have arrived correctly.

Session layer (Layer 5): The session between the sending and receiving devices manages the receipt confirmation.

Presentation layer (Layer 6): Data may be decrypted or decompressed back into its original format.

Application layer (Layer 7): The complete email is presented to the recipient in a usable format, typically visible within their email application.

This sequence demonstrates how each layer of the OSI Model plays a vital role in the journey of data from one device to another across a network.

IMPORTANCE OF THE OSI MODEL

The OSI model helps in not one but many tasks for a user.

Standardization: The OSI model helps standardize how network solutions are designed and evaluated, making it easier to create interoperable systems.

Troubleshooting: By understanding at which layer a networking issue is occurring, technicians can more effectively troubleshoot and resolve network problems.

Modularity: Each layer of the OSI model operates independently of the others. This modularity allows for easier updates and changes in one layer without affecting others.

Development: Developers can create network products aimed at the functionalities of specific layers, simplifying the development process and enhancing compatibility across different network technologies and architectures.

Understanding the OSI model is like having a map of a complex system. It provides the context and tools to manage and diagnose network systems, ensuring efficient communication and problem-solving within diverse IT environments.

BASIC NETWORKING HARDWARE

Let us understand about the connecting devices used to create a network.

Hubs: Simple devices connecting multiple Ethernet devices, acting as a single network segment. These are obsolete and hardly used these days.

Switches: Operate at the data link layer to create a network by connecting devices and managing node-to-node communication (Figure 2.4).

Figure 2.4 Black and white photo of a network switch with Ethernet ports, status lights, and a reflective surface.

Routers: Devices that forward data packets between computer networks, creating an "internetwork" (Figure 2.5).

Figure 2.5 Black and white photo of a wireless router with four antennas, status lights, and a gradient background.

FUNCTIONS AND KEY FEATURES OF HUB, SWITCH, AND ROUTER

Here are a few functions and key features of hubs, routers, and switches. Hubs, switches, and routers handle network traffic differently, affecting how Wireshark observes and captures data packets. Understanding each device's function helps correctly interpret the data captured during network analysis.

Hub

A hub is a basic networking device that connects multiple Ethernet devices, making them act as a single network segment. It broadcasts incoming data packets to all connected devices,regardless of the intended recipient, which can lead to collisions and network inefficiency.

Key features

Simplicity: Hubs are simple and have no software management tools. They are typically used in small, less complex networks.

Collision domains: All ports on a hub belong to the same collision domain, which can lead to data collisions if multiple devices transmit simultaneously.

Cost-effective: Generally cheaper than switches and routers, suitable for small setups or where network performance is not critical.

Switch

A switch is an intelligent networking device that connects devices within the same network (like within a single building). It receives incoming data packets and redirects them to their destination on a local network using MAC addresses. Unlike a hub, a switch only sends data to the device it is meant for, not to all connected devices.

Key features

Intelligent data handling: Switches use MAC addresses to learn and store the locations of connected devices, optimizing the data traffic flow.

Collision domains: Each port on a switch forms a separate collision domain, which means it can effectively reduce network congestion by allowing multiple packets to be transmitted simultaneously on different ports.

Performance: Typically offers better performance than hubs because traffic is directed only to relevant devices rather than all devices.

Note: Switches are far more advanced and have primarily replaced hubs in most network setups. They are more efficient because they manage traffic on a network by sending data only to the intended recipient, thereby reducing unnecessary traffic and virtually eliminating it.

Router

A router connects multiple networks, such as connecting a home network to the Internet. It determines the best path for data packets to travel across networks and can handle data using IP addresses.

Key features

Internetwork communication: Routers are the only one of the three devices that can facilitate data transfer between different networks.

Traffic direction: Uses routing tables and protocols to decide the best path for sending packets to their destinations.

Advanced functions: Provides additional features like firewall protection, traffic management, and, in some cases, Wi-Fi connectivity.

Note: A router connects the whole network to the Internet, and a switch connects various devices within the network, ensuring that data flows only to the correct devices. Switches are ideal for creating networks, routers for connecting networks, and hubs for simple tasks where high performance is not required (see Table 2.1).

Table 2.1 Comparison between Hub, Switch, and Router

Feature	*Hub*	*Switch*	*Router*
Definition	A hub is a basic networking device that connects multiple devices in a network and broadcasts data to all connected devices	A switch is a networking device that connects multiple devices and uses MAC addresses to forward data to the intended recipient	A router is a networking device that connects multiple networks and forwards data based on IP addresses
Layer	It operates at the OSI model's physical layer (Layer 1)	Operates at the data link layer (Layer 2) and sometimes at the network layer (Layer 3)	Operates at the network layer (Layer 3) of the OSI model
Data forwarding	Broadcasts data to all devices in the network	It forwards data only to the intended recipient device based on MAC addresses	Routes data to other networks based on IP addresses
Addressing	No addressing mechanism	Uses MAC addresses	Uses IP addresses
Performance	Low performance due to unnecessary data broadcasting	Better performance due to intelligent data forwarding	High performance with efficient routing mechanisms
Usage	Used in small, simple networks	Used in medium to large networks	Used to connect different networks, such as LAN to WAN
Security	It is less secure as data is broadcasted to all devices	It is more secure as data is sent only to the intended recipient	Highly secure with support for firewalls and encryption
Cost	Cheaper compared to switches and routers	Moderately priced	Expensive compared to hubs and switches

ABOUT MODEMS

Modems (modulator-demodulator) are used to modulate and demodulate signals for data transmission over telephone lines, cable systems, or satellites. In a home setting, a modem connects your home network to your Internet Service Provider (ISP), facilitating access to the Internet.

Note: Modems are not involved in network routing, switching, or traffic management within a local network. They primarily focus on providing a bridge between your local network and the service provided by your ISP.

Wi-Fi modems

A Wi-Fi modem is often called a modem-router combo or a gateway. It combines the functionalities of a modem and a wireless router into a single unit. This device serves as a critical component in home and small office networking, providing access to the Internet and local network connectivity (Figure 2.6). Here's a breakdown of what a Wi-Fi modem does:

Figure 2.6 Black and white photo of a wireless router with three antennas, status lights, and a reflective surface.

Modem functionality

Purpose: The modem part of the device connects to your Internet Service Provider (ISP) through a broadband connection like DSL, cable, or fiber. It modulates and demodulates the signals for communication over these services.

Note: It converts digital data from a computer to analog for transmission over telephone lines, cable systems, or satellites, and vice versa.

Router functionality

Purpose: The router part distributes the internet connection from the modem to various devices in your home or office, either through wired Ethernet connections or wirelessly via Wi-Fi.

Role: It assigns local IP addresses to each device on the network and manages the traffic within the network, ensuring data packets are sent to the correct devices. It also handles security functions like firewall protection.

Wi-Fi capabilities

Purpose: Provides wireless access to the network, allowing devices like smartphones, tablets, laptops, and smart home devices to connect to the Internet and each other without physical cables.

Role: Broadcasts a wireless signal that devices can connect to, secured with encryption protocols like WPA2 or WPA3 to protect the network from unauthorized access.

ADVANTAGES OF WI-FI MODEMS

The following are the advantages of Wi-Fi modems.

Convenience: Combining two devices into one reduces clutter and simplifies the setup and management of home networks.

Cost-effective: Usually cheaper than buying a separate modem and router.

Space-saving: Occupies less space than having two separate devices.

RELEVANCE OF NETWORKING BASICS AND THE OSI MODEL IN USING WIRESHARK

Understanding the basics of networking and the OSI model is crucial for effectively learning and using Wireshark, a powerful network protocol analyzer. Here's how this foundational knowledge aids in mastering Wireshark:

Layered approach to networking

A layered approach to networking refers to organizing the functions of a communication system into distinct layers, where each layer handles specific tasks and interacts only with the layers directly above and below it.

Understanding layers: Wireshark captures network data at different layers. Knowledge of the OSI model helps you understand which layer the specific data operates at. For instance, knowing that IP operates at the Network layer (Layer 3) and TCP at the Transport layer (Layer 4) helps you filter and analyze data packets accordingly.

Protocol analysis: Each OSI model layer corresponds to different network protocols that Wireshark can capture and dissect. Recognizing the functionality of each layer aids in comprehending the significance of each protocol's role in data transmission.

Data encapsulation and decapsulation

Packet details: Wireshark displays the details of each packet, including headers and payloads corresponding to different OSI layers. Understanding how data encapsulation works across these layers lets you interpret what each part of the packet represents and how data is structured as it moves through the network.

Error detection: Knowledge of how data is framed at the Data Link layer or segmented at the Transport layer helps identify common errors or issues like fragmentation or packet loss.

Traffic filtering and analysis

Layer-specific filters: With a solid grasp of networking basics, you can use Wireshark's powerful filtering capabilities to isolate traffic by layer-specific criteria, such as IP addresses (Network layer) or TCP ports (Transport layer).

Performance metrics: Analyzing traffic flow across different OSI layers enables you to assess network performance metrics such as throughput, latency, and error rates. It can help in network troubleshooting and optimization.

Troubleshooting and network diagnostics

Problem isolation: Knowing which layer a problem occurs in allows you to use Wireshark to isolate and troubleshoot issues efficiently. For instance, you would focus on Layer 3 information if there's a routing issue.

Real-time analysis: Wireshark provides real-time capture and analysis of network traffic. Understanding the OSI model helps make sense of dynamic data flows and pinpoint anomalies at specific layers.

Security analysis

Security features: Different OSI layers have different security protocols (like SSL/TLS at the Presentation layer). Understanding these layers helps monitor and analyze security features and detect potential threats.

Intrusion detection: Wireshark can detect unusual patterns that may indicate a security breach, such as unusual ports being used or spikes in traffic at specific layers.

CONCLUSION

The knowledge of networking fundamentals and the OSI model equips you with the necessary tools to navigate and utilize Wireshark effectively. It enhances your ability to analyze, diagnose, and resolve network issues, making your use of Wireshark more proficient and insightful. This foundational understanding improves your technical skills and enriches your capacity to maintain and secure networks.

MULTIPLE CHOICE QUESTIONS (MCQs)

1. What is the primary purpose of the Data Link Layer in the OSI model?
   A) To manage device addressing and routing across multiple networks
   B) To encrypt and compress data
   C) To establish, manage, and terminate sessions
   D) To ensure reliable data transfer between directly connected nodes

Answer: D)

2. Which OSI layer translates data between the application and the network?
   A) Session Layer
   B) Transport Layer
   C) Presentation Layer
   D) Network Layer

3. In the OSI model, which layer handles data routing using IP addresses?
   A) Transport Layer
   B) Network Layer
   C) Data Link Layer
   D) Application Layer

Answer: B)

4. Which of the following devices operates at the Data Link Layer of the OSI model?
   A) Routers
   B) Switches
   C) Modems
   D) Repeaters

Answer: B)

5. What is encapsulation in the context of the OSI model?
   A) The process of adding headers to data as it moves down the layers
   B) The removal of headers from data as it ascends the layers
   C) The process of error checking at each layer
   D) The management of session establishment and termination

Answer: A)

GLOSSARY

1. **Application Layer:** The Application Layer (Layer 7) is considered the last layer of the OSI model for the sender when describing how data flows from the sender to the receiver. At the receiver's end, the Application Layer is the last layer where the received data is processed and presented to the user or application. For example, the Application Layer processes and displays the email data to the user.
2. **Data Encapsulation:** The process of adding headers and trailers around some data. Each layer in the OSI model encapsulates the packet it receives from the layer above following the protocol being used.
3. **Data Link Layer (Layer 2):** Responsible for node-to-node data transfer and error correction in frames. It includes sublayers such as Media Access Control (MAC) and Logical Link Control (LLC).
4. **Decapsulation:** The process of removing headers and trailers as data passes up through the layers. Each layer removes the header and trailer information meant for it, processes the remainder, and passes it to the next layer.
5. **Layer-specific Filters:** Filters used in network analysis tools like Wireshark to isolate traffic by layer-specific criteria such as IP addresses (Network layer) or TCP ports (Transport layer)
6. **Network Layer (Layer 3):** Manages device addressing and determines the best path for data to reach its destination across multiple networks, using protocols like IP and ICMP.
7. **OSI (Open Systems Interconnection) Model:** A conceptual framework used to understand network interactions in seven layers, from the physical transmission of data to the applications that users interact with.

8. **Physical Layer (Layer 1):** Concerns the physical equipment involved in data transfer, such as cables, cards, and other hardware. It handles the transmission and reception of raw unstructured data over a physical medium.
9. **Presentation Layer (Layer 6):** Translates data between the application and network layers. It ensures that data from a network is in a usable format and is responsible for data encryption, compression, and translation.
10. **Protocol Analysis:** Examining various communication protocols within network traffic to ensure proper structure, troubleshooting, and network behavior analysis.
11. **Session Layer (Layer 5):** Establishes, manages, and terminates connections (sessions) between applications. It sets up, coordinates, and terminates conversations, exchanges, and dialogues between the applications at each end.
12. **Transport Layer (Layer 4):** Provides transparent data transfer between end systems. It is responsible for end-to-end error recovery and flow control. It ensures complete data transfer using protocols such as TCP and UDP.

Chapter 3

Installing and using Wireshark

INTRODUCTION

Wireshark is a powerful network protocol analyzer widely used for network troubleshooting, analysis, software and protocol development, and education. In this chapter, we'll cover Wireshark's installation and basic usage on Windows, macOS, and Linux platforms, focusing on its presence in Kali Linux for security professionals.

INSTALLING WIRESHARK ON WINDOWS

Follow the steps given to install the Wireshark on Windows OS.

1. Downloading the installer

Visit the official Wireshark website **at wireshark.org.** Click on the Windows Installer link suitable for your system (32-bit or 64-bit) (Figure 3.1).

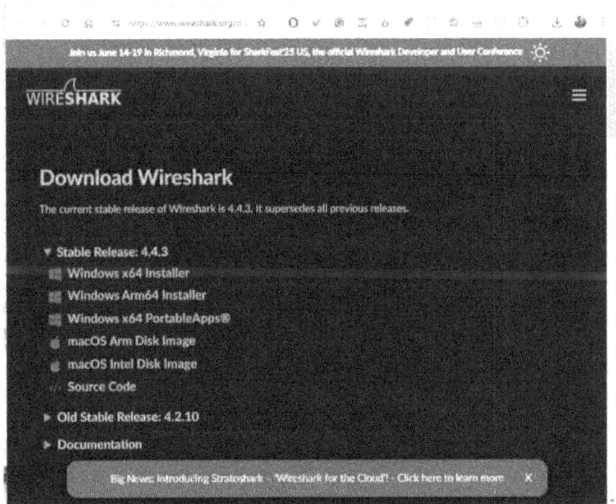

Figure 3.1 Wireshark download page showing stable releases and installers.

DOI: 10.1201/9781003539261-3

2. Running the installer

Open the downloaded file to start the installation process. Follow the installation wizard's prompts. Agree to the license terms, choose your desired components (such as USBPcap for capturing USB traffic), and select the installation directory (Figure 3.2).

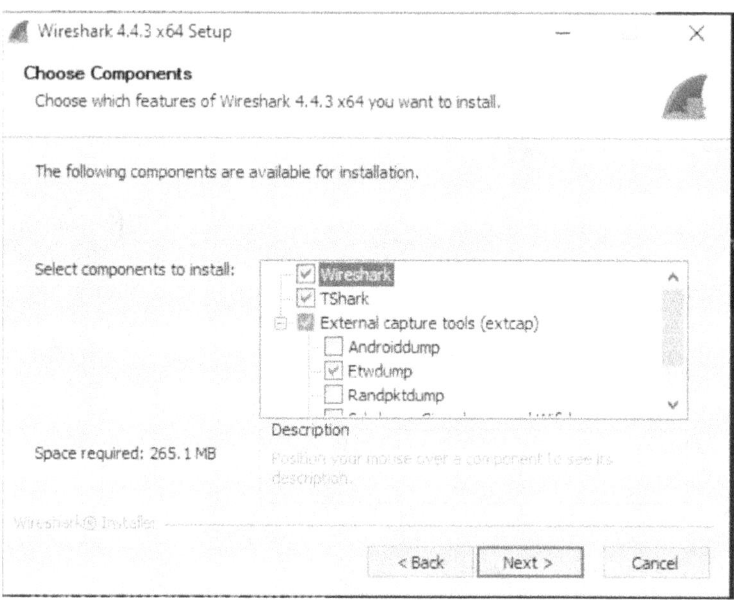

Figure 3.2 Wireshark 4.4.3 x64 Setup window at "Choose Components" step with feature selection.

3. Completing installation

Review the installation settings and click "Install" (Figure 3.3). Once the installation is complete, run Wireshark immediately or start it later via the Start Menu.

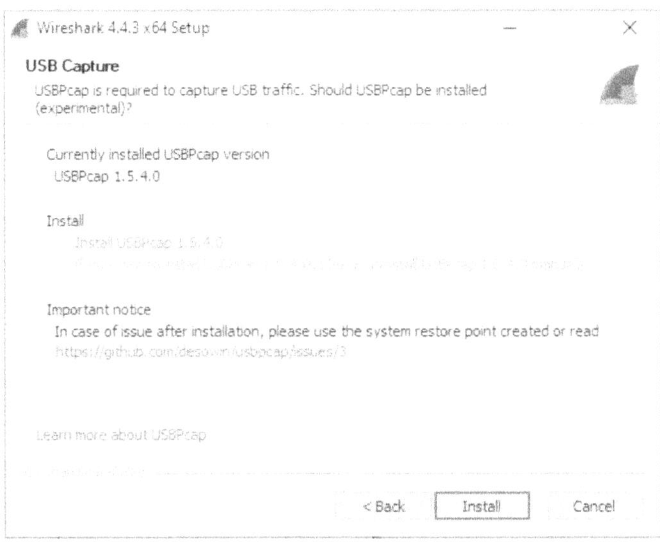

Figure 3.3 Wireshark 4.4.3 x64 Setup window at "USB Capture" step, showing USBPcap installation options.

NPCAP AND USBPCAP

While installing, do not forget to enable the download options for Npcap and USBPcap. Npcap and USBPcap are software libraries that serve as vital tools for capturing network traffic in different contexts, specifically tailored for use with network analysis tools like Wireshark. They are often referred to as "packet capture drivers" or "packet capture libraries".

In Wireshark, both Npcap and USBPcap are essential tools used for capturing network traffic, each serving distinct purposes:

Npcap

Npcap is a packet-sniffing library for Windows, providing the functionality necessary for Wireshark to capture live network traffic on Windows systems. It is an updated, more secure, and feature-rich version of the older WinPcap. Here are some key features and uses of Npcap:

1. *Packet capture*: Npcap lets Wireshark capture packets on network interfaces, including Ethernet and Wi-Fi.
2. *Loopback packet capture*: Unlike WinPcap, Npcap can capture and send loopback packets, allowing you to capture traffic that your computer is sending to itself, which is particularly useful for debugging and testing applications.

3. *Raw packet sending*: Npcap enables the sending of raw packets, which can be helpful in network testing and simulation of network conditions.
4. *Improved performance*: Npcap operates in WinPcap compatibility mode but also offers a native API mode that can have better performance and more features.
5. *Secure mode*: Npcap can be installed in a restricted mode, which limits its access to the administrator's group to the packet-capturing capabilities, enhancing security.

USBPcap

USBPcap is an open-source USB packet capture tool for Windows that captures USB traffic. USBPcap is used to analyze USB devices and their communication with the computer. It is invaluable for developing device drivers, debugging software, and forensic investigation. Key functionalities include:

1. *USB traffic capture*: USBPcap captures USB packet data transferred over USB hubs and devices connected to the computer. This data can include anything from data transfers to and from external storage devices to communications with peripheral devices like keyboards and webcams.
2. *Analysis and debugging*: Developers can use USBPcap to analyze the data flow between USB devices and the operating system, helping to debug and develop software and drivers for USB devices.
3. *Educational and forensic use*: For educational purposes, USBPcap can help students and researchers understand USB protocols and device communications. In forensics, it can capture data transfers that might include malicious activities or data exfiltration attempts.

Both tools are vital in their respective domains. Npcap focuses on network traffic, and USBPcap is dedicated to USB communications, providing comprehensive coverage of data flow analysis in Wireshark for various digital communications and environments.

FIRST LAUNCH AND INITIAL CONFIGURATION

Wireshark may request permission to download protocol and other updates for the first launch. Allow these updates to ensure you have the latest definitions. Configure the network interfaces for packet capturing by selecting "Capture" > "Options" and choosing the desired interfaces (Figure 3.4).

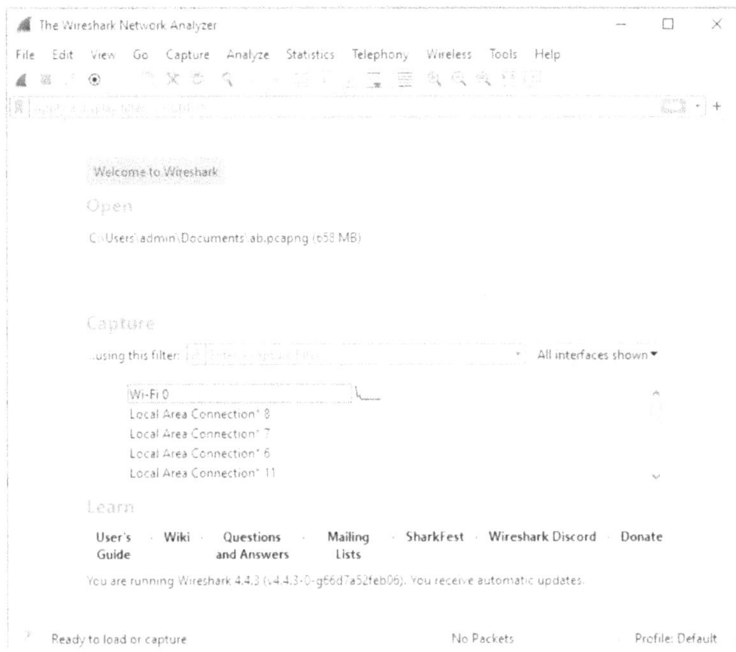

Figure 3.4 Wireshark interface with capture options.

INSTALLING WIRESHARK ON macOS

Follow the steps given to install Wireshark on macOS.

1. Downloading the installer
   Navigate to the Wireshark download page and select the macOS installer package.
2. Running the installer
   Open the downloaded .dmg file and drag Wireshark to your Applications folder. You may need to override security settings to open it the first time, as it's downloaded from the internet. Go to *System Preferences → Security & Privacy* and under the General tab, click "Open Anyway" .
3. Additional tools
   Installing command-line utilities (like dumpcap) might require additional steps. Open a terminal and run the install script in the .dmg file if needed.
4. First launch
   Open Wireshark from the Applications folder. You may be prompted to install additional components like ChmodBPF, which is necessary for capturing live data on macOS.

USING WIRESHARK ON LINUX (INCLUDING KALI LINUX)

Wireshark is exceptionally well-integrated into Linux environments, including popular distributions like Ubuntu and specialized platforms like Kali Linux, which security professionals favor. On most Linux distros, Wireshark can be installed via package managers (e.g., *sudo apt-get install wireshark*). During the installation, users may be prompted to configure permissions to allow non-superusers to capture packets. This setup enhances security by minimizing root access.

For Kali Linux users, Wireshark comes pre-installed, reflecting Kali's focus on advanced security and penetration testing tools. Launching Wireshark on Linux generally involves opening it from the command line with Wireshark or through the graphical user interface. The user interface and functionality remain consistent across platforms, ensuring a seamless experience for analyzing and troubleshooting network traffic.

INSTALLATION ON GENERAL LINUX DISTROS

For distributions like Ubuntu, use the package manager to install Wireshark. Open a terminal and run: sudo *apt-get install wireshark*. During installation, you may be asked if non-superusers should be allowed to capture packets. Choose according to your security policy.

1. Using Wireshark on Kali Linux
   Kali Linux comes with Wireshark pre-installed. You can start it from the command line by typing wireshark or through the menu in the GUI.
2. Basic usage
   a) Select the appropriate network interface under "Capture" > "Options" or click on the interface list in the main window to capture packets (Figure 3.5).

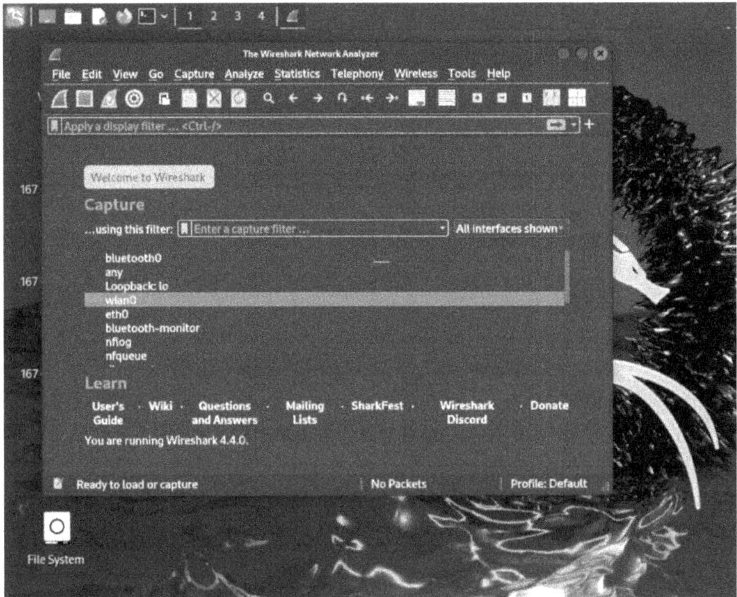

Figure 3.5 Wireshark 4.4.0 Network Analyzer interface on Kali Linux with interface capture option.

b) Use the display filter to narrow down to specific protocols or traffic types. For instance, *ip.addr == 192.168.1.1* to view all traffic involving that IP address.

ANALYZING CAPTURED DATA

The main window displays the packets. Clicking on a packet shows detailed information in the packet details pane. Use the packet bytes pane to examine the raw data.

Note: We will study all three panes in detail in upcoming chapters.

SAVING AND EXPORTING DATA

Captured data can be saved in various formats for later analysis or use as evidence.

Saving captured packets

1. **Save the capture:**
   a) Go to *File* → *Save As* to open the Save dialog box.
   b) Choose the location to save the file and enter a filename.
   c) You can choose different formats, but the default .pcapng format is recommended because it supports more information than the older .pcap format.
2. **Export specific packets** (optional):
   a) If you want to save specific packets or data, use *File* → *Export* Specified Packets.
   b) You can select which packets to export based on the current display filter or a range of packet numbers.
3. **Export packet data:**
   a) You might want to export packet details or packet bytes for deeper analysis or reporting.
   b) Use *File* → *Export Packet Dissections* to export packet details as plain text, CSV, or other formats.

CONCLUSION

Wireshark is an indispensable tool for network analysis, and its versatility across different operating systems makes it a valuable skill for any network or security professional. Whether you are working on Windows, macOS, or Linux, understanding how to install and begin using Wireshark is the first step toward mastering network troubleshooting and security analysis.

MULTIPLE CHOICE QUESTIONS (MCQs)

1. What is Npcap primarily used for in Wireshark on Windows?
   A) Exporting packet data
   B) Capturing live network traffic
   C) Installing USB drivers
   D) Managing user permissions

Answer: B)

2. Which component is necessary for capturing live data on macOS using Wireshark?
   A) Npcap
   B) USBPcap

C) ChmodBPF
D) dumpcap
Answer: C)

3. What is the recommended file format for saving captured packets in Wireshark because it supports more information?
A) .csv
B) .txt
C) .pcap
D) .pcapng
Answer: D)

4. Which of the following is NOT a use case for USBPcap?
A) Analyzing USB device communications
B) Capturing USB traffic for forensic investigations
C) Capturing network traffic via Ethernet
D) Developing USB device drivers
Answer: C)

5. How can one enable non-superusers to capture packets during Wireshark installation on Linux?
A) By enabling Npcap
B) Through the package manager installation settings
C) Installing USBPcap
D) Downloading the Linux installer
Answer: B)

GLOSSARY

1. **ChmodBPF:** A component on macOS required for capturing live data by providing appropriate permissions to access network interfaces.
2. **dumpcap:** A command-line utility included with Wireshark used to capture packet data.
3. **Ethernet:** A wired LAN technology that transmits data over cables, unlike Wi-Fi which uses wireless signals.
4. **Npcap:** A packet-sniffing library for Windows that captures live network traffic on Windows systems.
5. **Packet Capture:** The process of intercepting and logging traffic that passes over a digital network or part of a network.
6. **USBPcap:** An open-source USB packet capture tool for Windows that captures USB traffic and analyzes and debugs USB devices.
7. **Wireshark:** A network protocol analyzer used for network troubleshooting, analysis, protocol development, and educational purposes.

Chapter 4

Basics of packet capturing

INTRODUCTION

Packet capturing involves intercepting data packets that travel through a network, allowing network administrators, security experts, and IT professionals to monitor network traffic and diagnose network issues. This chapter introduces the fundamentals of packet capturing, focusing on how to set up captures, use filters for efficient analysis, and understand basic network traffic. This understanding is crucial for analyzing traffic from various sources, including Wi-Fi, Bluetooth, and other transmission methods.

SETTING UP PACKET CAPTURES

Setting up packet captures in Wireshark involves selecting the correct network interface and configuring capture options to suit specific monitoring needs.

The following are steps to set up a basic capture

1. *Open Wireshark*: Start the application and select the "List of available capture interfaces" option to see network interfaces.
2. *Choose the correct interface*: Select the network interface through which the traffic you want to monitor flows. This might be an Ethernet interface for wired connections and a Wi-Fi interface for wireless traffic.
3. *Start capturing*: Click the *Start capturing packets* button after selecting the interface (Figure 4.1). Wireshark begins capturing all packets that pass through the selected interface.

DOI: 10.1201/9781003539261-4

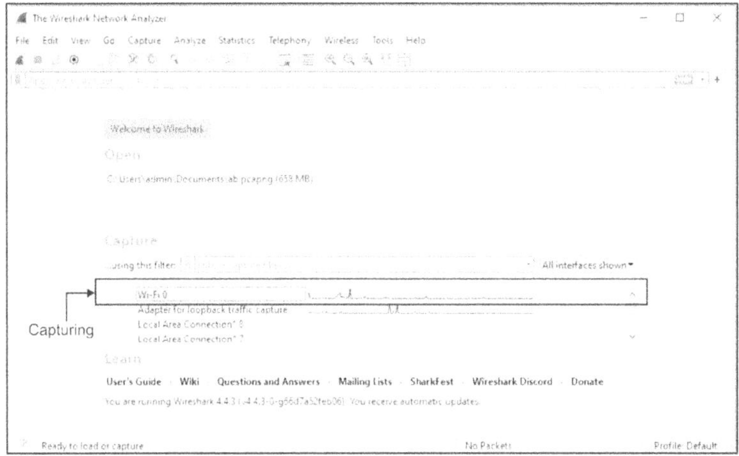

Figure 4.1 Wireshark 4.4.3 interface showing the welcome screen, file loading options, and available network interfaces (including Wi-Fi 0) for live packet capture.

For more flexibility, you can click on the *Capture* option (Figure 4.2).

You can see Promiscuous mode and monitor mode here. You can turn it on or off as you require.

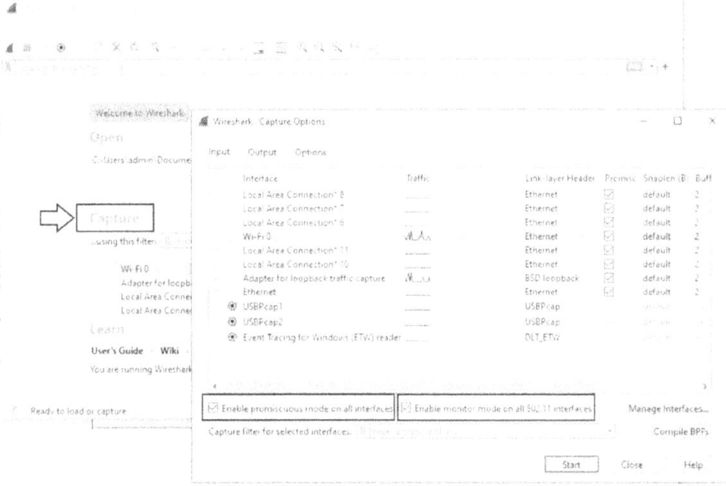

Figure 4.2 Wireshark "Capture Options" window displaying interfaces, traffic types, and configuration settings.

ABOUT PROMISCUOUS MODE

Promiscuous Mode in Wireshark is a network interface configuration that allows a device to capture all network traffic on the same network segment, regardless of whether the packets are addressed to the device. It works by bypassing the default behavior of only processing packets meant for the device's MAC address or broadcast/multicast packets.

Suppose you use Wireshark in Promiscuous Mode on a computer connected to an Ethernet network. In that case, you can see not only the data packets meant for your device but also those meant for other devices connected to the same switch or hub. This is because Wireshark captures all the traffic flowing through its connected segment, not just its own communications.

In Wi-Fi networks, it can capture packets within range. Still, its effectiveness may be limited by encryption, network segmentation, or hardware support. Promiscuous Mode is essential for analyzing network performance, troubleshooting issues, and performing security assessments.

Note: Multicast is like a teacher sending a group message to only the students in the debate club, not the entire class. Multicast is a network communication method where data is sent to a specific group of devices, not everyone. It's efficient for tasks like video streaming or online gaming, as only subscribed devices receive the message.

This mode can be beneficial in the following activities

Troubleshooting and diagnostics

Promiscuous Mode enables detailed troubleshooting of network issues by capturing all packets on a network segment.

Example: A network engineer suspects a misconfigured device on the network sends out corrupt packets. By capturing traffic in Promiscuous Mode, they can isolate these packets and identify the source device, even though it's not communicating directly with their own machine.

Security analysis

Promiscuous Mode is crucial for capturing potentially malicious packets that might be directed to other devices on the network.

Example: During a routine security check, a cybersecurity analyst uses Promiscuous Mode to capture all traffic and discovers a series of unrecognized ARP requests trying to resolve IP addresses that don't belong to any known device on the network, indicating a potential ARP spoofing attack.

Network performance optimization

Capturing all network traffic helps analyze overall network performance and optimize data flows.

Example: An IT consultant sets up Wireshark in Promiscuous Mode to monitor all traffic on a corporate network. They notice several large file transfers during peak hours, impacting network performance. Using this data, they recommend policy changes to schedule large transfers during off-peak times.

ABOUT MONITOR MODE

Monitor mode is a specialized mode of operation for wireless network interface cards (NICs). In this mode, the NIC can capture all wireless traffic within its range, regardless of whether the packets are addressed to it. This is different from promiscuous mode, which works at the Ethernet or IP layer and can capture traffic only within the same network (e.g., LAN or Wi-Fi it is connected to).

COMPARING TWO MODES

Let us understand the comparison between the two modes with the help of an example:

Example: Imagine sitting in a café with your laptop open and enjoying coffee. You're connected to the café's Wi-Fi and using Wireshark to analyze the network traffic.

In this scenario, let's compare the two modes available in Wireshark: promiscuous and monitor modes.

Promiscuous mode in Wireshark

In promiscuous mode, Wireshark can capture traffic sent to your laptop or broadcast to all devices on the café's Wi-Fi network. For example, in Promiscuous Mode, you can see the data packets sent between your laptop and the café's access point (AP), such as HTTP requests or other general traffic. However, suppose someone at another table sends data between their laptop and a different access point. In that case, Wireshark won't capture those packets unless they are broadcasted (e.g., ARP requests) or if your laptop is within range of the other device's transmission (should be close enough).

Monitor mode in Wireshark

Imagine you're in the same café, but this time, you switch your laptop to monitor mode in Wireshark. In this mode, your laptop can pick up all the traffic in the area, even from the nearby café's Wi-Fi network, to which you aren't connected. It means you can see packets from the other café's access point and the one you're connected to. This might include:

1. *Beacon frames*: These are sent by access points (APs) to announce their presence to nearby devices.
2. *Probe requests*: These are sent by nearby devices searching for available networks.
3. *Encrypted data packets*: These may be captured from other devices communicating with their own access points, but they appear as encrypted unless you have the correct keys.

In essence, monitor mode lets you capture traffic from multiple access points around you, including those outside your direct network in a Wi-Fi environment.

Let us conclude this particular case.

In this café scenario, promiscuous mode lets you capture traffic either directed at you or broadcasted within the same network. In contrast, monitor mode expands your visibility, allowing you to capture wireless traffic from other nearby networks, like the neighboring café's Wi-Fi. Monitor mode is much more powerful for understanding the broader wireless environment. It is helpful for network analysis or security auditing.

In switched networks

- Modern networks use switches, which forward packets only to the specific port where the destination device is connected, based on the MAC address table.
- In such cases, promiscuous mode alone cannot capture packets intended for other devices. Techniques like port mirroring (SPAN) or network tapping are required to direct traffic from multiple devices to the NIC.

In wireless networks

- In Wi-Fi networks, promiscuous mode may be combined with monitor mode to capture packets for all wireless devices, as Wi-Fi has additional layer-2 filtering and encryption mechanisms.

- In a Wi-Fi network, all devices communicate over the same radio frequencies. All traffic is inherently "broadcast" over the air and can theoretically be captured by any device within range. A Wi-Fi network doesn't rely on a physical switch like wired Ethernet, so the concept of "ports" and their mirroring is not directly applicable.

Note: SPAN (Switched Port Analyzer), commonly referred to as port mirroring, is a feature of network switches that allows administrators to duplicate or "mirror" network traffic from one or more switch ports (or VLANs) to another port where it can be analyzed using tools like Wireshark. So, SPAN is primarily used in Ethernet networks for traffic monitoring and analysis (In Table 4.1, you can see the comparison).

Table 4.1 Comparison of promiscuous mode, monitor mode, and port mirroring

Feature	*Promiscuous mode*	*Monitor mode*	*Port mirroring*
Use case	Captures traffic on the same segment (wired)	Captures raw 802.11 frames on Wi-Fi	Mirrors traffic from specific ports (wired)
Layer of operation	Data Link Layer (Ethernet)	Physical Layer (802.11)	Data Link Layer (Ethernet)
Traffic visibility	All unicast, multicast, and broadcast packets on the same segment (if supported)	All packets on the Wi-Fi channel (if supported)	Traffic flowing through mirrored ports
Network type	Wired/Wi-Fi (limited for Wi-Fi)	Wi-Fi only	Wired only
Encryption handling	Cannot bypass encryption	Captures encrypted and unencrypted frames	Not applicable (operates post-decryption)
NIC support	Supported by most NICs	Requires special NIC with monitor mode	No special NIC needed (switch configuration)
Configuration	Software setting in Wireshark or OS	Requires NIC and Wi-Fi driver support	Requires switch or router configuration
Traffic scope	Limited on Wi-Fi; effective for wired segments	Comprehensive for Wi-Fi analysis	Comprehensive for wired networks

SOME REASONS THE MONITOR MODE IS NOT ACTIVATED

Here are the key reasons why monitor mode might not be activating:

1. *Hardware compatibility*: Not all Wi-Fi adapters support monitor mode. Ensure your adapter is capable (e.g., Alfa AWUS036NHA, TP-Link TL-WN722N v1). TP-Link works best. Also, install ncap for Windows from https://npcap.com/
2. *Driver issues*: Ensure you have the correct or updated drivers for your adapter, as some drivers may not expose monitor mode functionality.
3. *Operating system limitations*: Monitor mode is better supported on Linux. On Windows, it may require specific drivers or third-party tools. Download npcap for Windows. That will most probably enable the monitor mode.
4. *Incompatible software/tools*: Ensure the software (Wireshark, Aircrack-ng, and similar) is compatible with your adapter and supports monitor mode.
5. *Incorrect configuration*: On Linux, you may need to manually configure your adapter to switch to monitor mode using commands like ifconfig or airmon-ng.

ABOUT NPCAP

We are using the TP-Link adapter and Windows 10 OS in this book. We installed Npcap, and the monitor mode started working. **Npcap** is a modern packet capture library developed by the Nmap Project, designed to replace the outdated WinPcap on Windows. It enables Wireshark to capture and analyze network traffic by providing access to packets on network interfaces, including support for promiscuous mode, monitor mode (for capturing raw wireless traffic), and loopback traffic. Npcap is compatible with modern Windows versions, offers improved performance, and supports advanced features like IPv6 and wireless packet analysis. Wireshark's functionality on Windows needs to ensure reliable and efficient network analysis.

CAPTURE OPTIONS

The first thing to work in Wireshark is setting the interface according to your convenience. Go to *Capture → Options* to work on options displayed under tabs of the dialog box.

Output tab

In Wireshark, the Output tab is where you can configure how the captured packet data is saved or displayed. It's primarily used when exporting or saving the captured network traffic (Figure 4.3).

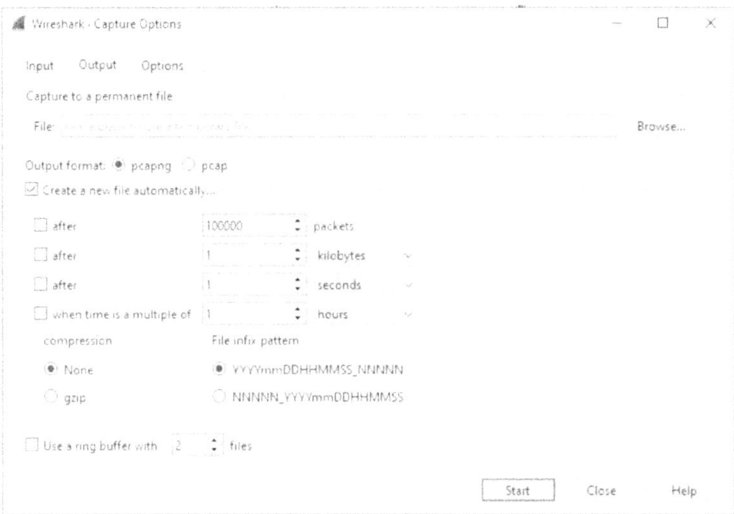

Figure 4.3 Wireshark "Capture Options" window (Output tab) showing settings for saving captured files, format, and compression.

Here's what the key features in the **Output** tab allow you to control:

1. *Capture to a permanent file*: It refers to the ability to continuously capture network traffic and save the captured packets to a file on your system without losing data, even if the capture session is interrupted or the application is closed.
2. *File format*: You can choose the format you want to save your capture (e.g., **pcap, pcapng,** or **csv**). The **pcap** format is the most common and is used by many network analysis tools. At the same time, **CSV** is useful if you want to open the data in a spreadsheet.
3. *File name*: You can specify the name and location of the file where the captured packets are saved. You can also configure Wireshark to automatically append a timestamp to the file name for sequential saving of capture files.
4. *Create a new file automatically*: If you want Wireshark to save captures in multiple files, you can set a size limit for each file. Once the limit is reached, Wireshark automatically starts a new capture file. This is useful for capturing large volumes of network traffic without losing data.

5. *Ring buffer*: Wireshark can create a ring buffer where older capture files are automatically overwritten once the buffer size limit is reached. This is helpful when you're continuously capturing data and want to avoid manually managing files.

Options tab

In Wireshark, name resolution and MAC address resolution are features that convert numerical addresses (like IP addresses or MAC addresses) into human-readable names. These features make it easier to analyze network traffic by displaying names instead of raw numbers. This can be done using the Options Tab (Figure 4.4). Let us learn about it.

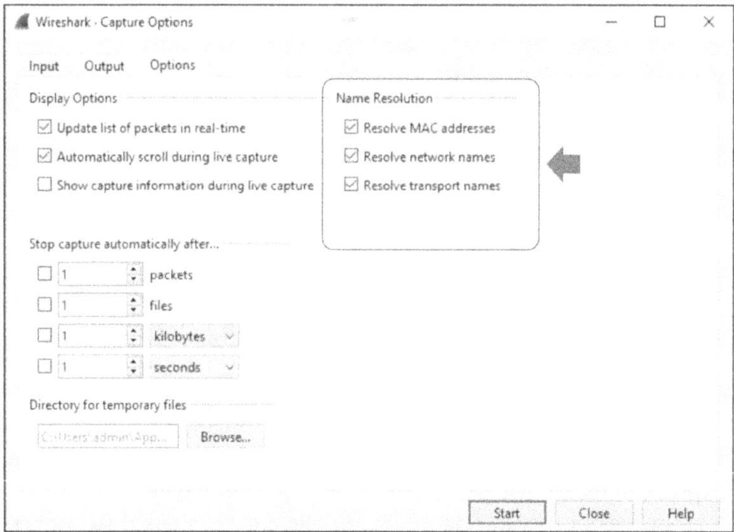

Figure 4.4 Wireshark "Capture Options" window (Options tab) showing display, name resolution, and stop capture settings.

1. *Resolve MAC addresses*: It converts raw MAC addresses (e.g., 00:1A:79:XX:XX:XX) into manufacturer names or device vendors (e.g., Apple Inc.). For example, a MAC address 00:1A:79:XX:XX:XX is resolved to Apple Inc. This helps identify which vendors' devices are involved in network traffic.
2. *Resolve network names*: It translates IP addresses (e.g., 192.168.1.1) into hostnames (e.g., *router.local* or *example.com*). It makes it easier to identify the source and destination devices or services in the network traffic. For example, instead of seeing 93.184.216.34, you might see example.com.

3. *Resolve transport names*: It maps port numbers (e.g., 80, 443, 22) to their corresponding protocol or service names (e.g., HTTP, HTTPS, SSH). For example, port 80 is displayed as HTTP, and port 443 is displayed as HTTPS. It provides context about the purpose of the traffic, such as identifying web browsing (HTTP/HTTPS) or file transfer (FTP).

CAPTURING TRAFFIC FROM WI-FI, BLUETOOTH, AND OTHER SOURCES

Capturing traffic from different sources like Wi-Fi and Bluetooth involves specific considerations due to the nature of these transmissions.

Capturing Wi-Fi traffic

1. Select the Wi-Fi adapter: Choose your wireless adapter from the list of network interfaces in Wireshark.
2. Enable monitor mode (if supported): This mode captures packets not explicitly addressed to your device, including management and control packets.
3. Start the capture: Monitor the wireless traffic as you would with a wired connection.

Capturing Bluetooth traffic

1. Setup Bluetooth monitoring: On some systems, like Linux, use tools like btmon alongside Wireshark to capture Bluetooth HCI (Host Controller Interface) packets.
2. Select Bluetooth interface in Wireshark: After setting up external tools, if necessary, select the Bluetooth interface from Wireshark and start capturing.

Considerations for other sources

Ensure compatibility: Make sure your network adapter supports capturing the specific type of traffic.

Legal and ethical considerations: Always ensure that you are authorized to capture network traffic, especially in networks not owned by you.

Mastering packet capturing with Wireshark opens up vast possibilities for network troubleshooting, security analysis, and understanding network behaviour.

USING FILTERS FOR EFFICIENT ANALYSIS

Filters are essential for isolating relevant data from the massive stream of packets captured during monitoring. There are two types of filters.

1) Capture filter

2) Display filter

CAPTURE FILTERS

Capture filters define which packets should be captured and saved to disk by Wireshark. These filters are applied in real time as the data flows into the capture tool, which can significantly reduce the amount of data written to the capture file. Capture filters are set before starting the packet capture. They are implemented at a low level, within Wireshark's capture engine or even deeper at the network driver level.

Key Characteristics:

- They operate on a lower level, often using syntax from libpcap/npcap.
- They are less flexible and complex than display filters because they can only test packet headers.
- They help in managing resources by reducing the amount of unnecessary data captured.

Note: Libpcap and npcap are packet capture libraries used for network monitoring and analysis, commonly used in tools like Wireshark. Libpcap is used on Unix-based systems. WinPcap (or its successor, Npcap) is used on Windows systems to enable packet capturing for network analysis applications.

Real-life scenario: Suppose you are monitoring a network and are only interested in HTTPS traffic. You could set a capture filter to only capture packets on TCP port 443, the default HTTPS port. The filter syntax might look like this: *tcp port 443*. It prevents all other data types from being captured, saves disk space, and reduces processing requirements.

Here, you can see how the Wireshark's screen is divided into various panes (Figure 4.5).

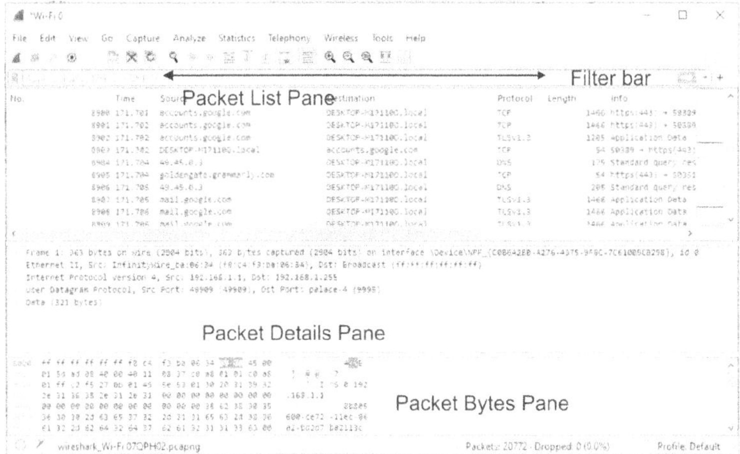

Figure 4.5 Wireshark capturing traffic on Wi-Fi 0, showing the packet list, details, and bytes panes.

Filter bar color indications

When you enter a filter (capture filter or display filter), the bar's color changes to green or red.

Green bar

Meaning: The filter syntax is correct.

Explanation: When you type a display filter into the filter bar, and it turns green, this indicates that the syntax of the filter is valid, and Wireshark recognizes it as a properly formatted filter. This means the filter effectively applies to the currently displayed or captured packet data.

Red bar

Meaning: The filter syntax is incorrect.

Explanation: If the filter bar turns red, it signifies a syntax error or unrecognized expression in your filter. It means Wireshark cannot parse the filter due to a typo, incorrect field name, or some other syntax issue, and no filtering action will be taken based on the current input.

Example of filter application

When you enter a filter like *ip.addr == 192.168.1.1*, the bar will:

- Turn green if the syntax is correct, indicating that the filter now highlights or hides packets based on whether their IP address field matches 192.168.1.1.
- Turn red if there is a mistake, such as a typo ip.adr == 192.168.1.1 (notice adr instead of addr), indicating an error that needs correction.

The immediate color feedback helps users quickly identify and correct mistakes in filter expressions, facilitating more efficient and accurate packet analysis. This feature is especially useful in complex filtering situations where multiple conditions are combined or specific protocol fields are targeted, helping to avoid the frustration of unresponsive or incorrect filter results.

Changing the layout of panes

If you want to change the layout of three windows, go to *Edit → Preferences*. Select the layout option from the left pane, and choose the layout that seems convenient (Figure 4.6).

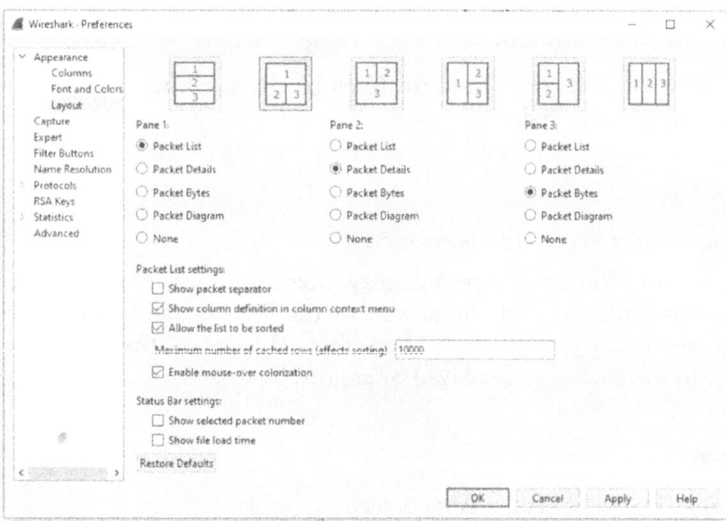

Figure 4.6 Wireshark "Preferences" window (Layout tab) configuring packet panes and display options.

THE THREE PANES

Wireshark, a powerful network protocol analyzer, displays packet data in a window divided into **three panes.** Each of these panes serves a specific function to help users inspect and analyze captured network traffic efficiently.

Here's an overview of the three panes, first in the table format (see Table 4.2), then in details.

Table 4.2 Comparison of Wireshark's three panes and their uses

Pane	*Description*	*Primary uses*
Packet list pane	It displays a summary of all captured packets in chronological order. It includes fields like packet number, time, source, destination, protocol, length, and info.	It provides an overview of all packets for quick navigation and filtering.
Packet details pane	It shows detailed, hierarchical information of a selected packet. Displays protocol layers such as Ethernet, IP, TCP/UDP, and application-level data.	Used to analyze packet contents layer by layer for troubleshooting or security analysis.
Packet bytes pane	It displays a selected packet's raw byte data in hexadecimal and ASCII formats.	Used for in-depth analysis, including payload inspection and identifying specific patterns or anomalies.

1. Packet list pane (top pane)

Purpose: This pane shows a list of all captured packets. Each row represents a single packet, and it displays key information about the packet, such as:

No.: Packet number (sequence in the capture).

Time: Timestamp indicating when the packet was captured (relative to the capture start time).

Source: The source IP address or MAC address.

Destination: The destination IP address or MAC address.

Protocol: The network protocol used (e.g., TCP, UDP, ICMP).

Length: The size of the packet.

Info: A brief description of the packet's contents or action (e.g., "HTTP request", "TCP handshake").

Usage: This pane helps users quickly scan through the captured traffic and find packets of interest based on their source, destination, protocol, or content.

The info column: In Wireshark, the Info column summarizes key details about each packet. The column can display TCP flags and other important information for TCP packets. Here are the common flags and details you might see in the Info column (see Table 4.3).

Table 4.3 Common flags and details in the Wireshark info column

Flag/detail	*Description*	*Significance*
SYN	A Synchronization flag is used to initiate a TCP connection	It indicates the start of a three-way handshake
ACK	An Acknowledgment flag confirms the receipt of data	It ensures reliable data delivery
FIN	A Finish flag signals the termination of a TCP connection	It marks the end of a connection
RST	The reset flag is used to terminate a connection immediately	Often indicates errors or abrupt termination
PSH	A push flag is used to instruct the receiver to process data immediately	Ensures real-time delivery of certain data
URG	An urgent flag indicates that the data in this segment should be prioritized	It is used in scenarios requiring urgent data processing
TCP retransmission	It Indicates a retransmission of a TCP segment	It can point to network congestion or packet loss
Duplicate ACK	A duplicate acknowledgment for the same packet	It may signal packet loss or network issues
Out-of-order	Indicates that a packet arrived out of the expected sequence	It may be caused by routing issues or network delay
Window size	Represents the amount of data the sender can receive without acknowledgment	Affects TCP throughput and flow control
Malformed packet	Indicates a packet that does not conform to protocol standards	It could be caused by corruption or attacks
ICMP echo (ping)	A request or reply message is needed to check connectivity	Used for basic network diagnostics
Keep-alive	A small packet is used to keep a connection active	It prevents idle connections from being closed
Zero window	Indicates that the receiver's buffer is full	This may cause delays in data transfer
Fast retransmission	Triggered by multiple duplicate ACKs	Used to quickly resend lost packets without waiting for a timeout
TCP spurious retransmission	Indicates retransmission that may not have been necessary	Can occur due to packet delay or misinterpretation

The TCP flags and details in Wireshark's Info column are invaluable tools for troubleshooting network issues and enhancing network security. Here's how each of these can be applied:

TROUBLESHOOTING NETWORK ISSUES

Connection establishment problems

[SYN], [SYN, ACK], [ACK]:

Used to identify whether the TCP three-way handshake completes successfully.

Example: If only [SYN] packets are visible without [SYN, ACK], it could indicate a server issue, firewall block, or network outage.

Connection termination

[FIN], [FIN, ACK], [RST]:

Analyzing these packets helps confirm if connections are being closed cleanly or abruptly.

Example: Frequent [RST] packets may indicate application errors or abrupt session drops.

Data transfer problems

[PSH, ACK], TCP segment:

It helps identify delayed or missing packets.

Example: If data transfer stalls, observing [PSH, ACK] can show whether the server pushed the data and whether the client acknowledged it.

Congestion and flow control

Zero window, keep-alive:

Detect flow control issues and idle connections.

Example: Zero Window packets suggest the receiver is overwhelmed, potentially indicating a need to optimize resource allocation.

Packet loss or reordering

Retransmissions, Out-of-order:

It highlights network reliability issues like dropped packets or misordered delivery.

Example: Repeated retransmissions may suggest congestion or faulty hardware.

NETWORK SECURITY

Detecting unauthorized connections

[SYN]: Excessive or unexpected [SYN] packets could signify port scanning or reconnaissance activity by an attacker.

Example: A spike in [SYN] packets on unused ports may indicate malicious probing.

Abnormal termination

[RST]: Frequent reset packets could indicate active attacks like session hijacking attempts.

Example: [RST] packets with mismatched source addresses may suggest spoofing.

Identifying data exfiltration

[PSH, ACK]: Monitoring [PSH] packets can help detect unauthorized data transfer.

Example: Large outbound [PSH, ACK] packets to unknown IPs may indicate that sensitive data is being sent out.

Replay or injection attacks

Out-of-order: Out-of-order packets may result from malicious injection into a session.

Example: These attacks can manifest as unusual packet behavior, helping detect attempts to overwhelm or disrupt services.

DoS and DDoS detection

Zero window: Excessive Zero Window packets may result from deliberate attempts to overload a server (DoS attack). A Zero Window Packet in networking refers to a specific TCP packet sent by a receiving device to the sender, indicating that the receiving device's buffer is full and cannot process more data. It is part of the TCP flow control mechanism, which ensures that data is transmitted at a rate the receiver can handle.

Example: Flooding a server with connections that immediately stall by sending Zero Window packets.

PROACTIVE MEASURES

- *Set alerts*: Wireshark allows you to filter and create alerts for flags such as [SYN] floods or [RST] spikes.
- *Baseline behavior*: Understanding standard traffic patterns helps distinguish legitimate activity from anomalies.
- *Capture filters*: Use capture filters to limit the data you collect, focusing only on potentially malicious activity. For example, if you want to capture TCP packets with the SYN flag using a capture filter (not a display filter), you can use:

2. Packet details pane (Middle Pane)

Purpose: The middle pane provides a detailed breakdown of the packet selected in the Packet List Pane. It shows the hierarchical structure of the packet's protocol layers:

1. **Frame information (Physical/Link Layer Metadata):**
   - General details about the captured packet as a whole.
   - Includes Layer 1 information:
     - Frame number.
     - Timestamp (when the packet was captured).
     - Packet size (captured size and on-the-wire size).
     - Protocols in the packet.

2. **Ethernet header (Data Link Layer):**
   - Includes Layer 2 information:
     - Source MAC Address.
     - Destination MAC Address.
     - EtherType (e.g., IPv4, IPv6, ARP).

3. **IP header (Network Layer):**
   - Layer 3 information:
     - Source IP Address.
     - Destination IP Address.
     - Protocol type (e.g., TCP, UDP, ICMP).
     - Time-to-Live (TTL).
     - Header checksum.

4. **TCP header (Transport Layer):**
   - Layer 4 information:
     - Source Port and Destination Port.
     - Sequence and acknowledgment numbers.

- TCP Flags (e.g., SYN, ACK, FIN).
- Window size.
- Header length and checksum

Usage: You can inspect each protocol layer in the Packet Details Pane by clicking on a packet in the Packet List Pane. Expanding different protocol layers reveals more granular information, helping with deep packet analysis.

About the rest of the layers

Layers 5–7 of the OSI model—Session, Presentation, and Application—are often combined in network analysis tools like Wireshark. These layers handle the establishment and management of sessions (Layer 5), data translation and encryption (Layer 6), and user-facing protocols like HTTP, DNS, and FTP (Layer 7). In Wireshark, they are represented by application-layer protocols, showing details such as HTTP requests, DNS queries, or TLS handshake data. If these layers are not visible, it may be due to encryption, no application payload in the packet, or unsupported protocol dissection. These layers are critical for understanding user-level communication in a network.

3. Packet bytes pane (bottom pane)

Purpose: This pane shows the selected packet's raw data in hexadecimal and *ASCII format*. The data is displayed in two sections:

- *Hexadecimal (left side)*: It shows the raw binary data of the packet in hexadecimal format.
- *ASCII (right side)*: The same data is converted into human-readable ASCII text.

Usage: The Packet Bytes Pane allows users to view the exact contents of the packet, which is particularly useful for inspecting non-text data (e.g., binary files, encryption) or understanding how specific protocols encode information.

Display filters

Display filters are used after the packets have been captured. They do not reduce the amount of data captured; instead, they filter the packets that have already been captured and are currently displayed in the Wireshark interface. Display filters are highly flexible and powerful, allowing for complex searches and fine-grained control over the visibility of packets in the capture file.

Key Characteristics:

- They operate within Wireshark after packets are captured
- They can test broader packet properties, including headers and payload content
- They allow users to change which packets are displayed without requiring a new capture

Real-life scenario: Imagine you've captured all traffic during a specific network event. Still, you're only interested in analyzing packets that contain DNS queries. You can apply a display filter to show only these packets: *dns*. Even though the capture contains all types of traffic, the display filter hides everything except DNS packets, simplifying your analysis.

STEPS TO APPLY DISPLAY FILTERS

Here are steps to apply display Filters (Figure 4.7):

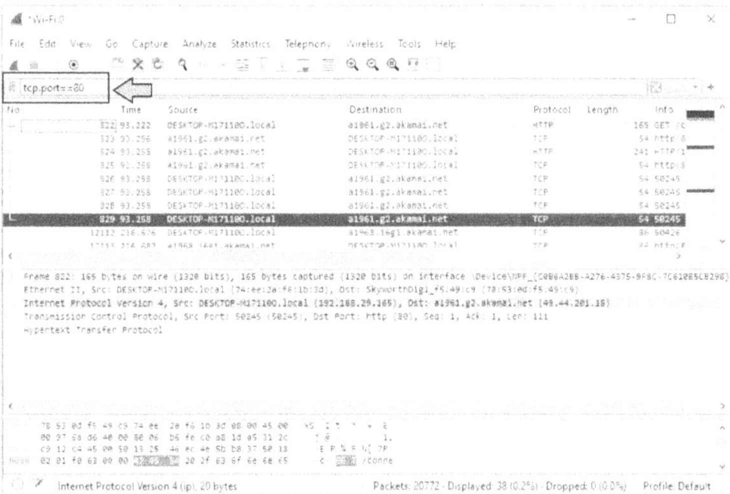

Figure 4.7 Wireshark capturing Wi-Fi 0 traffic with a filter (tcp.port==80), showing HTTP and TCP packets.

1. Start capturing traffic.
2. Access the filter bar: Located at the top of the Wireshark window.
3. Enter a filter expression: Type your filter criteria in the filter bar. For example, *tcp.port == 80* to view only TCP traffic over port 80 (it is a display filter).

4. Apply the filter: Press the Enter key to view the filtered results.

Working of this filter

The Wireshark display filter tcp.port == 80 captures all TCP packets where the source or destination port is 80, commonly used for HTTP traffic. This includes HTTP requests, responses, and any non-HTTP traffic that uses port 80. The filter focuses solely on the port number and does not verify the application-layer protocol. The http filter should be used instead to capture HTTP traffic strictly.

UNDERSTANDING BASIC NETWORK TRAFFIC

Understanding network traffic involves recognizing common protocols, analyzing packet flow, and identifying patterns or anomalies.

Key components to observe

In the context of analyzing network traffic using Wireshark, there are several key components to observe that can provide valuable insights into network behavior, potential issues, and security threats. Here's a brief explanation of these components:

Protocols used

Observing the protocols in use within network traffic is foundational. Protocols like TCP, UDP, HTTP, HTTPS, and others tell you about the nature of the traffic. For instance, TCP is often used for reliable communication, while UDP might be used for streaming or real-time communications. Knowing which protocols are in use can help you determine the purpose of the traffic and identify any unusual patterns.

Traffic direction

Analyzing the direction of traffic—incoming (download) or outgoing (upload)—is crucial for understanding how data flows through the network. This can help identify if a device sends out large amounts of data unexpectedly, which is a sign of a compromised system, or receives more data than usual, indicating a denial-of-service attack or other network abuse.

Check the Source and Destination IP addresses in the Packet List Pane.

- The packet likely represents upload traffic if the source is your device's IP and the destination is a server.
- The packet likely represents download traffic if the source is the server and your device's destination.

Frequency and size of packets

The packets' frequency and size can indicate the traffic volume and type on the network. A sudden increase in packet size or frequency might suggest a spike in activity, which could be benign (e.g., video streaming) or malicious (e.g., flood attacks). Large packets that regularly occur might be data transfers or backups. In contrast, small, frequent packets could be signaling or keep-alive messages. Monitoring these aspects can help in the early detection of anomalies and provide metrics for normal network behavior, establishing a baseline for future analysis.

The Length column gives a good high-level indication of packet size. Still, deeper analysis in the Packet Details Pane is needed to understand the actual data size.

By closely observing these key components, users can effectively utilize Wireshark to monitor network performance, ensure security, and troubleshoot issues more efficiently.

Note:

- **Protocols used:** Such as TCP, HTTP, UDP, and ICMP
- **Traffic direction:** Incoming (download) vs. outgoing (upload) traffic.
- **Frequency and size of packets:** Helps identify usage patterns and potential threats.

MOST COMMON CAPTURE FILTERS

Here are 10 of the most common capture filters, along with an explanation of what each does:

Here's a detailed look at ten primarily used Wireshark capture filters with real-life examples to illustrate how they might be used in practical network analysis or troubleshooting scenarios. These filters can help you focus on relevant traffic while capturing. For example, in a corporate network, you might use host [IP] to capture traffic to/from an important server or port 443 to focus on encrypted HTTPS traffic. You can combine these filters to capture more specific data.

1. *host [IP Address]*

- *Description*: Captures packets to or from a specific host (IP address).
- *Example*: host 192.168.1.1
- *Real-life scenario*: If you are troubleshooting network traffic to or from a particular server, this filter will help you capture only the relevant packets.

2. *src host [IP Address]*
   - *Description*: Captures packets where the source IP is a specific address.
   - *Example*: src host 192.168.1.5
   - *Real-life scenario*: Useful when you want to see traffic originating from a specific machine on your network.
3. *dst host [IP Address]*
   - *Description*: Captures packets where the destination IP is a specific address.
   - *Example*: dst host 192.168.1.10
   - *Real-life scenario*: If you're monitoring traffic destined for a particular server, use this filter.
4. *port [Port Number]*
   - *Description*: Captures packets on a specific port.
   - *Example*: port 80
   - *Real-life scenario*: Capturing HTTP traffic, commonly on port 80, to analyze web interactions.
5. *src port [Port Number]*
   - *Description*: Captures packets where the source port is a specific number.
   - *Example*: src port 22
   - *Real-life scenario*: Useful for capturing traffic originating from an SSH session (which uses port 22).
6. *dst port [Port Number]*
   - *Description*: Captures packets where the destination port is a specific number.
   - *Example*: dst port 443
   - *Real-life scenario*: Capturing HTTPS traffic, typically on port 443.
7. *tcp*
   - *Description*: Captures all TCP traffic.
   - *Example*: tcp
   - *Real-life scenario*: Useful when monitoring all TCP-based communications, such as web browsing, file transfers, or application protocols.
8. *icmp*
   - *Description*: Captures ICMP traffic (used for network diagnostics like ping).
   - *Example*: icmp

- *Real-life scenario*: Helpful when troubleshooting network reachability issues (e.g., using ping).

9. *net [Network address]*
   - *Description*: Captures packets to or from a specific subnet.
   - *Example*: net 192.168.1.0/24
   - *Real-life scenario*: Capturing traffic from an entire local network (e.g., to monitor internal communications).
10. *tcp port [Port Number]*
    - *Description*: Captures TCP packets on a specific port.
    - *Example*: tcp port 80
    - *Real-life scenario*: When you visit a website using HTTP, your browser communicates with the server over TCP port 80 to request and receive the webpage. Unlike HTTPS, this communication is unencrypted, making it less secure.

MOST COMMON DISPLAY FILTERS

Wireshark display filters are a powerful feature allowing users to narrow the packet view to display only those matching specific criteria. Here are fifteen familiar and easy-to-use display filters, their purposes and real-life examples. This is to practice the more complex cases we consider in the next chapter.

1. *ip.addr == 192.168.1.2*

Use: Filters all traffic to and from a specific IP address (Figure 4.8).

Figure 4.8 Wireshark capturing Wi-Fi 0 traffic with a filter (ip.addr==192.168.1.2), showing TLSv1.2 and TCP packets.

Example: Monitoring network traffic to and from a company's central file server to ensure no unauthorized access attempts.

2. *dns*

Use: Captures all DNS traffic to analyze queries and responses.

Example: Investigating slow internet issues by examining DNS traffic to see if there are delays in domain name resolution or frequent unresolved queries.

3. *tcp.port == 80 or tcp.port == 443*

Use: Monitors all HTTP and HTTPS traffic, essential for web data analysis.

Example: Analyzing web traffic during a marketing campaign to see the impact on server load and ensure SSL encryption is used for all secure transactions.

4. *ip.src == 192.168.0.0/16 and ip.dst == 192.168.0.0/16*

Use: Filters internal traffic within a specified IP range.

Example: Monitoring internal network traffic between departments for excessive or unusual data transfers that might indicate data leakage or misuse.

5. *ip.frag_offset > 0*

Use: Identifies fragmented IP packets.

Example: Diagnosing issues with VPN throughput by identifying fragmented packets, which can indicate MTU misconfigurations.

6. *tcp.length > 0*

Use: Filters TCP packets that contain a data payload.

Example: Focusing on non-empty TCP segments to analyze data throughput issues in application performance.

7. *udp*

Use: Captures all UDP traffic, including streaming and VoIP.

Example: Monitoring VoIP call quality by analyzing UDP traffic to detect packet loss and jitter issues.

8. *tcp.flags.push == 1*

Use: Identifies TCP packets with the PUSH flag set, indicating immediate data push to the receiving application. The OS or the network protocol stack typically does the PSH flag automatically, depending on the application and the nature of the data transfer. However, suppose you're working with raw sockets or a network tool like Scapy. In that case, you can manually set the PSH flag to ensure immediate data delivery.

Example: Troubleshooting latency in real-time applications, such as trading platforms, where timely data delivery is critical.

ADDING NEW COLUMNS

Sometimes, it becomes essential to add new columns, like to see the time elapsed since the previous packet in the capture.

Go to the menu: *Edit → Preferences* (on Windows/Linux) or *Wireshark → Preferences* (on macOS). Under *Appearance → Columns*, click the + button to add a new column. Name the column (e.g., "Time Elapsed"). Change the Field Type to "Custom". In the Field Name, enter *frame.time_delta*. This field shows the time elapsed since the previous packet in the capture (Figure 4.9).

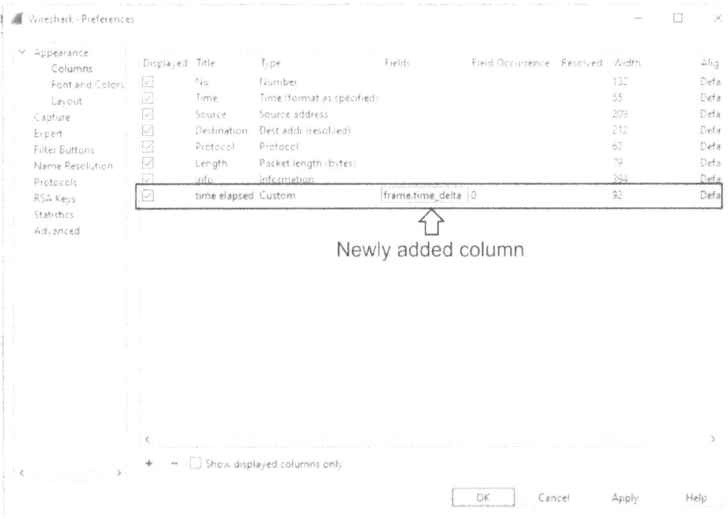

Figure 4.9 Wireshark "Preferences" window (Columns tab) configuring displayed columns, including a custom "time elapsed" column.

Here, you can see the latency in packet arrivals in the newly added *time elapsed* column (Figure 4.10).

Figure 4.10 Wireshark capturing Wi-Fi 0 traffic with a filter (tcp.flags.push==1), showing TLSv1.2 packets and time elapsed column.

The challenge remains to find which packet flag has been set and for which it is unset. For this, add a column with field type: *tcp.flags.push*. The *tcp .flags.push* field is a Boolean value indicating whether the **PSH** (Push) flag is set (i.e., **True/Set** or **False/Not Set**). Wireshark displays the string **set** when the flag is enabled and **not set** when the flag is disabled. **Set** means the PSH flag is enabled in the packet, and **Not set** means the flag is disabled (Figure 4.11).

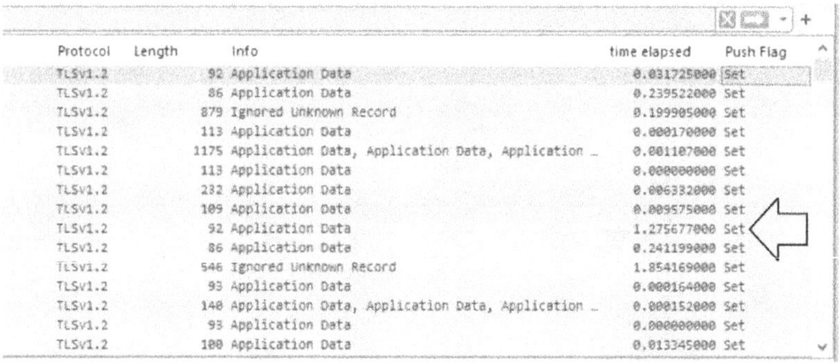

Figure 4.11 Wireshark capture of TLSv1.2 traffic with a "Push Flag" column, showing application data packets and time elapsed values. A black arrow highlights a specific packet with the Push Flag set.

9. tcp.flags.ack == 1 and ip.dst == 192.168.1.1

Use: Filters for ACK packets directed to a specific IP help track responses.

Example: Ensuring that all data requests to a critical internal application server are acknowledged promptly, helping diagnose potential disruptions or server issues.

10. *http.request.method == POST*

Use: Filters for HTTP POST requests, helpful for observing data submission activities like form uploads.

Example: Monitoring for excessive POST requests to a web server could indicate a brute-force attack attempting to guess passwords or submit forms repetitively.

11. *ip.addr == 192.168.1.1*

Use: Filters packets where the source or destination IP address matches the specified address.

Example: If you want to monitor all traffic to and from a server with the IP address 192.168.1.1 to troubleshoot connectivity issues or check for unauthorized access, you can use this filter (Figure 4.12).

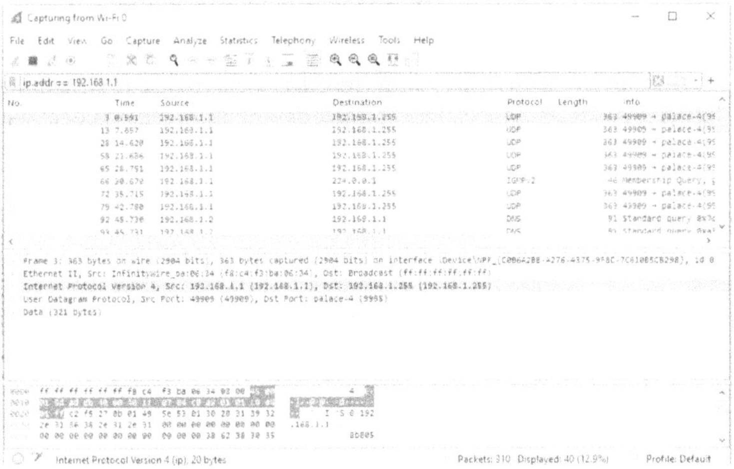

Figure 4.12 Wireshark capture of network traffic from Wi-Fi 0 filtered for IP 192.168.1.1, displaying UDP packets, an IGMPv2 membership query, DNS queries, detailed protocol information, and raw packet data.

12. *Filter*: *tcp.port == 443*

Use: Filter packets are where the TCP port (source or destination) matches the specified port commonly used for HTTPS traffic.

Example: To analyze secure web traffic or troubleshoot SSL/TLS issues on a website, you might filter on port 443 to isolate this traffic.

13. *Filter*: *udp*

Use: Displays all UDP packets.

Example: Useful in scenarios where you're troubleshooting VoIP issues or analyzing real-time streaming traffic, which often uses UDP for its lower overhead compared to TCP.

14. *dns*

Use: Filters all DNS (Domain Name System) traffic.

Example: If you suspect DNS issues are causing website resolution problems on your network, applying this filter would help you quickly isolate DNS queries and responses for further analysis.

15. *http.request.method == GET*

Use: Filters HTTP requests based on the method, specifically GET requests.

Example: When analyzing web traffic to understand the loading behavior of a website or to inspect which resources are being requested, filtering for GET requests can clarify what content is being fetched without modification.

Note: Wireshark's Capture and Display filters use different syntax and operate at different packet capturing and viewing stages.

APPLYING A SERIES OF DISPLAY FILTERS

In Wireshark, to apply a series of display filters sequentially, where each filter is based on the results of the previous filter, you can follow these steps:

1. Start by applying the first filter:
   a) Open Wireshark and start capturing packets, or open a saved packet capture file.
   b) In the display filter bar at the top, enter your first filter expression and press Enter to apply it.
2. Export the filtered packets:
   Once the first filter is applied and you have the desired packets, you can export these filtered packets to a new file. Go to *File → Export* Specified Packets. In the dialog box, choose to export displayed packets and save the file with a new name.
3. Open the exported file and apply the second filter:
   a) Open the newly created file in Wireshark.
   b) Now, apply your second filter in the display filter bar. This filters the already filtered packets from the first filter.

4. Repeat for additional filters:
   Repeat the process of exporting displayed packets and then apply the next filter on the new file for each subsequent filter.

5. Review final filtered packets:

After applying the last filter, review the packets that meet all your filtering criteria.
This method ensures that each filter is applied to an increasingly narrowed-down subset of packets, effectively implementing a chain of filters based on the results of the previous filters. This approach, however, involves multiple steps of exporting and opening files, which can be time-consuming but necessary to achieve sequential filtering without script automation.

CONCLUSION

Both types of filters are essential tools for anyone using Wireshark's arsenal for network diagnostics, security analysis, or educational purposes. Capture filters help manage the volume of data at the point of capture, making the process more manageable and efficient. Display filters provide flexibility in analysis, allowing detailed examination of traffic without the need for re-capture. Together, they enable powerful and efficient packet analysis and network troubleshooting.

MULTIPLE CHOICE QUESTIONS (MCQs)

1. What effect does the capture filter "host 192.168.1.1" have when set in Wireshark?
   A) It displays all packets to and from the IP address 192.168.1.1.
   B) It only captures packets to and from the IP address 192.168.1.1.
   C) It blocks all packets to and from the IP address 192.168.1.1.
   D) It highlights packets with the IP address 192.168.1.1.

   Answer: B

2. Using the display filter "tcp.port == 80 and ip.src == 10.0.0.1" in Wireshark will show you what type of traffic.
   A) All traffic from IP 10.0.0.1.
   B) Only HTTPS traffic to and from IP 10.0.0.1.
   C) HTTP traffic originating from IP 10.0.0.1.
   D) All TCP traffic passing through port 80.

   Answer: C

3. Which mode captures all wireless traffic within its range, not limited to the connected network?
   A) Managed Mode
   B) Switched Mode
   C) Monitor Mode
   D) Promiscuous Mode

Answer: C

4. What is the primary purpose of Promiscuous Mode in Wireshark?
   A) To capture traffic only directed at the device.
   B) To capture all packets within the device's network segment.
   C) To filter and display specific packet types.
   D) To decode encrypted traffic without keys.

Answer: B

5. What does the "tcp.port == 443" capture filter accomplish in Wireshark?
   A) Captures all UDP traffic on port 443.
   B) Displays all traffic over TCP port 443.
   C) Captures only HTTPS traffic over TCP port 443.
   D) Filters out all non-HTTPS traffic.

Answer: C

GLOSSARY

1. **Bluetooth Packet Capture:** This involves capturing packets transmitted over Bluetooth technology, which helps troubleshoot Bluetooth device communications.
2. **Capture Filters:** These filters are applied as data is captured and help reduce the volume of data by ignoring irrelevant packets.
3. **Display Filters:** Filters applied to data already captured to help sift through and display only the packets that meet specific criteria.
4. **Ethernet:** It is a standard technology used to connect computer and devices in a wired local area network (LAN).
5. **Filters:** Tools in Wireshark that allow users to include or exclude packets based on specific criteria, helping to focus on relevant data during analysis.
6. **MTU:** The Maximum Transmission Unit (MTU) is the largest amount of data that can be transmitted in a single packet on a network.
7. **Packet Capturing:** The process of intercepting and logging traffic that passes over a digital network or part of a network.
8. **Promiscuous Mode:** A mode in which a network card captures all traffic that passes through it, not just traffic addressed to it.

9. **TCP/IP (Transmission Control Protocol/Internet Protocol)**: The fundamental suite of protocols that supports the Internet and most private networks.
10. **UDP (User Datagram Protocol)**: A more straightforward, connectionless Internet protocol where error recovery services are not required, allowing data to be transferred before the receiving party provides an agreement.
11. **Wi-Fi Packet Capture**: Capturing data packets traversing a wireless network is crucial for analyzing and securing wireless communications.

Chapter 5

Utilizing display filters in Wireshark

INTRODUCTION

Display filters in Wireshark refine and narrow packet data during analysis. This lets users focus on specific traffic patterns or protocols of interest from captured data. Unlike capture filters (which apply before capturing data), display filters operate post-capture and offer powerful syntax for filtering based on fields, IP addresses, TCP flags, protocols, and more, making troubleshooting efficient.

Note: Display filters are applied to a dataset already captured to highlight specific packets or types of traffic.

MORE ON DISPLAY FILTERS

Display filters are used after the packets have been captured. They do not reduce the amount of data captured; instead, they filter the packets that have already been captured and are currently displayed in the Wireshark interface.

For example, imagine you've captured all traffic during a specific network event. Still, you're only interested in analyzing packets that contain DNS queries. You can apply a display filter to show only these packets: *dns*. Even though the capture contains all types of traffic, the display filter hides everything except DNS packets, simplifying your analysis.

Note: Capture filters cannot be directly used as display filters due to differences in syntax and capabilities. Similarly, display filters often reference details that are not accessible to capture filters.

TIPS FOR CRAFTING EFFECTIVE DISPLAY FILTERS

When crafting effective display filters in Wireshark, it's essential to understand how to specify the traffic you want to analyze precisely. Here are

DOI: 10.1201/9781003539261-5

some tips for creating effective display filters for various scenarios. Here are real-life scenarios for each of the tips on crafting effective display filters in Wireshark:

Use field names and operators

Scenario: Network access troubleshooting

A user reports that they are unable to access a specific server. The network administrator wants to verify that packets from the user's computer (192.168.1.4) are reaching the server.

To display packets involving 192.168.1.4 as either source or destination, use:

Filter: *ip.src == 192.168.1.4*

Usefulness: This filter shows all packets sent from the user's IP address, allowing the administrator to see if the packets are being sent correctly and if there are any responses from the server.

Combine filters with logical operators

Scenario: Identifying unauthorized access attempts

A security analyst suspects an unauthorized access attempt to a web server. They want to check if any packets from a specific IP (192.168.1.2) are attempting to connect to the server's HTTP port (80) (Figure 5.1).

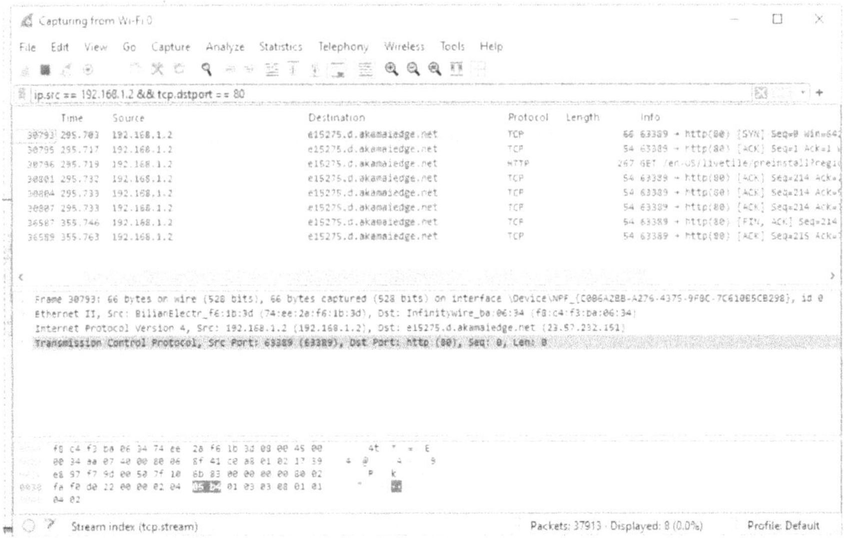

Figure 5.1 Wireshark capturing network traffic over Wi-Fi, showing TCP and HTTP details.

Filter: ip.src == 192.168.1.2 && tcp.dstport == 80

Usefulness: This filter is helpful in network security for monitoring or detecting unauthorized HTTP traffic originating from a particular IP address. If an IP address that shouldn't be sending traffic to a web server is doing so, it could indicate suspicious activity, like unauthorized access attempts or malware communicating with external web servers.

Filtering packets by IP ranges and content

Scenario: Monitoring internal subnet traffic

A network engineer must monitor all traffic from devices within a specific subnet (192.168.1.0/24) to ensure proper communication and detect anomalies.

Filter: ip.src == 192.168.1.0/24

Usefulness: Captures all packets from the subnet, which helps monitor internal communications and detect any unusual activities within the subnet.

Or

Use the *contains* keyword to search for packets containing specific data within fields.

Example: To find packets with HTTP headers containing the word "facebook" (Figure 5.2):

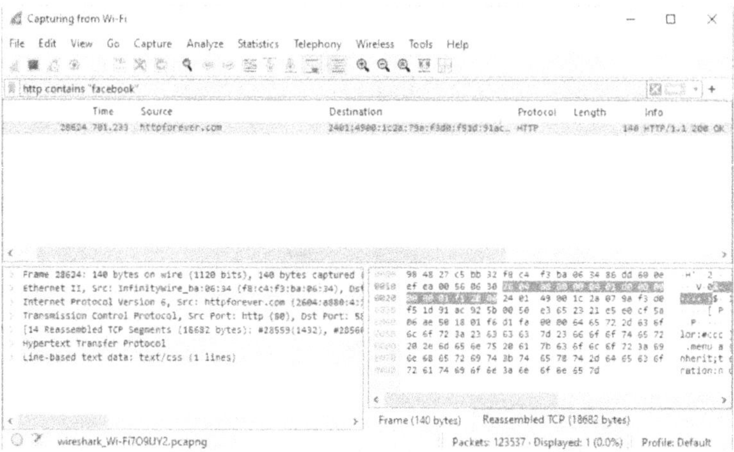

Figure 5.2 Wireshark filtering HTTP packets containing "facebook" in the response.

Filter: http contains facebook

Note: "facebook" in HTTP content doesn't always mean it's part of the user-visible text on the webpage. It might be present in the code for scripts, external links, or metadata. Use inspection tools to determine its exact role and location.

Filter by protocol

Scenario: HTTP traffic analysis

A web application developer is debugging issues with a website and needs to analyze only the HTTP traffic to understand what requests and responses are being exchanged

Filter: http

Usefulness: Shows only HTTP protocol traffic, allowing the developer to focus on web requests and responses without being distracted by other types of traffic (Figure 5.3).

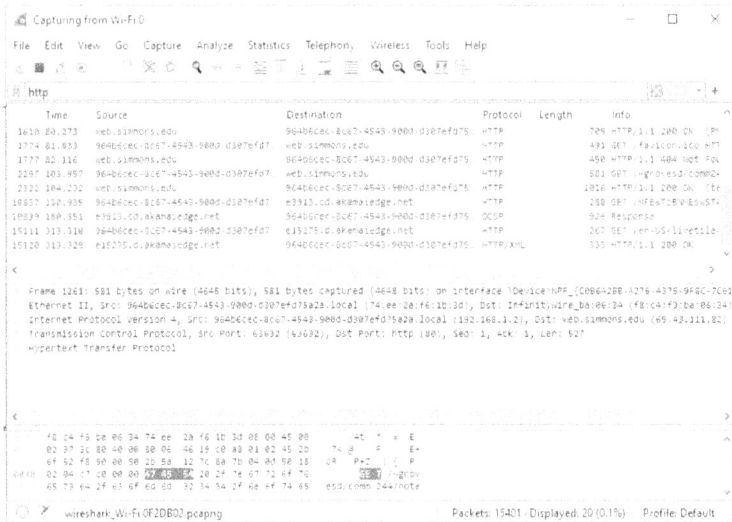

Figure 5.3 Wireshark filtering HTTP packets, showing GET requests and responses.

Filter by port numbers

Scenario: SSH connection monitoring

An IT security manager wants to monitor all SSH connections to a server for unauthorized access. SSH provides encrypted communication between a client and a remote device. This ensures that sensitive data like passwords and commands are secure. For example, a system administrator can log into a server from their laptop using SSH without exposing credentials to potential attackers.

Filter: tcp.dstport == 22

Usefulness: It displays only packets destined for port 22, typically used for SSH, allowing the security manager to monitor and analyze SSH traffic specifically.

Use comparison operators for ranges

Scenario: Detecting large file transfers

A network administrator wants to detect large file transfers over TCP, which may indicate unauthorized data exfiltration.

Filter: tcp.len > 1000

Usefulness: Filtering packets with a TCP payload size greater than 1000 bytes helps to identify large file transfers that could be unauthorized data transfers (Figure 5.4).

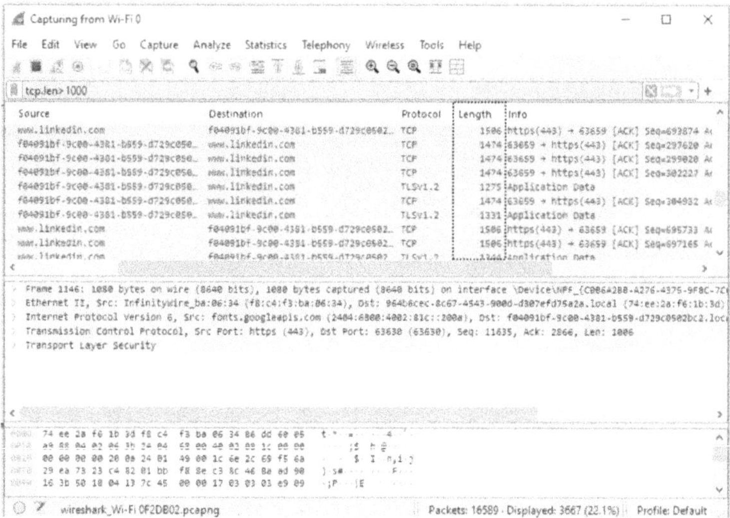

Figure 5.4 Wireshark filtering TCP packets with a length greater than 1000 bytes.

Match strings or text patterns

Scenario: Sensitive data leak detection

A cybersecurity analyst suspects that sensitive information is being leaked through HTTP requests. They want to find all packets containing the word "password" in the URL.

Filter: http.request.uri contains password

Usefulness: Displays HTTP requests where the URI contains the word "password," helping to identify potential data leaks involving sensitive information. Note that the display filter *http.request.uri* contains "password" works for **GET requests,** where parameters appear in the URL. However, for **POST**

requests or form submissions, you would need to analyze the body content using an appropriate filter, and decryption is required for HTTPS traffic.

Note: all URLs (addresses) are also URIs (identifiers), but not all are URLs. A URI can simply name something without showing where to find it.

Filter by MAC addresses

Scenario: Tracking device communication

A network administrator wants to monitor traffic from a critical device with a known MAC address (00:1A:2B:3C:4D:5E) to ensure it communicates properly.

eth.dst == 00:1A:2B:3C:4D:5E

Usefulness: Shows all packets destined for the specified MAC address, allowing the administrator to track the device's communication and detect any anomalies.

Filter by TCP/UDP flags

Scenario: Detecting port scanning

A security analyst wants to detect a possible port scanning attack on their network by identifying SYN packets commonly used in scanning attempts.

tcp.flags.syn == 1

Usefulness: Captures packets where the SYN flag is set, which helps detect the start of TCP connections and can indicate a port scan if multiple SYNs are detected without corresponding ACKs.

WHY MISSING ACKS INDICATE A PORT SCAN:

- When a system receives many SYN packets—either to different ports on the same device or to the same port across many devices—but never receives the final ACK to complete the connection, it suggests someone is scanning the network to find open ports or active machines without actually connecting to them.
- This is useful because legitimate clients usually initiate a full handshake, but in the case of an SYN scan, you only see SYN packets and potentially SYN-ACK responses. Still, there are no corresponding ACK packets to complete the connection.
- The purpose of this technique is to avoid establishing a full connection, which can help evade detection from intrusion detection systems (IDS) or firewalls. The absence of the final ACK is a key signature of a SYN scan.

Use exclusion filters

Scenario: Focusing on Non-HTTP traffic

A network engineer is interested in analyzing all non-HTTPS traffic to identify other services running on the network.

not tcp.port == 443

Usefulness: Analyse non-HTTPS traffic while ignoring encrypted web traffic. It helps investigate plaintext protocols like FTP or HTTP, ignoring secure connections (Figure 5.5).

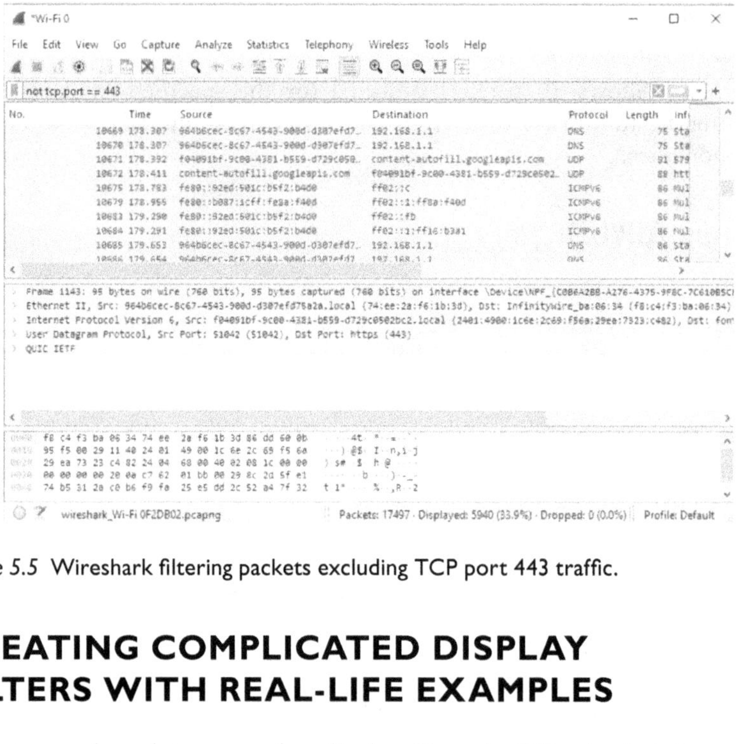

Figure 5.5 Wireshark filtering packets excluding TCP port 443 traffic.

CREATING COMPLICATED DISPLAY FILTERS WITH REAL-LIFE EXAMPLES

Creating and applying complex display filters in Wireshark is incredibly useful in real-life scenarios for network troubleshooting, security monitoring, and performance analysis. Below are examples of situations where each type of filter could be effectively used:

Combine multiple conditions

Scenario: Network troubleshooting

A network administrator suspects that a specific device (192.168.1.2.) is attempting to communicate with another device (192.168.1.10) using TCP, but the communication fails. To verify, the administrator uses:

ip.src == 192.168.1.2 and ip.dst == 192.168.1.10 and tcp

Usefulness: This filter helps identify whether packets are being sent correctly between these two IP addresses using TCP, aiding in troubleshooting connectivity issues (Figure 5.6).

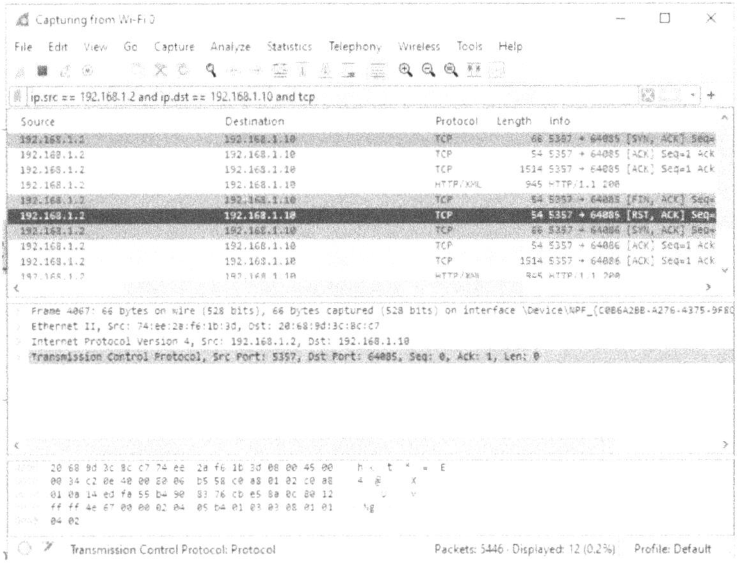

Figure 5.6 Wireshark filtering TCP traffic between two specific IP addresses.

Use parentheses for grouping

Scenario: Security incident investigation

An incident responder is analyzing network traffic for potential signs of a security breach. They suspect two internal IPs might be communicating over HTTP, which is unusual for internal traffic:

(ip.src == 192.168.1.4 or ip.src == 192.168.1.10) and tcp.dstport == 80

Usefulness: This filter identifies HTTP traffic from specific internal IPs, helping to investigate unauthorized web traffic that might indicate data exfiltration (Figure 5.7).

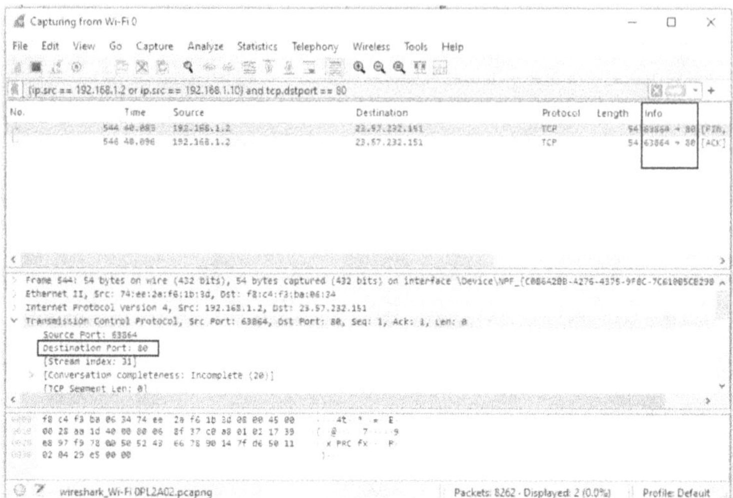

Figure 5.7 Wireshark filtering TCP traffic with destination port 80 from two IPs.

Filter by multiple protocol layers

Scenario: Malware analysis

A security analyst is investigating DNS traffic over UDP from a suspected compromised device (192.168.1.2). The filter is: *udp and dns and ip.src ==* *192.168.1.2*

Usefulness: This filter isolates DNS queries originating from the suspicious IP address, helping the analyst focus on identifying abnormal patterns. It could reveal potential attempts to communicate with a command-and-control (C2) server using techniques like DNS tunneling, where encoded data is hidden within DNS query payloads to exfiltrate information or establish covert channels (Figure 5.8).

This screenshot shows the starting point of such an investigation. While no tunneling is immediately apparent, the analyst would next look for signs like long/random subdomains, frequent queries, or encoded payloads.

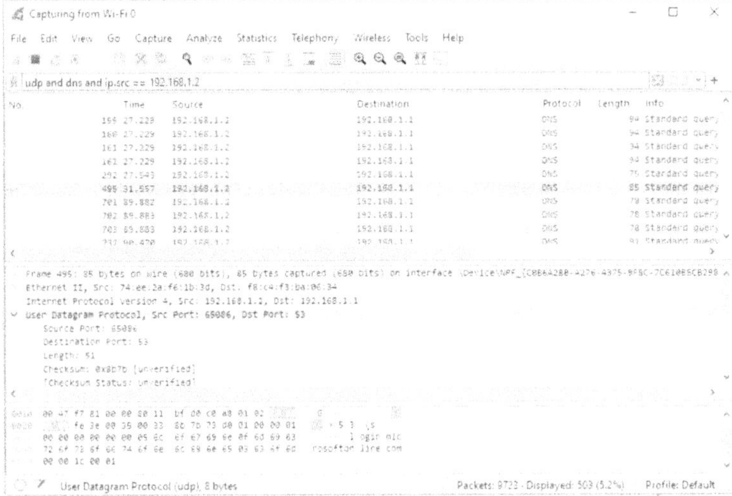

Figure 5.8 Wireshark filtering UDP and DNS packets from a specific IP source.

Note: DNS Tunneling is a technique that leverages the Domain Name System (DNS) protocol to transmit data covertly or bypass network restrictions. It involves embedding non-DNS traffic (such as HTTP, FTP, or even malicious data) into DNS queries and responses, using the DNS infrastructure as a "tunnel" for the data.

Signs of DNS tunneling in the middle pane

In the Packet Details Pane (Middle pane), DNS tunneling can be identified by analyzing the DNS query or response fields:

a. **Abnormally long query names**
   - DNS tunneling often involves unusually long domain names or subdomains.
   - Example:
     - Query: dGVzdC5kYXRhLmV4ZmlsdHJhdGVkLmNvbQ== .example.com
     - The long subdomain (dGVzdC5kYXRh…) may contain encoded or encrypted data (e.g., Base64).

b. **Frequent and repetitive queries**
   - Look for a high volume of DNS requests to the same or similar domains, especially with incremental subdomains.
   - Example:
     - 1.payload.example.com

- 2.payload.example.com
- 3.payload.example.com

Using subnet and port range expression

Scenario: Subnet monitoring

A network engineer wants to monitor all traffic from the 10.0.0.0/24 subnet, focusing on a specific range of source ports. The filter used can be:

ip.dst == 10.0.0.0/24 and tcp.srcport >= 1000 and tcp.srcport <= 2000

Usefulness: This filter allows the engineer to monitor traffic from a particular subnet and identify traffic patterns based on source port ranges, useful in performance monitoring or detecting abnormal traffic.

Combining filter expressions across fields

Scenario: **Web application analysis**

A web developer is debugging an application and needs to capture all HTTP GET requests containing a specific User-Agent string "Mozilla":

http.request.method == GET and http.user_agent contains Mozilla

Usefulness: This filter helps the developer isolate and analyze HTTP requests from a specific browser type or version, which is essential for troubleshooting browser-specific issues.

Filter by packet length or other numeric values

Scenario: **Performance bottleneck identification**

A network performance analyst is investigating large packet sizes that might be causing delays or performance issues:

frame.len > 1200

Usefulness: Identifies jumbo frames or large packets that could be causing issues on the network, helping pinpoint performance bottlenecks.

Note: The *frame.len* filter in Wireshark is not suitable for directly analyzing payload size because it includes the size of the entire frame, which consists of all protocol headers (like Ethernet, IP, and TCP/UDP) along with the actual payload data. However, it can provide an indirect hint if the payload size is expected to dominate the frame size.

Advanced string matching

Scenario: Data leak prevention

A security analyst suspects sensitive data is being sent out in HTTP requests. They use a filter to find URLs containing numbers (potentially account numbers or other sensitive data).

Remember that a URI (Uniform Resource Identifier) is a general term used to identify a resource by its location or name uniquely. A URL (Uniform Resource Locator) is a specific type of URI that identifies a resource and provides the means to locate and access it, usually including a protocol (e.g., http, ftp). For example, http://example.com/12345 is both a URI and a URL because it specifies where and how to access the resource, whereas urn:isbn:12345 is a URI that names the resource but doesn't indicate how to access it.

Filter: http.request.uri matches "/d+"

Usefulness: This filter helps identify URLs containing numeric patterns, which helps detect potential data leaks or unauthorized data transfers—for example, http://example.com/products/12345. Here, 12345 can be a product id, and other product details can be transferred to a third party.

Note: The pattern /d+ used in a Wireshark display filter represents a specific regular expression for matching URIs containing sequences of digits. It would not match: */abc* (no digits)

Negate specific conditions

Scenario: *Focus on Non-HTTP traffic*

A network administrator wants to analyze all TCP traffic except HTTP to identify other services running on the network:

Filter: tcp and not tcp.port == 80

Usefulness: This filter excludes HTTP traffic, allowing the administrator to analyze other TCP-based services, which can help identify rogue services or non-HTTP-related issues.

Use complex field matching

Scenario: Detect fragmented ping attacks

An incident response team is analyzing ICMP traffic for potential fragmentation, which might indicate a ping of death attack:

Filter: icmp.type == 8 and ip.flags.mf == 1

Usefulness: This filter detects fragmented ICMP Echo Requests, a standard method used in:

a. **Network diagnostics**: Fragmentation issues can lead to packet loss, delayed delivery, and reassembly problems at the destination. Identifying fragmented IP datagrams can help diagnose these issues.
b. **Performance monitoring**: Network professionals can ensure fragmented IP datagrams are properly reassembled without loss or delay by examining fragmented packets.

c. **Path MTU discovery:** Fragmentation can also indicate issues in Path MTU Discovery, where intermediate network devices might improperly handle fragmented packets

Fragmented IP datagrams refer to IP packets that have been divided into smaller parts, known as fragments, to fit within the Maximum Transmission Unit (MTU) of the network medium they are traveling over.

Note: MTU (Maximum Transmission Unit) is the largest size (in bytes) of a single packet in a network. A packet that exceeds this size must be broken into smaller fragments for transmission across the network.

d. **Types of fragmented attacks**

There is a need to monitor fragmented packets as there could be many types of fragmentation attacks.

- **Fragmentation attacks:** In a DDoS attack, attackers may send a flood of fragmented packets to exhaust the resources of a target. These fragmented packets can overwhelm devices like firewalls, Intrusion Detection Systems (IDS), and the victim's own network infrastructure.
- **IP fragmentation:** Since fragmented IP datagrams consume more processing power for reassembly, a DDoS attack that relies on fragmented packets can degrade the performance of the target's network devices and operating systems.
- **Anomalous fragmentation patterns:** Regular monitoring of fragmented IP datagrams can help identify irregular patterns or bursts of fragmented packets that do not align with typical network usage, potentially indicating a DDoS attack.

Note: Regularly monitor fragmented IP datagrams to detect unexpected spikes in fragmented traffic. These spikes can be indicative of a DDoS attack. Utilize network analytics to look for unusual patterns in traffic fragmentation, such as sudden increases in fragmented ICMP packets or TCP packets.

Breakdown of the filter:

1. icmp.type == 8:
   - *icmp.type* refers to the type field in the ICMP (Internet Control Message Protocol) header.
   - *icmp.type == 8* matches ICMP Echo Request (commonly known as "ping" requests). ICMP type 8 indicates a request to test connectivity to another device on the network.

2. ip.flags.mf == 1:
    - *ip.flags.mf* refers to the "More Fragments" bit in the IP header.
    - *ip.flags.mf == 1* matches IP packets where the More Fragments bit is set, indicating that this is not the last fragment of a fragmented IP datagram.

Chain filters for in-depth analysis

Scenario: Identify unauthorized SYN scans

A security team is monitoring for unauthorized network scanning activities. They want to find SYN packets from a specific subnet, excluding HTTP traffic:

tcp.flags.syn == 1 and ip.src == 10.0.0.0/24 and not http

Usefulness: Helps detect SYN scan activities from a particular subnet, which could indicate an unauthorized network scan or probing attempt.

Time-based filtering

Scenario: Event correlation

An analyst is trying to correlate network events with a specific incident reported within the first 10 seconds of the capture:

Filter: frame.time_relative <= 10

Usefulness: This filter isolates packets captured in the first 10 seconds, helping the analyst correlate and analyse traffic immediately preceding or following a known event, crucial for incident investigation and root cause analysis.

CASE STUDY: DETECTING A POTENTIAL EXFILTRATION ATTEMPT USING DNS AND HTTPS

Scenario: A case of data exfiltration

A cybersecurity analyst is investigating a potential data exfiltration attempt. The attacker might use DNS requests to communicate with a command-and-control server and exfiltrate data through encrypted HTTPS connections. The analyst suspects these activities happen within a specific time window and involve a particular internal subnet. The goal is to create a filter that identifies DNS queries with suspicious patterns and correlates them with outgoing HTTPS traffic to a suspicious external IP, all within a short time frame.

*(ip.src == 192.168.1.0/24 and dns and dns.qry.name matches ".*example.*" and frame.time_relative >= 5 and frame.time_relative <= 15) or*

(ip.src == 192.168.1.0/24 and ip.dst == 203.0.113.5 and tls.handshake.type == 1 and frame.time_relative >= 5 and frame.time_relative <= 15)

EXPLANATION

a. **Source IP within a specific subnet:**
   Both parts of the filter begin with *ip.src == 192.168.1.0/24*, focusing on traffic originating from the internal subnet 192.168.1.0/24.
b. **Suspicious DNS queries:**
   - *dns*: Filters for DNS traffic.
   - *dns.qry.name matches ".*example.*"*: Uses a regex pattern to match any DNS query names containing the string "example", which might indicate communication with a suspicious domain.
   - *frame.time_relative >= 5 and frame.time_relative <= 15*: Limits the DNS traffic to the time window between 5 and 15 seconds relative to the start of the capture, focusing on activity within this specific period.
c. **Outgoing HTTPS traffic to a suspicious IP:**
   - *ip.dst == 203.0.113.5*: Specifies a particular external IP address suspected to be used for data exfiltration.
   - *tls.handshake.type == 1*: Filters for TLS Client Hello messages, indicating the start of an HTTPS connection.
   - *frame.time_relative >= 5* and *frame.time_relative <= 15*: Applies the same time window as the DNS filter to correlate activities occurring within the same timeframe.
d. **Combining both conditions with or:**
   The "or" operator combines these two complex conditions, effectively capturing traffic that meets the DNS query pattern or the HTTPS connection criteria within the same time window.

Usefulness: This filter is highly specific and helpful in detecting potential exfiltration attempts by focusing on DNS queries to suspicious domains and correlating them with outgoing encrypted traffic to a suspicious IP address. Narrowing the focus to a particular subnet and time frame enables the analyst to pinpoint suspicious activities quickly, aiding in rapid threat detection and response.

CATEGORY-WISE CLASSIFICATION OF DISPLAY FILTERS

An expanded list of Wireshark display filters is divided into various categories. You can try these to expand your horizons.

Network monitoring and analysis

Filters designed for comprehensive monitoring and detailed analysis of network traffic:

1. *ip.addr == 192.168.1.10*: Filters all traffic involving the specific IP address.
2. *dns*: Captures all DNS traffic to analyse queries and responses.
3. *tcp.port == 80 or tcp.port == 443*: Monitors all HTTP and HTTPS traffic.
4. *ip.src == 192.168.0.0/16 and ip.dst == 192.168.0.0/16*: Filters internal network traffic within a specified subnet.
5. *ip.frag_offset > 0*: Identifies fragmented packets.
6. *tcp.length > 0*: Filters TCP packets that contain a data payload.
7. *udp*: Captures all UDP traffic, including streaming and VoIP.
8. *tcp.flags.push == 1: Identifies TCP packets with the PUSH flag set.*
9. *tcp.flags.ack == 1 and ip.dst == 192.168.1.1*: Filters for ACK packets directed to a specific IP, useful for tracking responses.
10. *http.request.method == POST*: Filters for HTTP POST requests help observe data submission activities like form uploads (Figure 5.9).

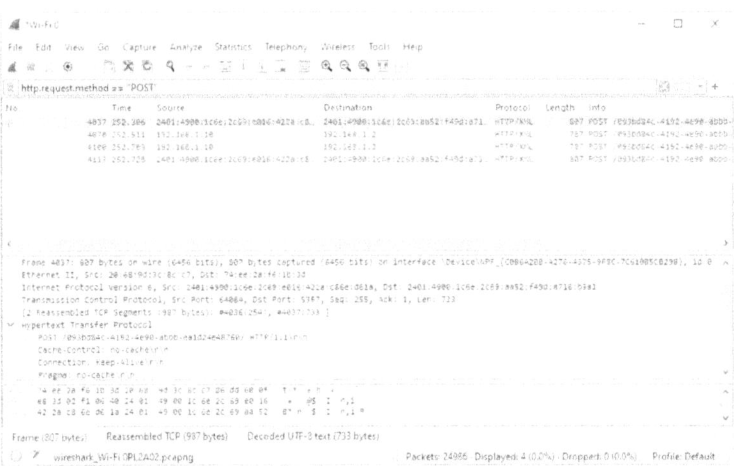

Figure 5.9 Wireshark filtering HTTP packets with POST requests.

Note: the payload in an HTTP POST request represents the data sent through a form or transmitted from the client to the server. It can include form fields, file content, or structured data like JSON or XML. In Wireshark, this data is visible in the bottom pane (Hex/ASCII view) as part of the captured HTTP traffic. To see the payload, you can use *Follow→Http stream*

Troubleshooting network issues

Filters useful for diagnosing and troubleshooting network performance or configuration issues:

1. *tcp.duplicate_ack*: Identifies duplicate TCP acknowledgments.
2. *tcp.analysis.retransmission*: Captures retransmitted packets.
3. *tcp.flags.reset == 1*: Highlights TCP resets.
4. *bootp.type == 2*: Monitors DHCP Offer messages to detect rogue DHCP servers.
5. *tcp.analysis.lost_segment*: Detects lost segments, which can indicate packet drops (Figure 5.10).

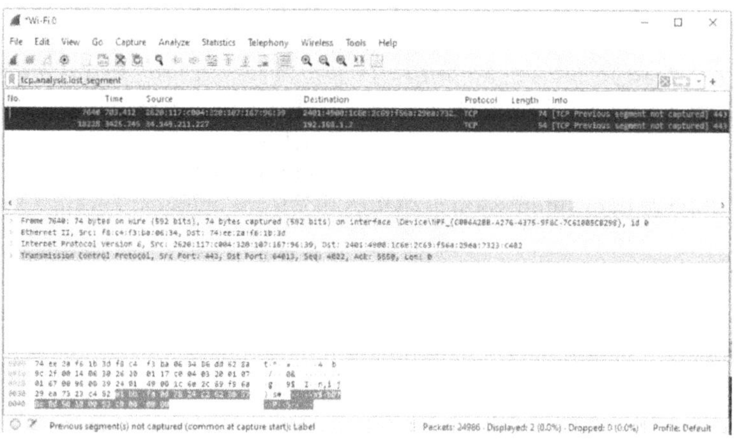

Figure 5.10 Wireshark filtering TCP packets with lost segments.

Note: In the colored version of the image, there is red text on a black background, indicating something is wrong with these packets, like lost segments.

DDoS attack detection

Filters for identifying potential DDoS attack patterns:

1. *tcp.flags.syn == 1 and tcp.flags.ack == 0*: is used to identify packets where a client is attempting to initiate a TCP connection (SYN) but has not yet received an acknowledgment from the server.
   - This filter is commonly used to detect SYN flood attacks where an attacker sends a large number of SYN requests to a server, overwhelming its resources and preventing legitimate clients from establishing connections.

- Network administrators can identify potential SYN flood attempts by filtering for SYN requests without corresponding ACKs.
- Network analysts might use this filter to troubleshoot connection issues, such as identifying sessions that are not being acknowledged by the server, which could indicate issues with server availability or TCP configuration (Figure 5.11).

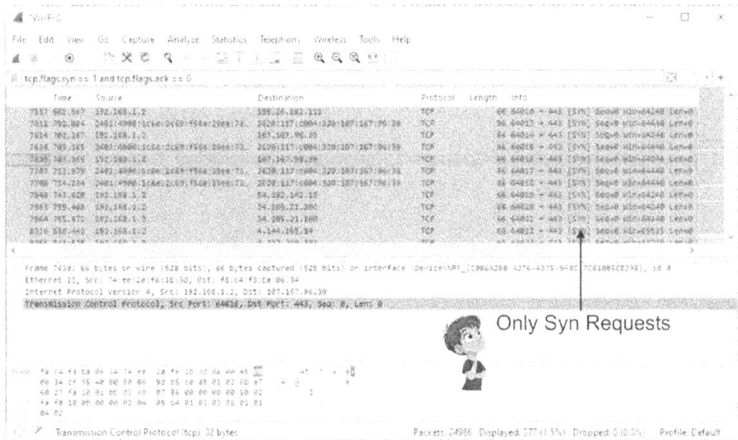

Figure 5.11 Wireshark filtering TCP packets with the SYN flag set but no ACK Note: to confirm an actual DDoS, you'd need to verify volume, duration, lack of responses, and possible intentional IP spoofing.

2. *icmp.type == 8*: Captures ICMP Echo Requests used in ping floods.
3. *http.response.code == 503*: Indicates that the HTTP response received from a server has a status code of 503 Service Unavailable. This status code means that the server can temporarily not handle the request. The server is temporarily overburdened or undergoing maintenance and cannot immediately respond to the client's request. Its Implications are:
   - The server might be experiencing high traffic, a temporary overload, or maintenance activities.
   - It could indicate issues like server hardware problems, excessive client requests, or misconfigurations.
4. *udp.length > 1400*: Detects huge UDP packets, often used in flooding attacks.

MITM and spoofing detection

Filters used to detect signs of Man-In-The-Middle (MITM) attacks or spoofing activities:

1. *arp.isgratuitous*: Identifies gratuitous ARP messages. In the context of networking and ARP (Address Resolution Protocol), a gratuitous ARP message is a special type of ARP packet sent voluntarily by a device to update other devices' ARP caches about its new IP address. It serves the following purposes:
   - Detect malicious ARP spoofing attacks where an attacker sends a gratuitous ARP to alter the ARP cache entries of nearby devices to redirect traffic.
   - Network administrators can spot unauthorized IP changes by monitoring for gratuitous ARP messages.
2. *ssl.handshake.cipher_suite == 0x0004 or ssl.handshake.cipher_suite == 0x0005*: Filters SSL/TLS sessions with weak cipher suites.

Note: Weak cipher suites refer to encryption algorithms and protocols considered insecure or inadequate by modern standards. These suites are vulnerable to attacks due to outdated cryptographic algorithms, poor key management, or weaknesses that can be exploited to compromise data security.

3. *eth.addr == ff:ff:ff:ff:ff:ff*: Captures frames sent to the Ethernet broadcast address. The **Ethernet broadcast address** is a special MAC (Media Access Control) address used in Ethernet networking to send a frame to all devices on a local network. It is represented as ff:ff:ff:ff:ff:ff in hexadecimal format. This can be useful for diagnosing network issues, understanding broadcast traffic, and monitoring ARP or DHCP requests.
4. *arp.opcode* == 2: Monitors for ARP replies, which can be part of ARP poisoning.

Security threats and vulnerabilities

Filters for detecting exploitation attempts and security threats:

1. *http.request.method == GET and http.request.uri contains "cmd.exe"*: Searches for command injection attempts.
2. *http.request.uri contains "login" and http.request.uri contains "password"*: Identifies URLs that might be harvesting credentials.
3. *ssl.alert_message.level* == 2: Monitors fatal SSL/TLS alerts.
4. *http.request.full_uri matches ".*\\.php\\?.*=http.*"*: Detects potential PHP Remote File Inclusion attempts.
5. *tcp.flags* & *0x29* == *0x29*: Identifies packets with suspicious flag combinations used in Xmas tree scans.

Explanation:

Flags in hexadecimal:

FIN: 0x01 (bit 0)

PSH: 0x08 (bit 3)

URG: 0x20 (bit 5)

Combined mask:

To check for FIN, PSH, and URG, their hexadecimal values are combined: 0x01 | 0x08 | 0x20 = 0x29.

Filter logic:

tcp.flags & 0x29: This checks if the bits for FIN, PSH, and URG are set in the tcp.flags field.

== *0x29*: Ensures that all three flags are set.

Note: Ensure you have packets with all three flags (FIN, PSH, URG) set; otherwise, no results appear.

ABOUT XMAS TREE SCAN

An Xmas tree scan is a network scan used by attackers to map out open ports and services on a target system. It gets its name from the pattern of TCP flags used in the packets, resembling a Christmas tree's lights (with FIN, PSH, and URG flags set).

This scan aims to send TCP packets to a target with these three flags set to probe for open ports. The scan elicits responses from the target system, indicating that specific ports are open and vulnerable.

These expanded and organized filters enable users to apply Wireshark more effectively for network monitoring, troubleshooting, attack detection, and security assessments.

CONCLUSION

The chapter effectively breaks down the complexities of network protocols and packet analysis, illustrating how display filters can be applied in real-world scenarios to streamline the troubleshooting process. The versatility of Wireshark's filtering capabilities is thoroughly explored, from simple protocol-based filters to more complex conditional statements involving logical, comparison, and string operators. Additionally, the discussion on the strategic use of wildcards, port numbers, and exclusion filters further enhances the reader's ability to tailor the analysis to precise requirements.

By mastering the techniques discussed in this chapter, network professionals can improve their workflow and ability to respond swiftly to network anomalies and security incidents.

MULTIPLE CHOICE QUESTIONS (MCQs)

1. What is the primary purpose of using display filters in Wireshark?
   A) To limit the amount of data captured during the capture process.
   B) To analyse and refine data that has already been captured.
   C) To save captured data to disk.
   D) To encrypt sensitive packet data.

Answer: B

2. Which display filter in Wireshark would you use to view all HTTP traffic that includes “facebook” in the payload?
   A) http.request.uri contains “facebook”
   B) http contains “facebook”
   C) tcp contains “facebook”
   D) ip contains “facebook”

Answer: B

3. If you want to identify large file transfers over the network, which Wireshark display filter would be most effective?
   A) tcp.len > 1000
   B) frame.len > 1000
   C) ip.len > 1000
   D) data.len > 1000

Answer: A

4. To monitor all SSH connections to a server using Wireshark, which display filter should you apply?
   A) tcp.dstport == 22
   B) tcp.srcport == 22
   C) ip.port == 22
   D) ssh.port == 22

Answer: A

5. How would you filter Wireshark to display only the DNS traffic from a specific IP address?
   A) ip.src == 192.168.1.2 && dns
   B) dns && ip.dst == 192.168.1.2
   C) dns && ip.addr == 192.168.1.2
   D) ip.src == 192.168.1.2 && udp.port == 53

Answer: A

GLOSSARY

1. **Capture Filters:** Filters that are set before capturing network traffic with Wireshark or any packet-sniffing tool. These filters prevent unwanted packets from being captured, thus reducing the amount of data that needs to be stored and analyzed.
2. **Comparison Operators:** Operators used in display filters to define conditions for filtering packets, such as >, <, >=, <=, ==, and !=, which help identify packets based on specific criteria like port numbers, packet sizes, or other protocol-specific fields.
3. **Display Filters:** Filters applied to a dataset already captured to highlight specific packets or types of traffic. They do not reduce the amount of data captured; instead, they filter the packets that have already been captured and are currently displayed in the Wireshark interface.
4. **Exclusion Filters:** A method used in Wireshark to explicitly exclude certain types of traffic from analysis, helping to narrow down the dataset to more relevant packets for specific investigations.
5. **Field Names:** In Wireshark, these are the names that access data from the packet layers. Each protocol has a set of field names defined for accessing its data within packets.
6. **Logical Operators:** These are used in Wireshark filters to combine multiple conditions. Examples include (*and, or not*), which help craft complex queries to precisely isolate the desired network traffic.
7. **MAC Addresses:** Unique identifiers assigned to network interfaces for communications on the physical network segment. Filters may specify MAC addresses to track packets from or to specific hardware devices.
8. **Port Numbers:** In networking, ports serve as communication endpoints for each specific application or service on a system. Display filters often use port numbers to isolate traffic intended for specific services.
9. **Protocol Filters:** Display filters specific to a protocol, such as http or tcp, used to isolate all traffic of a particular protocol type within the captured data.
10. **TCP/UDP Flags:** Specific bits are set in the header of TCP or UDP packets to control how the protocols communicate. Examples include SYN, ACK, or FIN flags in TCP, which are crucial for establishing or terminating sessions and ensuring reliable data transfer.
11. **Wildcards:** Used in display filters to match partial data strings within packets, including traffic that meets specific pattern criteria without needing an exact match.

Chapter 6

Analyzing protocols with Wireshark

INTRODUCTION

This chapter provides a detailed exploration of how to dissect common protocols such as TCP, UDP, and HTTP using Wireshark's protocol analysis features. Understanding these protocols and their representation in Wireshark is essential for effective network analysis and troubleshooting. Here, we explore the structure of these protocols, the typical issues that can be detected, and how to use Wireshark's tools to analyze them in real-world scenarios.

ANALYZING TCP (TRANSMISSION CONTROL PROTOCOL)

We need to understand and gain an overview of the TCP protocol structure to analyze TCP.

TCP (Transmission Control Protocol) is a core protocol of the Internet Protocol Suite that provides reliable, ordered, and error-checked delivery of a stream of bytes between applications running on hosts communicating via an IP network. The protocol ensures that data is transmitted accurately and in the correct sequence.

TCP FLAGS AND THEIR IMPORTANCE

TCP (Transmission Control Protocol) uses flags to manage communication between two devices and ensure reliable data transfer. These flags are 1-bit fields within the TCP header that indicate specific control messages, such as connection initiation, acknowledgment, or termination.

DOI: 10.1201/9781003539261-6

TCP flags are essential for:

- **Managing TCP connections** (establishment, data transfer, termination).
- **Error handling** (e.g., resetting connections).
- **Flow control** and ensuring proper sequencing of data packets.
- **Troubleshooting and analysis** (e.g., with Wireshark)

TCP FLAGS LIST AND THEIR FUNCTIONS

There are **9 TCP flags**, each with a unique purpose:

1. SYN (Synchronize)
   Purpose: Initiates a new connection between a client and server.
   Importance: Used in the **three-way handshake** to synchronize sequence numbers between two devices.
   Example: The first packet sent during connection setup contains the SYN flag.
2. ACK (Acknowledgement)
   Purpose: Confirms the receipt of data.
   Importance: TCP is a reliable protocol; every data segment (except the first SYN) must be acknowledged. The **ACK flag** ensures data integrity.
   Example: After receiving data, the receiver returns an ACK packet to the sender.

ABOUT TCP THREE-WAY HANDSHAKE

The **TCP three-way handshake** is a process used to establish a reliable connection between a client and server. It involves three steps: the client sends an SYN request, the server responds with SYN-ACK, and the client replies with ACK, confirming the connection is established (Figure 6.1).

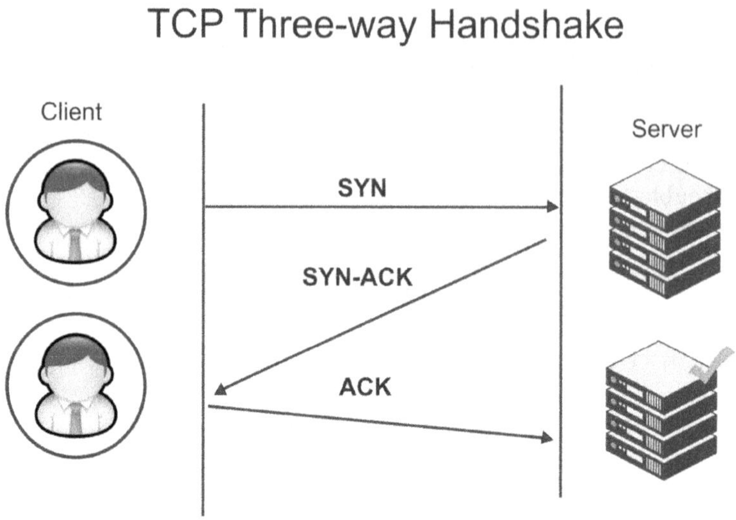

Figure 6.1 Diagram of TCP three-way handshake showing SYN, SYN-ACK, and ACK messages between client and server.

Note: The SYN (Synchronize Sequence Number) flag is used in the initial step of the handshake. It informs the server that the client wants to establish a connection and specifies the sequence number for subsequent segments.

3. FIN (Finish)
   Purpose: Indicates that a device wants to terminate the connection gracefully.
   Importance: Ensures that all remaining data is transmitted before closing the connection.
   Example: Both parties exchange FIN and ACK packets during connection termination.
4. RST (Reset)
   Purpose: Abruptly reset the connection.
   Importance: Used to handle **errors or unexpected issues,** like when a packet reaches a closed port.
   Example: A server might send an RST if it receives data for a non-existent connection.
5. PSH (Push)
   Purpose: Instruct the receiver to process the data immediately instead of buffering it.
   Importance: Ensures low-latency communication by delivering data to the application without delay.

Example: Used in real-time applications, like chat or voice over IP (VoIP).

6. URG (Urgent)
   Purpose: Marks data as urgent, requiring immediate attention.
   Importance: Ensures that time-sensitive data is processed before other queued data.
   Example: Rarely used today but was initially designed for scenarios where certain data must be prioritized (e.g., system alerts).
7. ECE (Explicit Congestion Notification Echo)
   Purpose: Indicates network congestion, allowing devices to react without packet loss.
   Importance: Helps control congestion by notifying the sender to slow down.
   Example: Seen in modern networks implementing congestion avoidance techniques.
8. CWR (Congestion Window Reduced)
   Purpose: Inform the receiver that the sender reduced its sending rate due to network congestion.
   Importance: Works alongside **ECE** for efficient congestion management.
9. NS (Nonce Sum)
   Purpose: Used for protection against certain types of packet duplication attacks.
   Importance: It ensures **reliability and security** by verifying whether retransmissions occur correctly.

IMPORTANCE OF TCP FLAGS

Let us see how these flags are combined for tasks like connection management, reliable data transmission, and error handling.

Connection management

SYN, ACK, and FIN manage **connection setup and termination** through a well-defined handshake process.

Reliable data transmission

ACK ensures that each segment is acknowledged, and retransmissions occur if necessary.

Error handling

RST allows quick correction of issues like packet delivery to a closed port.

Flow and congestion control

ECE and CWR enable efficient handling of network congestion.

Immediate data delivery

PSH and URG facilitate real-time communication, and data must be processed immediately.

HOW TCP FLAGS APPEAR IN WIRESHARK

Wireshark provides visibility into these flags for troubleshooting:

tcp.flags.syn == 1 → Shows all packets with SYN flags (connection attempts).
tcp.flags.rst == 1 → Displays reset packets (abrupt terminations).
tcp.flags.fin == 1 → Shows termination packets.

Note: TCP flags ensure **connection management, reliability, and error handling.** Using tools like Wireshark, network engineers can analyze these flags to diagnose connectivity issues and optimize communication processes.

TCP HEADER FIELDS

In Wireshark, the TCP header is dissected into several fields:

- **Source port and destination port:** Identify the sending and receiving applications
- **Sequence number:** Specifies the position of the first data byte in the segment relative to the data stream
- **Acknowledgment number:** Indicates the next expected byte from the other side of the communication
- **Flags:** Control bits that manage the state of the connection (e.g., SYN, ACK, FIN, RST)
- **Window size:** The amount of data that can be sent before an acknowledgment must be received

ANALYZING TCP STREAMS

Wireshark's "Follow TCP Stream" feature allows analysts to reconstruct the data exchange between two endpoints. This is useful for troubleshooting issues like incomplete file transfers, broken connections, or unauthorized data transmission.

Real-life scenario: Troubleshooting slow network performance

A network administrator notices slow performance on a network and suspects packet loss. By applying a display filter for a specific TCP session (*tcp .stream eq X*) and examining the sequence and acknowledgment numbers, the administrator can identify retransmissions, indicating packet loss or network congestion. The administrator can then further analyze the Time-Sequence Graph (Stevens) to visualize retransmissions and identify the root cause of the network slowdown.

TCP ANALYSIS IN WIRESHARK

Wireshark offers built-in tools for analyzing TCP streams:

1) **TCP analysis flags:** Wireshark marks packets with analysis flags, such as *tcp.analysis.retransmission,* to identify potential issues like packet loss. This filter identifies regular retransmissions in TCP traffic. A retransmission occurs when a TCP segment is sent again because the sender did not receive an acknowledgment (ACK) within the expected time frame. This typically indicates packet loss in the network (Figure 6.2).

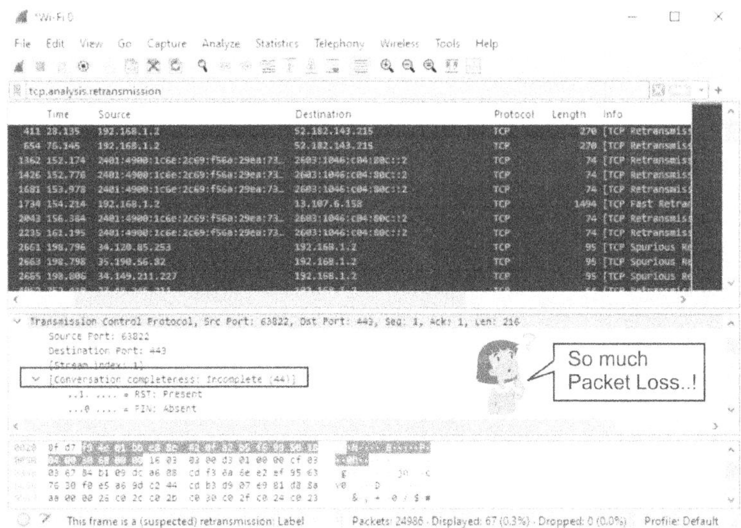

Figure 6.2 Wireshark capture of TCP retransmission packets with source, destination, protocol, and retransmission details.

Note: if you see the above image in color, it is red text over black, indicating packets with issues.

2) **Round trip time (RTT):** RTT can be analyzed using the *tcp.analysis.ack_rtt* filter to measure the time between sending a segment and receiving the corresponding acknowledgment. This helps diagnose latency issues.

What should the time elapsed be?

The expected time depends on your network's characteristics:

- **Local network (LAN):** RTT values are typically very low, often less than **1 millisecond (ms).**
- **Wide area network (WAN):** RTT values can range from **10 ms to 100 ms** or more, depending on the geographical distance and the connection quality.
- **High-latency networks:** RTT can be much higher for networks like satellite links, often exceeding **500 ms.**

Before moving further, as shown in the image below, add "tcp.analysis.ack_rtt" as a field by adding a column using *Edit→Preferences* and selecting the "column" option. Check Figure 6.3.

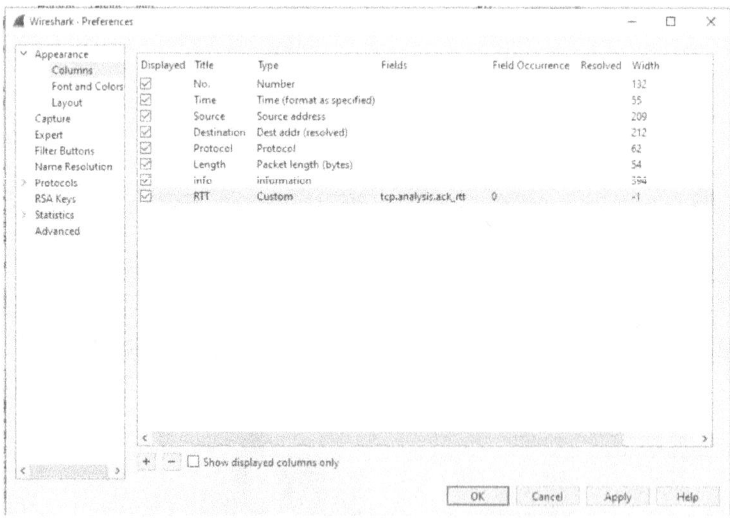

Figure 6.3 Wireshark preferences window (Columns tab) showing configurable columns like Time, Source, Destination, Protocol, and RTT.

In Figure 6.4, you can see values in the RTT column.

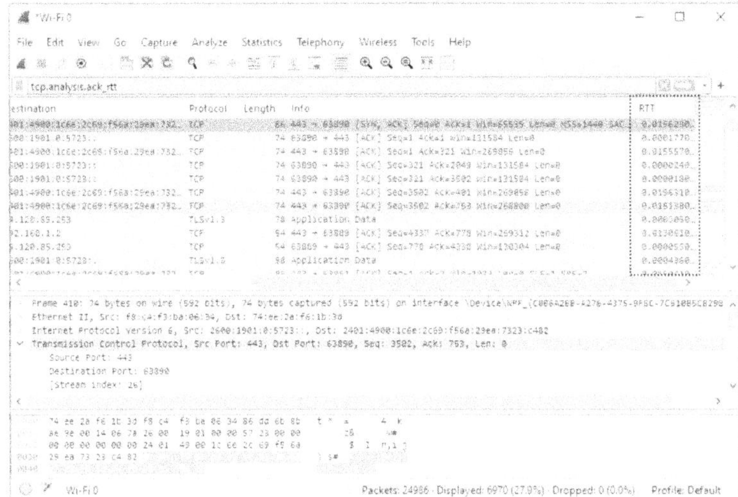

Figure 6.4 Wireshark capture of TCP acknowledgment round-trip time (RTT) with detailed packet and sequence number information.

Note: In the figure 6.4, you can also give the display filter as *tcp*

Scenario: Look for packet loss

A user downloads a large file (e.g., a software update or a video file) from a server over a network using the **Transmission Control Protocol (TCP)**. TCP ensures reliable data delivery by retransmitting lost or corrupted packets. However, the file download is slower than expected due to network issues.

1. Apply a filter to see **TCP retransmissions:**

   tcp.analysis.retransmission

2. Wireshark marks retransmissions as tcp.analysis.retransmission in the **Info** column. If you see many retransmissions, this could indicate packet loss in the network, causing slow communication between the client and server.

Note: High retransmissions often point to network congestion or issues with the quality of the network connection (e.g., faulty hardware or poor Wi-Fi signal). Addressing network congestion or replacing hardware might resolve the issue.

ANALYZING UDP (USER DATAGRAM PROTOCOL)

We need to understand and gain an overview of the UDP protocol structure to analyse UDP.

Overview of UDP protocol structure

UDP (User datagram protocol) is a simpler, connectionless protocol than TCP. It is used when low latency and reduced protocol overhead are more critical than reliability. UDP is commonly used for real-time applications like voice over IP (VoIP), online gaming, and video streaming.

UDP header fields

The UDP header in Wireshark consists of the following fields:

- **Source port and destination port:** Identify the sending and receiving applications.
- **Length:** Specifies the length of the UDP header and payload.
- **Checksum:** Provides error-checking for the header and data, although this is optional in IPv4.

Analyzing UDP streams

Unlike TCP, UDP does not have a stream reconstruction feature due to its connectionless nature. However, Wireshark provides several tools and features for analyzing UDP traffic, such as filtering by port numbers and inspecting payload content.

Relation between VOIP and UDP

Monitoring VoIP Traffic for Quality Issues is directly related to UDP (User Datagram Protocol) because VoIP (Voice over Internet Protocol) relies heavily on UDP for transmitting voice data over the network. Here's how they are connected:

1. VoIP and UDP: Connectionless communication
    - **UDP protocol:** VoIP applications often use UDP as the transport layer protocol because it is connectionless, so it does not require a handshake process (like TCP) to establish a connection before data transmission. This is crucial for real-time applications like VoIP, where speed and low latency are essential.

- **Low overhead:** UDP has a minimal protocol overhead because it lacks TCP's error recovery and retransmission features. This makes UDP ideal for VoIP, where maintaining a constant flow of voice packets is more important than ensuring every single packet arrives perfectly.

2. Real-time communication and UDP's suitability
   - **Real-time requirements:** VoIP requires the transmission of voice data in real-time. Any delay or interruption can lead to poor call quality, such as jitter, echo, or dropped calls. UDP's ability to send packets without establishing a connection or waiting for acknowledgments helps minimize delays.
   - **Tolerating packet loss:** VoIP applications are designed to tolerate some packet loss because human speech can still be understandable even if a few packets are lost. UDP's lack of error correction means it won't retransmit lost packets, which avoids further delays that would degrade the real-time voice experience.
3. Quality issues in VoIP and UDP traffic
   - **Jitter and latency:** Quality issues in VoIP often arise due to jitter (variability in packet arrival times) and latency (delay in packet delivery). Since UDP does not guarantee delivery order or timing, monitoring these parameters in UDP traffic is essential for assessing VoIP quality.
   - **Packet loss:** VoIP quality can also suffer from packet loss, where some voice packets do not reach their destination. Since UDP does not handle retransmissions, monitoring UDP traffic for packet loss helps identify issues that affect voice quality.
4. Monitoring VoIP Traffic with Wireshark
   - **Analyzing UDP traffic:** To monitor VoIP traffic quality, a network engineer uses Wireshark to capture UDP packets on ports typically associated with VoIP protocols, such as SIP (Session Initiation Protocol) on port 5060 and RTP (Real-Time Transport Protocol) on dynamic ports.

   Note: The Session Initiation Protocol (SIP) is a communication protocol used to establish, modify, and terminate multimedia communication sessions. These sessions can include voice calls, video calls, instant messaging, and other real-time communication over Internet Protocol (IP) networks. Dynamic ports are temporary network ports automatically assigned by a computer's operating system when an application requests any network communication. See Table 6.1 for the comparison.

Table 6.1 Dynamic ports vs. well-known ports

Aspect	*Dynamic ports*	*Well-known ports*
Port range	49152-65535 (default range)	0-1023
Usage	Temporary, client-side	Reserved for common services
Examples	Browsers, applications	HTTP (80), HTTPS (443)

Assessing QoS metrics: By analyzing captured UDP packets, the engineer can assess Quality of Service (QoS) metrics such as jitter, latency, and packet loss. Wireshark provides features like RTP stream analysis to evaluate these metrics, helping diagnose and resolve VoIP quality issues.

Note: Monitoring VoIP traffic for quality issues closely relates to analyzing UDP traffic. UDP is the transport protocol commonly used for VoIP due to its low latency and minimal overhead. Understanding and analyzing UDP traffic is essential for ensuring high-quality VoIP communications and quickly identifying and addressing any issues.

Real-life scenario: Monitoring VoIP traffic for quality issues

A company uses VoIP for internal communication, and users complain about poor call quality. By capturing UDP traffic on the network and applying a filter for the specific VoIP port (e.g., *udp.port == 5060* for SIP signaling), the network engineer can analyse the packets for jitter, delay, and packet loss, which are critical factors in VoIP quality. The engineer can use the RTP Streams feature in Wireshark to analyse Real-time Transport Protocol (RTP) streams, checking for packet loss and jitter that might degrade the call quality.

VoIP traffic is captured and analyzed to troubleshoot using Wireshark, focusing on **SIP** (Session Initiation Protocol) and **RTP** (Real-Time Transport Protocol) streams. Key areas of analysis include **jitter, packet loss,** and **latency,** which are identified as the root causes of poor call quality. Filters such as udp port 5060 for SIP traffic, rtp for voice streams, and *tcp.analysis.retransmission* for retransmissions are used to isolate the problem. After identifying high jitter, significant packet loss, and excessive latency, solutions like implementing **Quality of Service (QoS)** and upgrading network infrastructure are recommended to enhance VoIP performance.

UDP analysis in Wireshark

Checksum errors: UDP relies on checksums for error-checking. Wireshark flags packets with incorrect checksums using the *udp.checksum.bad* filter, helping analysts identify corrupted packets. A bad checksum indicates that the packet's data may have been corrupted during transmission.

The bad checksum information is displayed in the UDP layer within the Packet Details Pane:

Expand the User Datagram Protocol (UDP) section.

Look for a line labeled Checksum as: *Checksum: 0x1234 [incorrect] should be 0xabcd*

This means the packet was likely corrupted, as the transmitted Checksum does not match the calculated one.

- **Traffic patterns:** Analysts can use the *Statistics -> Conversations* feature to analyse UDP conversations and determine the amount of traffic generated by each source and destination. This can be useful for detecting unusual activity or potential security threats. Wireshark provides a detailed overview of conversations (sessions) between end-points. It can help you analyse issues like bad checksums or other anomalies by narrowing down problematic communication between specific IP addresses, ports, or protocols.

In this particular scenario, one question arises. How is VOIP related to UDP? Let us go into depth about this, as VOIP and UDP play an essential role in our lives. First of all, you should know that:

- VoIP relies on (Real-Time Transport Protocol): RTP to handle audio and video streams.
- RTP typically uses UDP as its transport layer protocol to ensure fast delivery of packets.

WHY UDP IS PREFERRED FOR VOIP

Low latency

VoIP requires packets to arrive quickly, even if some are lost. UDP does not wait for acknowledgments, avoiding delays.

Tolerance for packet loss

VoIP applications can handle minor packet loss using techniques like **jitter buffers** and **error concealment**, making reliable delivery (offered by TCP) unnecessary.

Efficient bandwidth usage

UDP has lower overhead than TCP because it doesn't maintain connection states or retransmit lost packets, saving bandwidth for real-time streams.

No retransmissions

Retransmissions in TCP can lead to delays and out-of-order packets, which are disruptive for real-time audio and video.

Real-life scenario: Detecting a DDoS attack

A sudden increase in UDP traffic might indicate a Distributed Denial-of-Service (DDoS) attack. Using Wireshark's conversations and endpoint statistics, a security analyst can identify the attack's top talkers and potential sources. By filtering the suspected malicious traffic (*udp.dstport == 123* for NTP amplification attacks, for example), the analyst can quickly confirm the presence of a DDoS attack and take steps to mitigate it.

To detect a UDP-based DDoS attack using Wireshark, begin by capturing traffic on the affected interface and focusing on UDP traffic. Analyze the volume of traffic using the *Statistics -> Summary* feature and look for sudden spikes. Investigate the source IPs and destination ports using *Statistics -> Conversations* and check for large numbers of unique source IPs targeting specific ports, often indicating a DDoS attack. Examine the packet sizes and identify any patterns of small requests followed by large responses, typical of amplification attacks like NTP or DNS floods. By analyzing traffic patterns, you can confirm the presence of a UDP flood attack and take appropriate steps to mitigate it, such as blocking malicious IP addresses or rate limiting the traffic.

High traffic volumes from a specific source with minimal requests and large responses indicate an amplification attack.

- You can see this by comparing **request** sizes and **response** sizes in the **Length** column of Wireshark.
- Large responses that overwhelm your server could indicate that your server is being used in an amplification DDoS attack.

ABOUT NTP AND NTP APPLICATION ATTACK

Network Time Protocol (NTP) is a protocol used to synchronize clocks across devices in a network to a precise time standard, typically Coordinated Universal Time (UTC). It operates over UDP port 123 and ensures that systems maintain accurate time, which is critical for functions like logging, authentication, and scheduling in distributed systems (Figure 6.5).

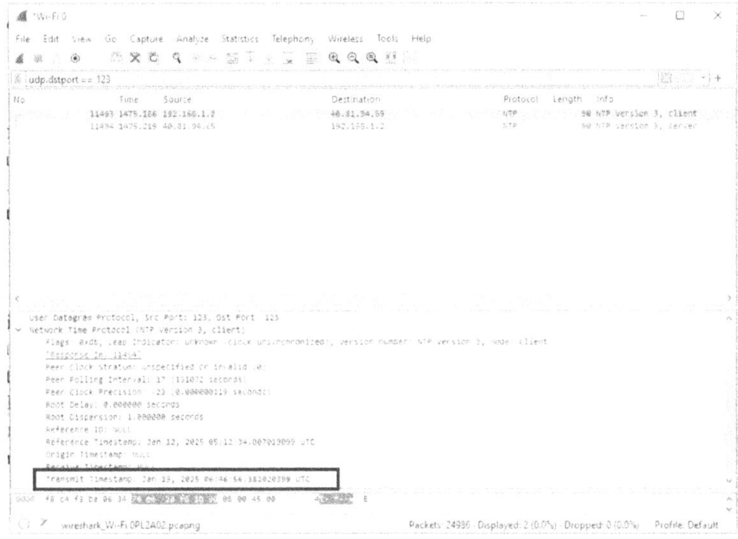

Figure 6.5 Wireshark capture of NTP traffic showing request and response between a client and server over UDP port 123.

However, NTP is vulnerable to NTP amplification attacks, a type of Distributed Denial-of-Service (DDoS) attack. In this attack, malicious actors exploit the protocol's monlist command, which returns an extensive list of the last clients that queried the server. By sending spoofed requests with a fake source IP (the target's IP), the attacker tricks the NTP server into sending significant responses to the target, amplifying the traffic. This can overwhelm the target's resources and cause service disruption. Proper server configuration, including disabling the monlist command and implementing rate limiting, is essential to mitigate such attacks.

Note: The monlist command is a diagnostic command used in older Network Time Protocol (NTP) versions. It retrieves a list of the last 600 clients connected to an NTP server. This command is part of the NTP server's monitoring functionality, hence the name "monlist" (short for "monitor list"). It is designed for debugging and monitoring purposes to provide insight into network activity related to the NTP server.

ANALYZING HTTP (HYPERTEXT TRANSFER PROTOCOL)

We need to understand and gain an overview of the TCP protocol structure to analyse TCP.

Overview of HTTP protocol structure

HTTP (Hypertext Transfer Protocol) is the foundation of data communication for the World Wide Web. It is an application-layer protocol for transmitting hypermedia documents, such as HTML. HTTP is designed for distributed, collaborative, and hypermedia information systems.

HTTP message structure

HTTP traffic in Wireshark is dissected into requests and responses:

- **HTTP requests:** Include methods like GET, POST, PUT, DELETE, and headers that define the request's parameters.
- **HTTP responses:** Include status codes (e.g., 200 OK, 404 Not Found) and headers that provide details about the response, such as content type and length.

HTTP analysis in Wireshark

This is how HTTP Analysis helps.

1. Identifying malicious domains or URLs: Many types of malware communicate with command-and-control (C&C) servers via HTTP. You can detect communication with known malicious domains or URLs by monitoring outgoing HTTP requests.
2. Detecting suspicious downloads: Malware often downloads additional payloads via HTTP. Analyzing file downloads or unexpected GET/POST requests can reveal malicious files being transferred over the network.
3. Analyzing user-agent strings: Malware often disguises its traffic by mimicking legitimate web browsers but may use suspicious or non-standard User-Agent strings. Analyzing these strings can help detect anomalous behavior.
4. Exfiltration of data: Malware may use HTTP to exfiltrate sensitive data. You can detect and prevent data breaches by monitoring unusual outbound POST requests containing large amounts of data.
5. Unusual HTTP headers: Anomalous or non-standard HTTP headers may indicate communication with malicious actors. For example, malware could disguise or encode malicious data using HTTP headers.

SCENARIO: MALWARE ANALYSIS THROUGH HTTP TRAFFIC

A network security team suspects that a machine on their network is infected with malware that communicates with a command-and-control server over

HTTP. The team can extract files downloaded over HTTP by analyzing the HTTP traffic and using the "Export Objects" feature. By examining these files, they can identify the malware and understand its behavior, enabling them to mitigate the threat and prevent future infections.

Situation 1: Detecting a malicious file download

1. **Capture HTTP traffic:** Use Wireshark to capture HTTP traffic on the network by applying the display filter *http*.
2. **Identify suspicious requests:** Monitor the HTTP requests for suspicious URLs or unusual domains. In the case of malware, you might see a request to download an executable or suspicious file format (e.g., .exe, .zip, .js) from an unknown source.
3. **Follow the HTTP stream:** Right-click on the suspicious HTTP request and select "Follow -> HTTP Stream". It shows you the entire HTTP conversation, allowing you to see the requested file and any additional data being transmitted.
4. **Check for abnormal user-agent strings:** Malware may use custom or non-standard User-Agent strings that differ from typical browsers. You can examine these in the HTTP headers to detect anomalies.

Situation 2: Detecting exfiltration attempts

An organization suspects that sensitive data is being leaked through HTTP. By capturing traffic and using a display filter (http.request.method == "POST"), a security analyst can focus on HTTP POST requests, which often carry sensitive data in the body. By examining the payload of these requests, the analyst can identify unauthorized data transfers and take necessary actions to prevent further leaks.

DO WE NEED TO ANALYSE HTTPS TOO?

Today, many malware families and threat actors use **encrypted HTTPS connections** to communicate with their command-and-control (C&C) servers, deliver payloads, and exfiltrate data. As a result, inspecting HTTP traffic alone might miss significant threats, as they hide within encrypted traffic.

While the content of HTTPS traffic is encrypted, you can still monitor unusual traffic patterns, such as:

- Frequent or significant outbound HTTPS connections.
- Connections to known malicious or uncommon IP addresses/domains.
- Abnormal or irregular data transfers (timing, size, frequency).

DDOS ATTACKS ON VARIOUS PROTOCOLS: TCP, UDP, AND HTTP

A **DDoS (Distributed Denial-of-Service) attack** overwhelms the target's resources—servers, bandwidth, or applications—making services unavailable. These attacks exploit specific weaknesses in protocols like **TCP**, **UDP**, and **HTTP**. Below is an overview of how these protocols are targeted and the relevant **Wireshark filters** to detect such attacks.

TCP-based DDoS attacks

TCP (Transmission Control Protocol) involves a three-way handshake to establish connections. Attackers exploit this to exhaust the server's resources by initiating many incomplete or malicious connections.

Common TCP attacks

Here are some common TCP attacks

- **SYN flood:** Sends many SYN packets without completing the handshake.
- **RST flood:** Bombards the target with reset packets to disrupt ongoing connections.
- **ACK flood:** Sends excessive ACK packets, consuming the server's processing power.

Impact:

- Resource exhaustion (CPU, memory) or connection slot depletion leads to service downtime.

UDP-based DDoS attacks

UDP (User Datagram Protocol) is connectionless, which makes it easy to spoof source IPs and flood the target with packets. Attackers also leverage **amplification attacks** by abusing open servers (like DNS or NTP) to generate massive traffic.

Common UDP attacks

- **UDP flood:** Sends large numbers of UDP packets to random ports, exhausting the target's processing power.
- **DNS/NTP amplification:** Amplifies small requests into large responses to overwhelm the target.

Impact:

- Bandwidth exhaustion or resource overload, resulting in disruption of network services.

Note: An NTP (Network Time Protocol) amplification attack is a Distributed Denial-of-Service (DDoS) attack. It leverages the Network Time Protocol to amplify the size of the attack traffic directed at the victim.

HTTP-BASED DDOS ATTACKS (LAYER 7)

HTTP is used for web-based services. Attackers flood websites with a high volume of legitimate-looking requests to exhaust application resources or perform slow request attacks to keep server threads occupied.

Common HTTP attacks

- **HTTP GET/POST flood:** Sends large volumes of GET or POST requests to the web server.
- **Slowloris attack:** Sends incomplete HTTP requests to keep connections open, exhausting server threads.

Impact:

- Application or website downtime, leading to lost business and degraded user experience. The Table 6.2 shows the attack mapping by protocol.

Table 6.2 Attack probability and impact

Protocol	*Attack type*	*Attack probability*	*Ease of execution*	*Impact*
TCP	SYN, ACK, RST Flood	Moderate	Medium	Resource exhaustion (memory, CPU)
UDP	Flood, amplification (DNS/NTP)	Very high	Easy	Bandwidth and resource exhaustion
HTTP	GET/POST flood, slowloris	High	Medium	Application downtime

WIRESHARK FILTERS TO DETECT DDOS ATTACKS

DDoS attacks target different protocols based on their unique vulnerabilities. UDP is the most commonly exploited due to its connectionless nature, while HTTP attacks focus on exhausting web servers at the application level. TCP attacks are slightly harder to execute but can cause significant damage by exhausting connection resources. Using Wireshark filters, network administrators can detect abnormal traffic patterns and take timely action to mitigate DDoS attacks. The Table 6.3 shows DDos and Traffic Anomalies using Wireshark filters.

Table 6.3 Protocol, Wireshark filters, purpose, and usage example

Protocol	*Wireshark filter*	*Purpose*	*Usage example*
TCP	tcp.flags.syn == 1 && tcp.flags.ack == 0	Detect SYN flood	Identifies SYN packets without corresponding ACKs
TCP	tcp.flags.rst == 1	Detect RST flood	Monitors excessive reset packets
TCP	tcp.flags.ack == 1	Detect ACK flood	Identifies high volumes of ACKs consuming resources
UDP	udp	General UDP traffic monitoring	Use to detect unexpected UDP traffic spikes
UDP	udp.length >= 512	Detect amplification attack	Finds large UDP packets, often used in DNS/NTP attacks
UDP	ip.src == <IP_ADDRESS> && udp	Track specific IP activity	Monitors UDP packets from a specific IP
HTTP	http.request.method == "GET"	Detect HTTP GET flood	Identifies excessive GET requests
HTTP	http.request.method == "POST"	Detect POST flood	Monitors POST requests, often used in application-layer attacks
HTTP	tcp && frame.time_delta < 0.01	Detect flood patterns	Finds bursts of TCP packets arriving too quickly

Note: After applying these filters, you might need to to deep inspect the packets.

CONCLUSION

This chapter provided a comprehensive understanding of analyzing and dissecting protocols such as TCP, UDP, and HTTP using Wireshark. By exploring these protocols' structure, features, and functionalities, readers gained insights into their roles in network communication and how to troubleshoot issues effectively. The chapter also highlighted the importance of using Wireshark's advanced tools, such as filters and stream analysis, to detect and mitigate common problems like packet loss, retransmissions, and network congestion.

Additionally, the chapter delved into the challenges posed by DDoS attacks on TCP, UDP, and HTTP protocols, providing practical guidance on detecting and addressing these threats using Wireshark. Through real-world scenarios and examples, it emphasized the critical role of protocol analysis in ensuring reliable network performance and security. With these skills, readers can confidently navigate complex network environments, optimize communication processes, and safeguard systems against emerging threats.

MULTIPLE CHOICE QUESTIONS (MCQs)

1. What does the ACK flag in a TCP header indicate?
   A) Start of a connection
   B) End of a connection
   C) Acknowledgment of received data
   D) Indication of congestion

Answer: C)

2. Why is UDP preferred for real-time applications like VoIP?
   A) It guarantees reliable data transfer
   B) It uses encryption
   C) It has low latency and minimal overhead
   D) It always retransmits lost packets

Answer: C)

3. What is the purpose of the RST flag in TCP?
   A) Establish a new connection
   B) Gracefully terminate a connection
   C) Abruptly reset a connection
   D) Acknowledge receipt of a packet

Answer: C)

4. Which filter would you use in Wireshark to identify retransmitted packets in a TCP stream?
   A) tcp.flags.fin == 1
   B) tcp.flags.syn == 1
   C) tcp.analysis.retransmission
   D) udp.port == 5060

Answer: C)

5. What is a key feature of QoS (Quality of Service) in networking?
   A) Encrypting traffic for security
   B) Managing traffic to reduce packet loss and latency
   C) Resending lost packets in real time
   D) Increasing bandwidth usage for faster performance

Answer: B)

GLOSSARY

1. **Checksum:** A method to detect errors in data by generating and comparing a calculated value.
2. **Command-and-Control Server (C&C):** A server used by attackers to control and manage infected systems remotely
3. **DDoS (Distributed Denial-of-Service) Attack:** Overloading a target with massive traffic to disrupt its services
4. **HTTP (Hypertext Transfer Protocol):** This protocol is used to transfer web pages and resources over the Internet
5. **HTTPS (HTTP Secure):** A secure version of HTTP that encrypts data for safe transmission.
6. **Latency:** Delay in data transmission from one point to another in a network.
7. **Packet Loss:** When data packets fail to reach their destination due to errors or network issues.
8. **QoS (Quality of Service):** Technology to manage traffic and ensure data delivery with minimal loss and delay.
9. **RTP (Real-Time Transport Protocol):** Protocol for real-time audio and video over IP networks.
10. **SIP (Session Initiation Protocol):** Protocol for starting and managing real-time multimedia communication sessions.
11. **TCP (Transmission Control Protocol):** A reliable protocol ensuring error-free data delivery over a network.
12. **Three-Way Handshake:** A three-step process (SYN, SYN-ACK, ACK) to establish a TCP connection
13. **UDP (User Datagram Protocol):** A simpler, faster protocol for applications needing low latency tolerating packet loss.
14. **User-Agent Strings:** Data in HTTP headers identifying the client software to the server.

Chapter 7

Network troubleshooting techniques using Wireshark

INTRODUCTION

Wireshark is one of the most widely used network analysis tools, enabling network specialists to capture, analyze, and resolve various network issues. Whether it's identifying performance bottlenecks or isolating security threats, Wireshark offers deep insights into the network's behavior. This chapter explores some common network problems, provides detailed scenarios, and walks through step-by-step solutions using Wireshark.

TROUBLESHOOTING NO INTERNET ACCESS

Here, we discuss the various Internet issues and how to troubleshoot them.

Problem: No Internet access

Scenario: A user complains that they cannot access the internet. They are connected to the local network but can't reach any websites.
Solution using Wireshark:

Follow the given steps:

For diagnosing why a user connected to the local network cannot access the internet, the following filters can be helpful in Wireshark

1. **Capture traffic from the affected device**
   Apply a filter to capture traffic from the user's device (Figure 7.1):
   ip.addr == <device_IP_address>

DOI: 10.1201/9781003539261-7

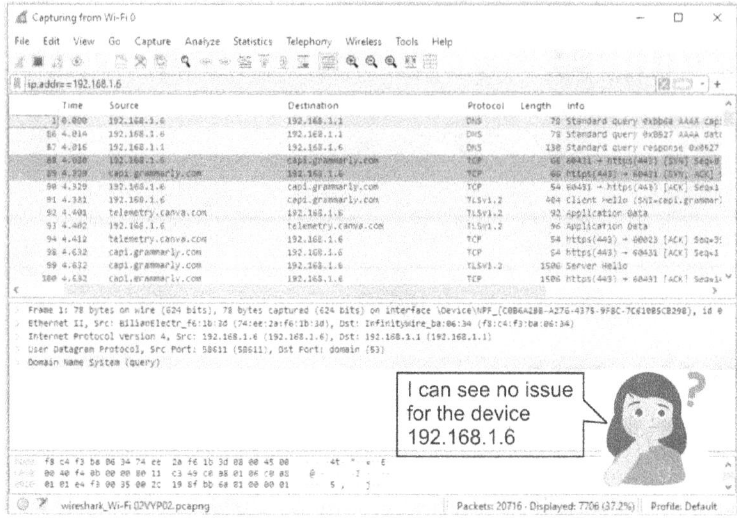

Figure 7.1 Wireshark capturing traffic from Wi-Fi 0 with a filter (ip.addr==192.168.1.6), showing DNS, TCP, and TLSv1.2 packets.

2. **Analyze DNS requests**

   dns.time in Wireshark signifies the duration taken for a DNS query to be sent and for the corresponding DNS response to be received. It represents the time interval between when the client sends a DNS request and when the DNS response is received.

   You can filter DNS traffic to see if DNS queries are being sent and responded to promptly. Also, add a column (Edit→Preferences) and Fields as *dns.time* as shown below. A good baseline is that most DNS lookups within a LAN should ideally be less than 5 milliseconds (Figure 7.2).

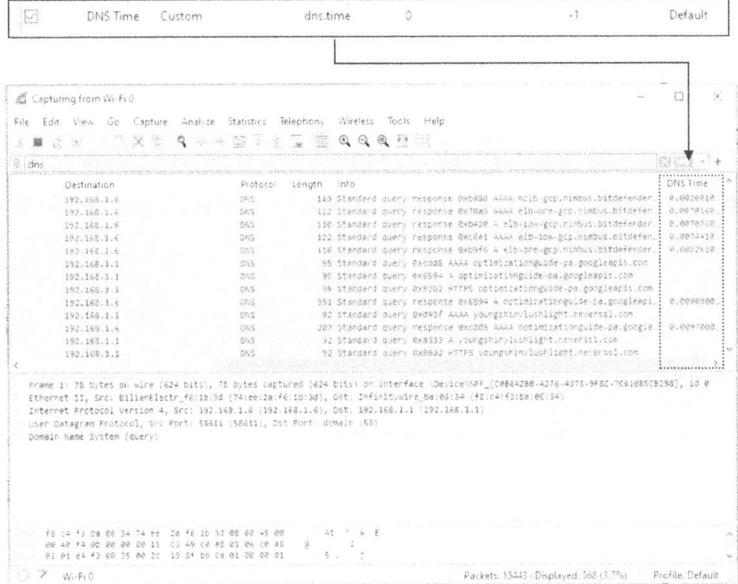

Figure 7.2 Wireshark capturing traffic with a custom DNS time column (dnstime) and displaying DNS queries and responses.

dns

Note: You can also set the filter as *dns.time>5* to check for all packets taking DNS time of more than 5 milliseconds.

3. **Ping test via ICMP**

   8.8.8.8 is a public DNS server operated by Google and is known for its high uptime and global availability.

   Use the ICMP filter to check if the device can ping 8.8.8.8. Pinging 8.8.8.8 is a simple and effective way to verify internet connectivity. If the ping succeeds, the network setup is fine. If it fails, you can investigate further with tools like *Tracert* or by examining your local network configuration (Figure 7.3).

```
C:\Users\admin>ping 192.168.1.7

Pinging 192.168.1.7 with 32 bytes of data:
Reply from 192.168.1.7: bytes=32 time=14ms TTL=128
Reply from 192.168.1.7: bytes=32 time=17ms TTL=128
Request timed out.
Reply from 192.168.1.7: bytes=32 time=140ms TTL=128

Ping statistics for 192.168.1.7:
    Packets: Sent = 4, Received = 3, Lost = 1 (25% loss),
Approximate round trip times in milli-seconds:
    Minimum = 14ms, Maximum = 140ms, Average = 57ms

C:\Users\admin>_
```

Figure 7.3 Using the Ping command in Windows at command prompt.

Or
You can also check by applying the filter:
ip.src == <ip_address_1> and ip.dst == <ip_address_2>

General solution

- Check the device's network configuration or gateway settings if ARP or DNS issues are detected.
- If DNS fails, switch to public DNS servers like Google DNS (8.8.8.8).

SLOW WEB APPLICATION ACCESS

Problem: Slow performance with a web application

Scenario: A web-based application that was previously fast is now very slow, and users are experiencing timeouts or long load times.

Solution using Wireshark:

Follow the given steps:

1. **Capture application traffic**
   Capture traffic between the user's device and the web server:
   ip.addr == <server_IP_address>
2. **Check for retransmissions**
   Use this filter to identify TCP retransmissions:
   tcp.analysis.retransmission
3. **Monitor RTT (Round trip time)**
   Use the RTT analysis filter to track packet delays:
   tcp.analysis.ack_rtt

4. **Visualize throughput**
   Use *Statistics→I/O Graphs* to monitor throughput and check for bandwidth limitations.

The **I/O Graph** in Wireshark visualizes network traffic over time, helping you analyze data flow patterns and detect anomalies. It plots metrics like packets, bytes, or bits per second. It supports multiple graph lines with customizable filters for specific protocols (e.g., ICMP, HTTP). You can adjust time intervals and Y-axis units to focus on key details. This tool is invaluable for identifying traffic spikes, troubleshooting bandwidth issues, detecting latency or packet loss, and monitoring protocol-specific behavior. The I/O Graph provides insights for effective network analysis by correlating graph trends with network events. Figure 7.4 shows an I/O graph.

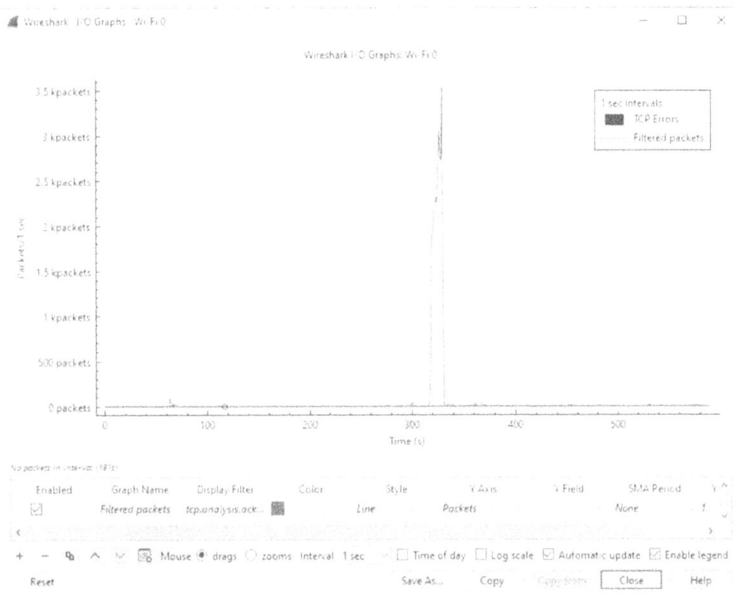

Figure 7.4 Wireshark I/O Graphs interface showing packet counts over time, highlighting TCP errors.

This graph from Wireshark's I/O Graph feature displays the packet rate (packets per second) over time for a network capture. It highlights two types of data: "TCP errors" and "filtered packets," with the latter being represented by the applied display filter tcp.analysis.ack_rtt. The Y-axis represents the packet rate, and the X-axis represents time in seconds. A spike in the graph around the 300-second mark indicates a significant increase in network activity, likely due to an error or high packet flow during that interval. This type of graph is useful for identifying periods of unusual activity, such as congestion, errors, or potential attacks.

General solution

- High retransmissions point to packet loss or network congestion. Check server and network paths.
- If high latency is observed, optimize routing or use a CDN.

DNS RESOLUTION ISSUES

Problem: Domain names not resolving

Scenario: Users report that they can access websites via IP addresses but not through domain names, indicating a DNS resolution issue.

Solution using *Wireshark*

Follow the given steps:

1. **Capture DNS traffic**
   Apply a filter to capture DNS traffic:
   dns
2. **Analyze DNS requests and responses**
   Check if DNS requests are being made and whether the server is returning proper responses.
3. **Check DNS response time**
   Use *Statistics -> Service Response Time* to analyze the response time of DNS servers.

General solution

If DNS requests are not responding, troubleshoot the DNS server or switch to a public DNS server like **8.8.8.8**.

Note: DNS not "resolving" refers to a situation where the Domain Name System (DNS) fails to translate a domain name (e.g., www.google.com) into its corresponding IP address (e.g., 142.250.190.78). When this happens, your computer or device cannot connect to the intended website or service, even though the site may be online and accessible from other networks.

HIGH BANDWIDTH USAGE

Problem: Network congestion due to high bandwidth usage

Scenario: The network is slow, and several users are experiencing poor performance. You suspect that some devices or applications are consuming too much bandwidth.

Solution using Wireshark:

Follow the given steps:

1. **Capture all network traffic**
   Use Wireshark to capture traffic across the affected network segment. Use this general capture filter:
   ip
2. **Analyze conversations**
   Go to *Statistics* -> *Conversations* to find the top talkers on the network. Do Sort by Bytes to identify devices or applications using the most bandwidth.
3. **Check protocol distribution**
   Use Protocol Hierarchy to view the breakdown of traffic by protocol, identifying whether streaming, file transfers, or other services are consuming bandwidth.

General solution

When a device or application consumes excessive bandwidth, it can degrade network performance for other users or critical services. To prevent this, network administrators can implement techniques such as Quality of Service (QoS) or Bandwidth Throttling. These methods help prioritize, limit, or allocate network resources efficiently to maintain consistent performance across the network. Table 7.1 compares both QoS and Bandwidth Throttling.

Table 7.1 QoS vs. Bandwidth Throttling

Aspect	*Quality of Service (QoS)*	*Bandwidth Throttling*
Purpose	Prioritize certain traffic based on importance	Limit bandwidth for specific devices/applications
Use case	Ensuring real-time services (VoIP, video calls) run smoothly	Preventing heavy apps (e.g., downloads) from overwhelming the network
Traffic type	Selectively prioritizes (VoIP > Downloads)	Reduces bandwidth for specific devices/apps
Dynamic adjustment	Can adjust priorities based on traffic conditions	Fixed bandwidth limits for specific cases
Example	Giving video calls higher priority over web traffic	Throttling streaming services to 2 Mbps

BROADCAST STORMS

Problem: Excessive broadcast traffic (broadcast storm). A broadcast storm is an overwhelming flood of broadcast traffic on a network, which can degrade or disable network performance.

Scenario: The network slows down periodically, and after investigation, it seems broadcast traffic is overwhelming the network.

Solution using Wireshark:

Follow the given steps:

1. **Capture broadcast traffic**
   Filter for broadcast traffic to capture only broadcast packets:
   eth.dst == ff:ff:ff:ff:ff:ff
   The Wireshark filter *eth.dst == ff:ff:ff:ff:ff:ff* captures Ethernet frames with the destination MAC address set to all ones, representing broadcast traffic sent to all devices in the local network. This filter is useful for analyzing protocols like ARP (IP-to-MAC resolution), DHCP (IP address assignment), and other network service discovery protocols. It helps troubleshoot issues like missing ARP replies, monitor DHCP communication, or diagnose excessive broadcast traffic that may indicate misconfigured devices or network loops. Broadcast traffic is confined to the local network (Layer 2) and does not traverse routers (Figure 7.5).

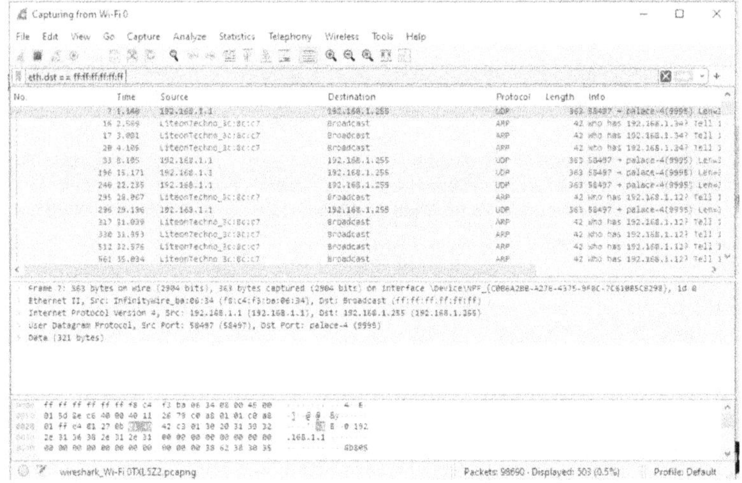

Figure 7.5 Wireshark capturing broadcast traffic (eth.dst == ff:ff:ff:ff:ff:ff), showing ARP and UDP packets.

2. **Check conversations**
   Go to *Statistics -> Conversations -> Ethernet* to see which devices are sending or receiving a large number of broadcast packets (Figure 7.6).

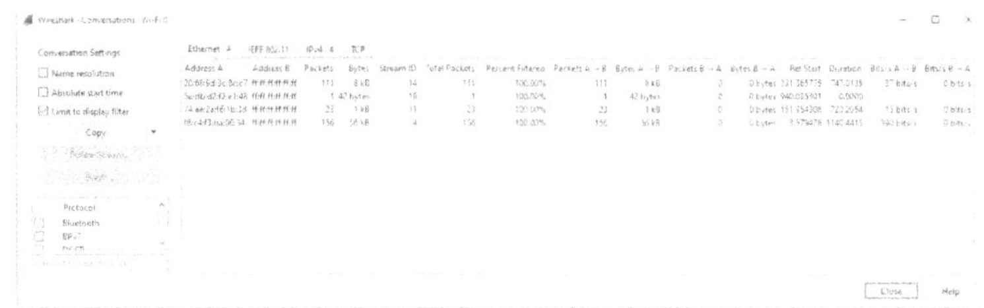

Figure 7.6 Wireshark Conversations interface displaying Ethernet and IPv4 conversation statistics.

This image displays the **Conversations** window in Wireshark, which summarizes network conversations based on selected protocols (e.g., Ethernet, IPv4, TCP). The table lists details of conversations, including source and destination addresses (Address A and Address B), packet counts, total bytes transferred, and stream IDs. It also breaks down data transferred in both directions (A→B and B→A). The settings on the left allow toggling options like name resolution, absolute start time, or applying filters. This view is typically used to analyze traffic patterns, identify high-traffic streams, or diagnose communication issues between devices.

3. **Look for loops**
   Capture **Spanning Tree Protocol (STP)** packets to check if loops are forming due to improper switch configuration:
   stp

General solution

- If a specific device generates excessive broadcast traffic, isolate it and check its configuration.
- Enable **Spanning Tree Protocol (STP)** on switches. The Spanning Tree Protocol (STP) is a network protocol used in Ethernet networks to prevent loops that could occur when there are multiple active paths between switches. STP ensures that only one logical path exists between two devices, eliminating the risk of broadcast storms and network failures caused by redundant links.

Note: STP prevents layer 2 loops by placing redundant ports in a blocking state. These extra links act as a backup that can enter a forwarding state if an active interface fails.

VLAN MISCONFIGURATION

Problem: VLAN tagging issues.

A VLAN (Virtual Local Area Network) is a logical grouping of devices on a network that appear to be on the same physical network, even if they are physically distributed across different switches. VLANs allow network administrators to segregate traffic within a larger network, improving security, performance, and manageability by creating smaller broadcast domains.

Note: VLAN tagging is a process where a VLAN ID is added to the header of an Ethernet frame to identify which VLAN the packet belongs to. It allows multiple VLANs to share the same physical network infrastructure (such as switches or routers) while logically separating their traffic.

Scenario: Devices on different VLANs cannot communicate with each other, even though they should. This could be due to VLAN misconfiguration.

Solution using Wireshark:

Follow the given steps:

1. **Capture VLAN traffic**
   Apply a filter to capture VLAN-tagged traffic:
   vlan
2. **Analyze VLAN tags**
   Check the **VLAN tags** in the packet details to ensure that traffic is being tagged with the correct VLAN ID.
3. **Look for incorrect VLAN IDs**
   If communication is failing, check for mismatched VLAN IDs between the source and destination.

General solution

- Correct VLAN assignments on switches.
- Ensure that the proper VLANs are allowed on trunk ports and that devices are correctly assigned to the correct VLANs.

TCP WINDOW SIZE AND FLOW CONTROL ISSUES

Problem: Slow Throughput Due to TCP Window Size Issues. Remember, the TCP window size refers to the amount of data (in bytes) a sender can send without requiring an acknowledgment from the receiver. It plays a critical role in flow control and network performance by regulating the amount of unacknowledged data allowed on the network at any given time.

Scenario: A file transfer between two devices is extremely slow, even though the network connection appears stable.

Solution Using Wireshark:

Follow the given steps:

1. **Capture TCP traffic**
   Apply a filter to capture the relevant TCP traffic:
   tcp
2. **Analyze TCP window size**
   - Check the *TCP window size* field in the packet details. A small window size can cause a bottleneck in data transmission.
   - Look for *Window Full* messages, indicating the receiver's buffer is full.
3. **Check for zero window conditions**
   Filter for zero window size (Figure 7.7):

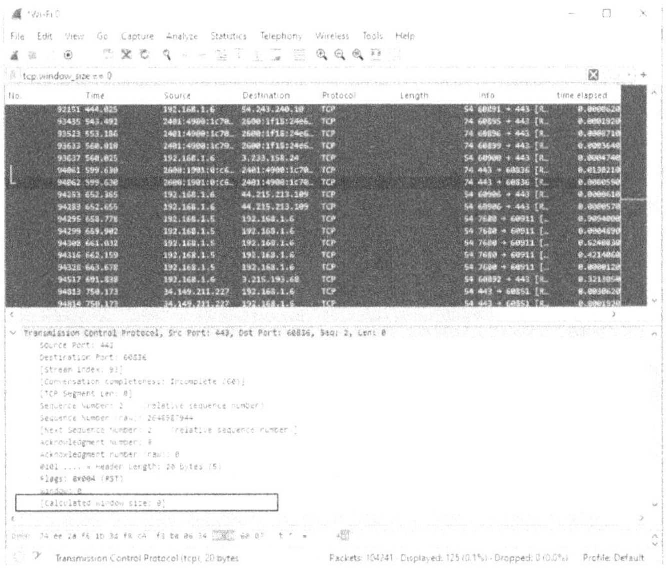

Figure 7.7 Wireshark capturing TCP traffic with a filter (tcp.window_size == 0), showing reset (RST) packets.

tcp.window_size == 0

Note: A larger window size allows more data to be sent before waiting for an acknowledgment, which can reduce transmission time for larger data transfers but may also lead to increased network congestion if not managed correctly. Too small a window size can lead to underutilization of network bandwidth since the sender must wait for acknowledgments frequently before sending more data.

General solution

If the window size is consistently small, it may indicate a problem with the receiving device's buffer settings or network load. Increasing the window size or adjusting buffer settings on the receiver may solve the issue.

DUPLICATE IP ADDRESS CONFLICT

Problem: Devices with duplicate IP addresses

Scenario: Users are experiencing intermittent connectivity issues, and after investigation, it appears that two devices are using the same IP address.

Solution using Wireshark:

Follow the given steps:

1. **Capture ARP traffic**
   Apply a filter to capture ARP packets and detect duplicate IP address responses:
   arp
2. **Analyze ARP requests and responses**
   Look for multiple devices responding to the same ARP request with the same IP address but different MAC addresses.
3. **Identify conflicting devices**
   Cross-check the MAC addresses in the ARP responses to find which devices use the same IP address.

General solution

Resolve the IP conflict by assigning a unique IP address to one of the devices or reconfiguring the DHCP server to avoid issuing the same IP to multiple devices. You can also restart devices to force them to obtain new IP addresses via DHCP.

PACKET LOSS

Problem: High packet loss

Scenario: Users report intermittent connectivity issues, with frequent drops in the connection. The network appears to have packet loss, impacting real-time VoIP or video conferencing applications.

Solution Using Wireshark:

Follow the given steps:

1. **Capture traffic to monitor packet flow**
   Capture traffic between the affected devices and the network. Apply filters for specific IP addresses (Figure 7.8):

ip.addr == 192.168.1.6 && ip.addr == 192.168.1.10

Source	Destination	Protocol	Length	Info
192.168.1.10	192.168.1.6	ICMP	74	Echo (ping) request id
192.168.1.10	192.168.1.10	ICMP	70	Destination unreachable
192.168.1.10	192.168.1.6	ICMP	74	Echo (ping) request id
192.168.1.10	192.168.1.10	ICMP	70	Destination unreachable
192.168.1.10	192.168.1.6	ICMP	74	Echo (ping) request id
192.168.1.10	192.168.1.10	ICMP	70	Destination unreachable
192.168.1.10	192.168.1.6	ICMP	74	Echo (ping) request id
192.168.1.10	192.168.1.10	ICMP	70	Destination unreachable

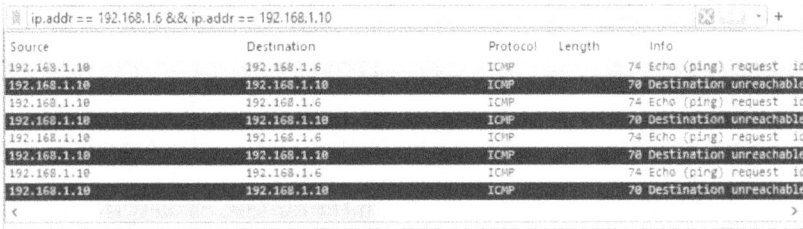

Figure 7.8 Wireshark capturing ICMP traffic between 192.168.1.6 and 192.168.1.10, showing ping requests and unreachable responses.

ip.addr == <source_IP> && ip.addr == <destination_IP>

This filter shows only those packets which have both IP addresses. In the following screen, you can see that there is some issue in communicating between these devices.

2. **Check for retransmissions**
   Apply this filter to identify TCP retransmissions (Figure 7.9):
   tcp.analysis.retransmission

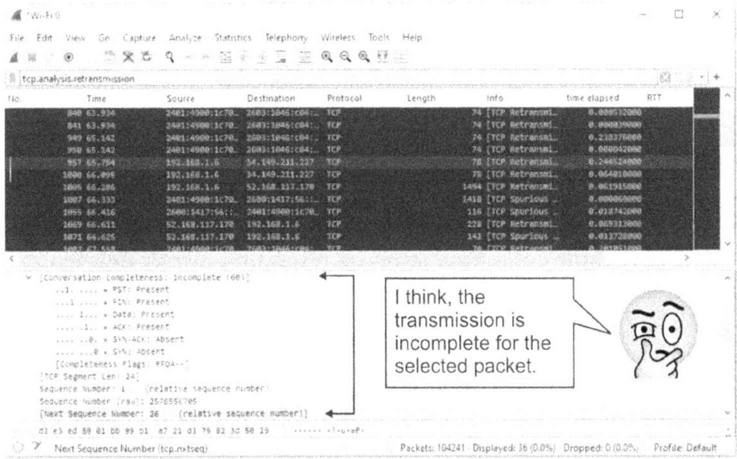

I think, the transmission is incomplete for the selected packet.

Figure 7.9 Wireshark capturing TCP retransmissions (tcp.analysis.retransmission), indicating incomplete transmission.

CONVERSATION COMPLETENESS (MIDDLE PANE)

You can check the completeness by observing the presence or absence of the following indicators,

RST: Present: A TCP RST flag indicates the connection was abruptly reset, suggesting incomplete or failed communication.
FIN: Present: The presence of a FIN flag means one side attempted to close the connection gracefully. However, the connection remains incomplete.
Data: Present: Indicates data was sent, but the conversation did not proceed as expected.
ACK: Absent: Indicates the acknowledgment for sent packets is missing, a sign of communication failure.
SYN-ACK: Absent: The absence of SYN-ACK indicates that the handshake may not have been completed correctly.
SYN: Absent: No SYN packets were captured, which is unusual unless this capture started mid-connection.

SEQUENCE NUMBERS

Sequence Number: *1 (Relative Sequence number)*: Indicates the first byte of the payload in the TCP stream.
Next Sequence Number: *26 (Relative Sequence number)*: Indicates that 25 bytes of payload were sent (26 – 1 = 25 bytes).

So, we can conclude that the conversation is incomplete due to missing acknowledgments (ACK: Absent) and the presence of a reset (RST: Present).

Note: In Wireshark, when the Info column shows "Retransmission," it indicates that a packet was resent because the sender did not receive an acknowledgment (ACK) within the expected time. This does not always mean the transmission is incomplete, as TCP's retransmission mechanism ensures reliable communication by resending lost or delayed packets. Retransmissions can occur due to network congestion, packet loss, or high latency. While a few retransmissions are normal in a busy network, frequent retransmissions may indicate underlying issues, such as poor network conditions, misconfigured devices, or hardware failures, which should be investigated further.

ANALYZE SEQUENCE NUMBERS

Apply this filter to monitor the TCP sequence numbers to identify missing packets or out-of-order delivery (Figure 7.10).

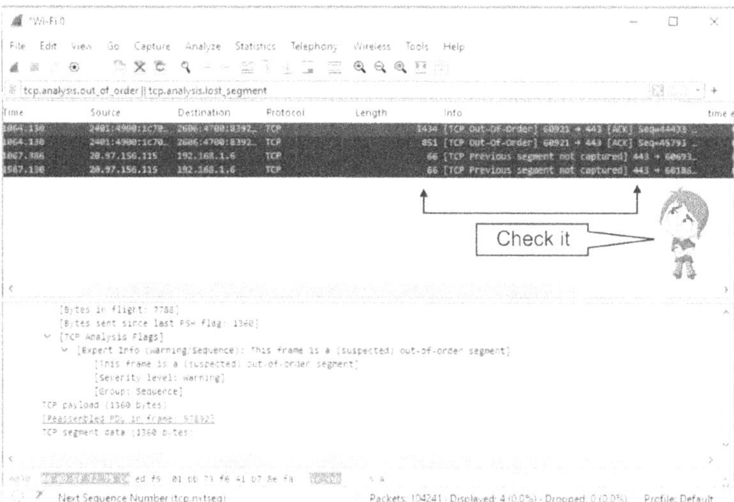

Figure 7.10 Wireshark capturing HTTPS traffic (tcp.port==443), displaying TCP and TLSv1.2 packets.

tcp.analysis.out_of_order || *tcp.analysis.lost_segment*

Check the Info column for messages like:

- "Out-of-order"
- "Previous segment not captured"
- "Retransmission"

General solution

If packet loss is detected, check for faulty hardware (such as network cables or switches) or issues with the network configuration. It may also be due to network congestion or interference in wireless networks.

LATENCY ISSUES

Problem: High latency

Scenario: Users experience delays in real-time VoIP calls or video conferencing applications. Upon investigation, it appears that there is high latency on the network

Solution using Wireshark:

1. **Capture traffic on the affected segment**
   Capture traffic on the relevant network segment using filters to isolate specific flows:
   ip.addr == <source_IP> || ip.addr == <destination_IP>
2. **Measure round trip time (RTT)**
   Use the following filter to measure RTT:
   tcp.analysis.ack_rtt
3. **Check for delays in packet delivery**
   Analyze the **Delta Time** between packets to identify transmission delays. You can see the delta time by adding a column Delta Time, with the field name *frame.time_delta*

Note: Delta time in networking refers to the time difference between consecutive packets captured in a network traffic analysis tool like Wireshark. It helps measure the delay or gap between two packets, which helps identify transmission delays, network congestion, or performance issues.

General solution

If high RTT values are observed, troubleshoot network paths for routing inefficiencies or congestion. Check network load and bandwidth utilization to ensure that traffic is flowing smoothly.

JITTER IN VOIP TRAFFIC

Problem: Poor voice quality in VoIP calls (Jitter)

Scenario: Users complain about poor voice quality during VoIP calls, with frequent distortions, echoes, or delays.

Solution using Wireshark:
Follow the given steps:

1. **Capture VoIP traffic**
   Apply a capture filter to capture **RTP** and **SIP** traffic:
   udp.port == 5060 || rtp
   The filter captures:
   - **SIP signaling traffic** on UDP port 5060 (used to set up VoIP calls).
   - **RTP packets**, which carry the actual voice or video data during the call.

   Note: SIP handles call setup and management, while RTP transports the media (audio/video) once the call is established.
2. **Analyze RTP stream**
   Go to *Telephony -> RTP -> Show All Streams* and analyze the RTP stream for jitter and packet loss.

3. **Monitor jitter**
   If jitter values are high, it indicates variability in packet arrival times, leading to poor voice quality.

General solution

If high jitter is present, prioritize VoIP traffic using **Quality of Service (QoS)** settings on routers and switches. Investigate potential network congestion or buffer settings on VoIP endpoints.

TROUBLESHOOTING SLOW FILE TRANSFERS

Problem: Slow file transfers between two devices

Scenario: A user reports that transferring files between their device and a file server takes much longer than usual. The network seems to be performing fine for other tasks.

Solution using Wireshark:

Follow the given steps:

1. **Capture file transfer traffic**
   Start capturing traffic between the two devices involved in the file transfer:
   ip.addr == <device_IP> && ip.addr == <server_IP>
2. **Check for TCP window size**
   Use the TCP filter to analyze the window size during the file transfer: *tcp.window_size*
3. **Look for retransmissions and out-of-order packets**
   Apply this filter to check if there are retransmissions, which can slow down file transfers: *tcp.analysis.retransmission*
   Use *tcp.analysis.out_of_order* to check if packets are arriving out of sequence.
4. **Monitor bandwidth usage**
   Use *Statistics -> I/O Graphs* to visualize the file transfer bandwidth in real time and detect if the transfer is being throttled.

General solution

- If the TCP window size is too small, check if the receiver cannot handle large amounts of data and adjust its buffer settings.
- If there are excessive retransmissions, inspect the physical network (like cables, switches, and routers) or potential congestion on the network.
- Optimize network routes or inspect the transport layer if packet reordering is observed.

WI-FI INTERFERENCE

Problem: Wi-Fi signal drops and slow speeds

Scenario: Users report that the Wi-Fi connection frequently drops or slows down, especially in certain office areas. Upon investigation, it seems like there is interference or congestion on the wireless network.

Solution using Wireshark:

Follow the given steps:

1. **Capture Wi-Fi traffic**
   Capture traffic on the specific Wi-Fi channel experiencing the issue. Use Wireshark in **Monitor Mode** (on compatible Wi-Fi adapters) to capture all traffic, including frames from specific channels.

   Set capture filter in Wireshark:

- Open **Wireshark** and go to **Capture Options** (Ctrl + K).
- Choose your Wi-Fi interface (e.g., wlan0, Wi-Fi, etc.).

   Set display filter in Wireshark:
   Set the display filter to capture traffic on the specific channel, like *wlan.channel == 6. If wlan.channel==6* is unavailable (giving error), use the corresponding frequency for channel 6 (2437 MHz) with this filter: *wlan_radio.frequency == 2437*

Note: On Windows, even with **Npcap** and monitor mode, channel information is often not captured due to system or driver restrictions. Linux systems generally provide more robust support for monitor mode and include channel information in the capture.

2. **Analyze signal strength and channel utilization**
   Perform the following steps:

- Use *Statistics -> WLAN Traffic* to see how much traffic is on the channel and how it compares to other channels.
- Check the **RSSI (Received Signal Strength Indicator)** in the Wi-Fi packet headers to determine the signal strength of the wireless access points.

3. **Check for channel overlap**
   Filter and analyze beacon frames to check if multiple access points or networks are operating on overlapping channels:
   wlan.fc.type_subtype == 0x08
4. **Look for retransmissions due to interference**

Use the following filter to check for retransmissions caused by interference:
wlan.fc.retry == 1

Note: If you want to capture filter SSID Wise, use the display filter like *wlan .ssid == "SSID"*

General solution

- If the signal strength is weak, consider relocating the access point or using a signal booster.
- If channel overlap is detected, change the access point to a less congested Wi-Fi channel (e.g., using 1, 6, or 11 for 2.4 GHz).
- If retransmissions due to interference are frequent, check for other nearby devices (like microwaves, Bluetooth, or other wireless networks) and minimize their impact.

TCP CONNECTION DROPS

Problem: TCP Connection Dropping Randomly. When a TCP connection drops, the connection between two communicating devices has been unexpectedly interrupted. It can occur due to network issues, device failures, timeouts, or packet loss.

Scenario: A server application intermittently drops connections with clients. Users report getting disconnected from services, and you suspect there is an issue with TCP connections randomly being terminated.

Solution using Wireshark:

Follow the given steps:

1. **Capture TCP traffic between client and server**
   Capture TCP traffic on the affected port (Figure 7.11):
   tcp.port == <application_port>

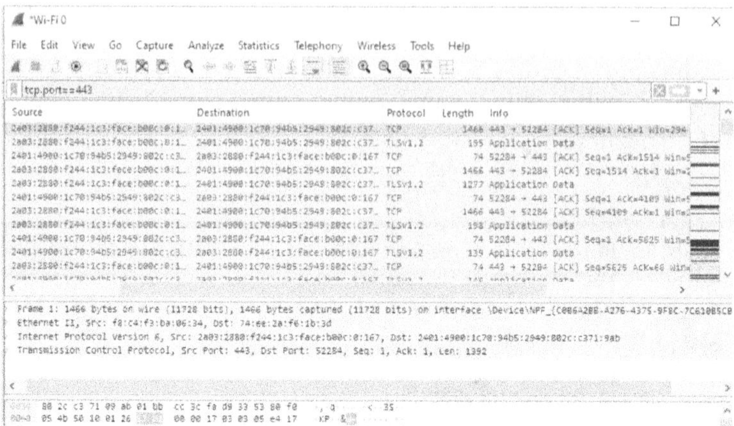

Figure 7.11 Wireshark capturing TCP reset packets (tcp.flags.reset == 1) with RST flags.

2. **Look for TCP RST (reset) packets**
   Apply this filter to check if the TCP session is being forcefully reset (Figure 7.12):
   tcp.flags.reset == 1

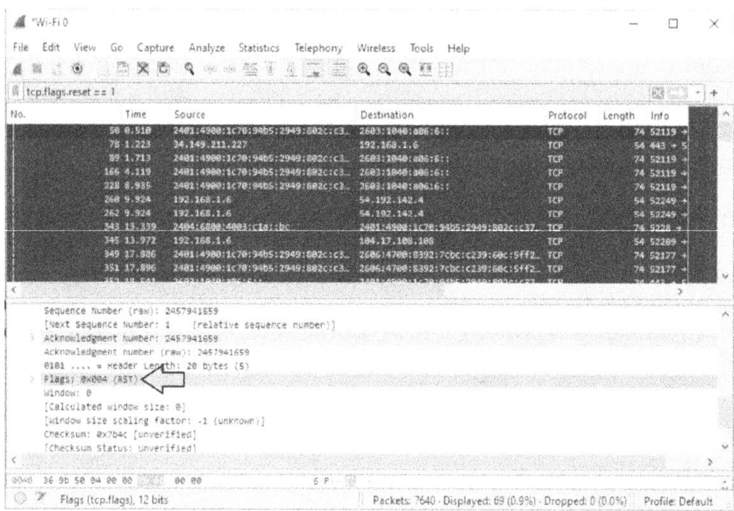

Figure 7.12 Wireshark capturing TCP connection termination (tcp.flags.fin == 1), showing FIN and ACK packets.

Note: The server or client may reject a connection attempt by sending a TCP Reset (RST). It is also possible that applications may terminate TCP connections prematurely, causing a Reset flag to appear.

3. **Check for TCP FIN (finish) packets**
   Look for TCP FIN packets to see if the connection is being closed gracefully (Figure 7.13):
   tcp.flags.fin == 1

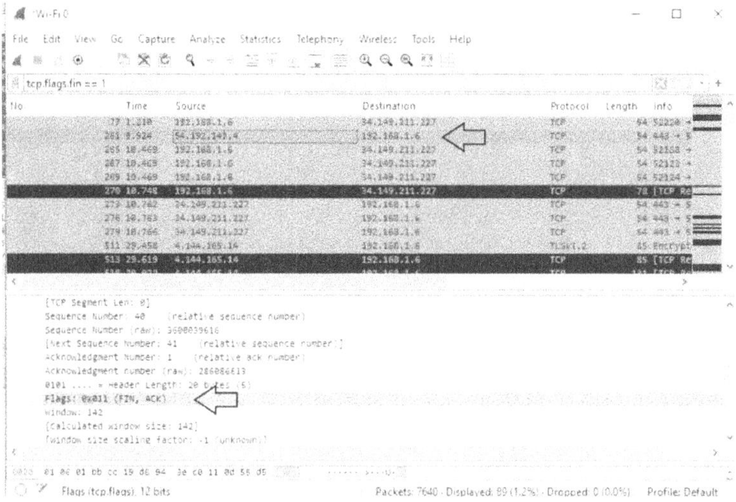

Figure 7.13 Wireshark capture showing TCP FIN packet used to indicate graceful connection termination.

4. **Inspect connection termination timing**
   Use *Statistics -> Conversations -> TCP* to analyze the conversation duration and determine if there are premature terminations or dropped packets. The Flows column counts the number of TCP packet exchanges (or flows) between the two endpoints during the conversation (Figure 7.14).

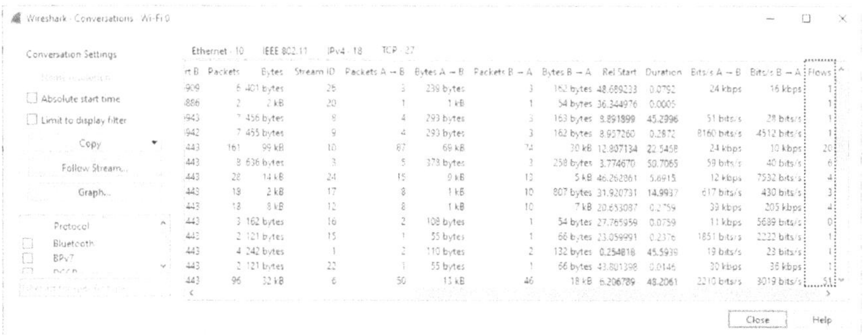

Figure 7.14 Wireshark Conversations view showing TCP stream details, including packets, bytes, duration, and flow count.

OBSERVATIONS

- Rows with Flows = 0: These are likely incomplete connections. Investigate for possible network issues or dropped responses.
- Rows with Flows =1: These are half-open connections (e.g., SYN sent, no ACK received). Potential dropped packets.
- High Packet Counts: Some conversations like Packets A → B = 219 indicate significant data flow.

Next steps:

1. **Analyze flows = 0 and flows = 1** rows:
    - Apply a filter like *tcp.flags.syn == 1* to identify half-open connections.
    - Check for tcp.analysis.retransmission to see if SYN packets were retried.
2. **Follow TCP stream:**
    - Right-click on a conversation and select "**Follow TCP Stream**" to view the complete exchange.
3. **Investigate firewall/network issues:**
    - If responses are missing (Flows = 0 or 1), check for firewalls or dropped packets.

General solution

- If TCP RST packets are present, check the server's or application's timeout settings or load balancing configuration that may prematurely terminate the connection.
- If TCP FIN packets are seen too early, the issue may be due to resource exhaustion on the server, so check the system or application logs for clues.
- Ensure no firewalls or security appliances are causing sessions to reset along the path.

CONCLUSION

Wireshark is an essential tool for network troubleshooting, enabling deep network traffic analysis to diagnose many problems. From detecting duplicate IP addresses and resolving DHCP issues to identifying packet loss and jitter in VoIP calls, Wireshark is also a versatile tool for issues like diagnosing slow file transfers and Wi-Fi interference and resolving TCP connection drops. It provides the visibility necessary to resolve complex network challenges. Network administrators can ensure efficient and effective network performance by applying the appropriate filters and using Wireshark's built-in tools.

MULTIPLE CHOICE QUESTIONS (MCQs)

1. What does the dns.time field in Wireshark indicate?
   A) The time taken to capture DNS traffic
   B) The time between sending a DNS query and receiving its response
   C) The delay caused by DNS server congestion
   D) The time required to establish a DNS connection

Answer: B)

2. Which Wireshark filter can be used to monitor traffic from a specific device?
   A) tcp.analysis.retransmission
   B) ip.src == <device_IP>
   C) eth.dst == ff:ff:ff:ff:ff:ff
   D) udp.port == 5060

Answer: B)

3. Which method in Wireshark helps identify devices consuming excessive bandwidth?
   A) Use the filter tcp.analysis.retransmission
   B) Use the filter ip.src == <device_IP>
   C) Use Statistics -> Conversations
   D) Use the filter udp.port == 5060

Answer: C)

4. Which Wireshark filter captures broadcast traffic on a network?
   A) ip.addr == <device_IP>
   B) eth.dst == ff:ff:ff:ff:ff:ff
   C) tcp.analysis.out_of_order
   D) wlan_radio.frequency == 2437

Answer: B) eth.dst == ff:ff:ff:ff:ff:ff

5. What does a high number of retransmissions in a TCP stream typically indicate?
   A) A well-performing network
   B) Packet loss or network congestion
   C) Faster data delivery
   D) Normal behavior in a Wi-Fi network

Answer: B)

GLOSSARY

1. **ARP (Address Resolution Protocol):** A network protocol used to map an IP address to a physical machine address that is recognized in the local network
2. **Broadcast Storm:** A network condition with many broadcast frames causing congestion and network slowdown.
3. **DHCP (Dynamic Host Configuration Protocol):** A network management protocol used to dynamically assign IP addresses and other network configuration parameters to devices on a network, enabling them to communicate on an IP network.
4. **DNS (Domain Name System):** A system that translates human-friendly domain names like "www.example.com" into numerical IP addresses necessary for locating and identifying computer services and devices on the internet.
5. **ICMP (Internet Control Message Protocol):** Used by network devices, like routers, to send error messages indicating that a requested service is not available or that a host or router could not be reached.
6. **I/O Graphs:** A feature in Wireshark that provides a graphical representation of data flow over time, useful for analyzing traffic patterns, trends, and potential anomalies.
7. **Jitter:** Variability in packet arrival times, which can affect the quality of streaming audio and video.
8. **Packet Loss:** Occurs when one or more packets of data traveling across a computer network fail to reach their destination, which errors in data transmission, network congestion, or other problems can cause.
9. **QoS (Quality of Service):** A set of technologies used to manage network traffic to reduce packet loss, latency, and jitter on the network.
10. **Retransmissions:** The resending of packets which have been either lost or damaged.
11. **Round Trip Time (RTT):** The duration of time it takes for a signal to be sent plus the duration of time it takes for an acknowledgment of that signal to be received
12. **Spanning Tree Protocol (STP):** A network protocol that ensures a loop-free topology for any bridged Ethernet local area network.
13. **TCP (Transmission Control Protocol):** A core protocol of the Internet Protocol Suite. It originates and manages the connection-oriented communications between computers.
14. **UDP (User Datagram Protocol):** A simpler message-based connectionless protocol than TCP.

15. **VLAN (Virtual Local Area Network)**: A group of host computers and servers configured to communicate as if they were attached to the same broadcast domain, regardless of their physical location.
16. **Window Size**: In TCP connections, the size of the window determines the number of bytes that can be transmitted without receiving an acknowledgment.

Chapter 8

Enhancing network security with Wireshark

INTRODUCTION

Enhancing network security with Wireshark involves using it to monitor, analyze, and troubleshoot network traffic in real time. Wireshark inspects packet-level data and helps security professionals identify suspicious activities, such as unauthorized connections, malware communication, or Distributed Denial-of-Service (DDoS) attacks. It can detect anomalies like ARP spoofing, DNS poisoning, or TCP SYN floods by applying filters and analyzing flags or patterns. Its detailed analysis capabilities make it essential for strengthening network visibility and security posture.

IDENTIFYING AND ANALYZING MALWARE TRAFFIC

Malware often communicates with external command-and-control (C&C) servers to receive instructions or exfiltrate stolen data. This communication is often disguised as legitimate traffic, making it difficult to detect with standard network monitoring tools. Wireshark provides the packet-level visibility needed to uncover this traffic and identify potential malware infections.

Problem: Detecting malware traffic

Scenario: A company's security team suspects that a device in their network is infected with malware, as unusual outbound traffic to unknown IP addresses has been reported.

Step-by-step solution using Wireshark:

1. **Capture traffic from the suspected device**
   To begin your investigation, start Wireshark on the network segment where the affected device is located. You'll want to focus on the traffic from the specific device to monitor its communication. Apply a capture filter to monitor traffic to and from the suspected device's IP address:

DOI: 10.1201/9781003539261-8

Capture filter: *ip.addr == <suspected_device_IP>*
This filter ensures that Wireshark captures traffic related to the IP address of the suspected device, making your capture more focused and efficient.

2. **Look for suspicious DNS requests**
Malware often uses DNS to resolve domain names for Command and Control (C&C) communication or to download additional payloads. You can look for suspicious or unusual DNS requests using a display filter.
dns
Once you apply the DNS filter, look for any unusual DNS requests, such as requests for unknown or suspicious domains. Malware often tries to resolve domain names that don't belong to legitimate services. Pay particular attention to non-standard domains, especially those related to suspicious or newly registered domains.

3. **Analyze HTTP/HTTPS traffic**
Many types of malware use HTTP or HTTPS to communicate with C&C servers or to download malicious payloads. To capture and analyze this traffic, use the following display filters:
http
Display filter for HTTPS (SSL/TLS): *ssl or tls*

It would help to be careful when looking at the Server Name Indication (SNI) field in the TLS/SSL handshake. The SNI indicates which domain the client (the infected device) is trying to connect to during an encrypted connection. Malicious traffic often connects to unusual or untrusted domains.

Note: The Server Name Indication (SNI) field in a TLS handshake allows a client (e.g., the infected device) to tell the server which hostname it tries to connect to, especially when multiple websites are hosted on the same IP address. This is important because malware often connects to servers hosting suspicious or malicious domains via HTTPS.

To inspect the SNI field, you can apply this display filter to look for the SNI in TLS traffic:
tls.handshake.extensions_server_name
It shows you the hostname the device is attempting to contact. It could indicate malicious activity if it seems suspicious or out of place. For example, Let's say you're capturing traffic from a suspected infected device, and you see several TLS handshakes when you apply the display filter *tls.handshake.extensions_server_name.* You may see results like this as seen in Table 8.1 and Figure 8.1:

Table 8.1 TLS protocol table

No.	*Time*	*Protocol*	*Info*
32	12.345678	TLS	Client Hello, SNI: maliciousdomain.com
45	12.567890	TLS	Client Hello, SNI: example.com
58	13.123456	TLS	Client Hello, SNI: anotherdomain.com

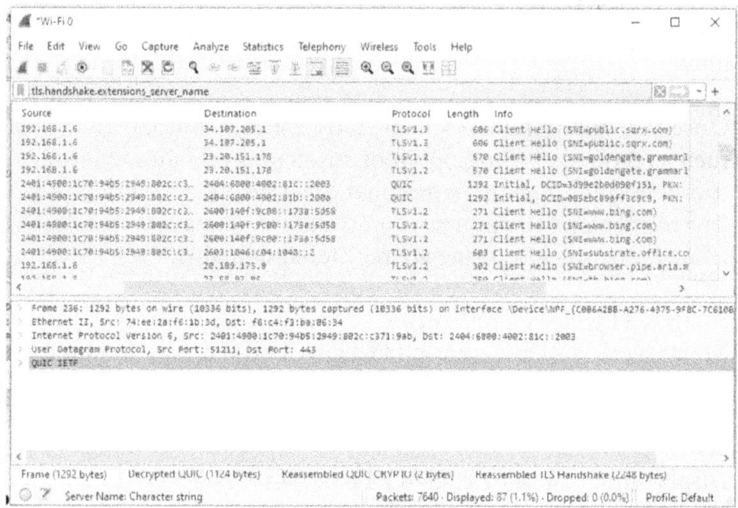

Figure 8.1 Wireshark Packet Capture displaying TLS handshake with Server Name Indication (SNI).

The captured traffic primarily shows **TLS** and **QUIC** communication with domains like www.bing.com and goldengate.grammarly .com, which appear legitimate, though public.sqrx.com warrants further investigation. Tools like VirusTotal, AbuseIPDB, and IPVoid can be used to verify the reputation of domains and destination IPs, while services like Whois Lookup or DomainTools provide details about domain registration and ownership.

Additionally, Shodan or Censys can help analyze the characteristics of the destination IPs or servers. Applying filters such as quic and tls in Wireshark allows for a more granular analysis of handshake patterns and anomalies in server responses. Using *Statistics --> Conversations* in Wireshark can also help identify unusual connection behavior. Persistent monitoring using tools like Zeek or Splunk can provide further insights into the network behavior if any suspicious activity is detected.

4. **Detect suspicious protocols**

   Malware sometimes uses uncommon or less frequently used ports and protocols to evade detection. For example, malware might use non-standard HTTP ports, or communicate over DNS (UDP port 53) to avoid detection.

You can look for suspicious traffic using **display filters** targeting uncommon protocols and ports that malware might use. Consider the following display Filter for Suspicious Protocols:

- *tcp.port == 8080* (Some malware uses port 8080 for HTTP-like communication)
- *udp.port == 53* (DNS is commonly used for C&C communication)

You can add more protocols to the filter depending on the network traffic you suspect is being used by the malware. For example, **port 443** is commonly used by malware for encrypted communication over HTTPS.

GENERAL SOLUTION

If you detect suspicious DNS queries, HTTP/HTTPS traffic, or unusual protocol usage, here's the next step to take:

- **Isolate the device:** Disconnect the suspected infected device from the network to prevent further communication with the malware's C&C server.
- **Perform a deeper forensic analysis:** Once isolated, perform a deeper investigation, including scanning the device for malware, checking for unusual processes, and analyzing any files or payloads that might have been downloaded.
- **Use Wireshark to track initial infection:** Wireshark can help identify when the malware first contacted an external server. By filtering for **timestamps** and **specific communication patterns**, you can pinpoint when the infection occurred, which can help you trace back to its source.

Using Wireshark's powerful **capture** and **display filters**, you can focus on suspicious network traffic, such as DNS requests, HTTP/HTTPS traffic, and uncommon protocols, to detect malicious behavior. This process aids in identifying the malware's C&C communication, and Wireshark can provide crucial data for further forensic investigation. Once the infected machine is isolated, a more in-depth analysis can begin to eradicate the threat and prevent further damage.

DETECTING UNAUTHORIZED ACCESS ATTEMPTS

Unauthorized access attempts, whether external (such as brute-force attacks) or internal (unauthorized insider access), pose significant risks to network security. Wireshark can monitor network activity for signs of these attempts by inspecting failed login attempts, connection spikes, or attempts to access restricted areas.

Problem: Detecting brute-force login attempts

Scenario: A web server is under a brute-force attack as an external attacker attempts to guess login credentials by sending multiple failed login requests. The server responds slowly, and you suspect an attacker is trying to gain unauthorized access.

Step-by-step solution using Wireshark:

1. **Capture traffic on the server's network interface**
   Start capturing traffic from the server that is the target of the brute-force attack. Use a filter to monitor login attempts by filtering for specific ports (e.g., SSH or RDP):
   tcp.port == 22 (for SSH)
   tcp.port == 3389 (for RDP)
   tcp.port == 22 || tcp.port == 3389

Note: Both SSH and RDP provide remote administrative access to systems. Compromising these protocols often gives attackers complete control of the target machine. Attackers prioritize these protocols as they are gateways to servers and networks.

2. **Look for failed login attempts**
   Brute-force attacks generate many failed login attempts. Analyze the login protocol (e.g., **HTTP POST** for web-based login or **SSH traffic** for command-line logins):
   http.request.method == "POST"
   Or:
   ssh
3. **Identify a high volume of login requests**
   Use **Statistics -> Conversations** to identify a large number of login attempts from a single IP address. If one IP address repeatedly attempts logins within a short time frame, it may indicate an ongoing brute-force attack.
4. **Check for TCP reset (RST) flags**
   Attackers might trigger resets after failed login attempts. You can filter for TCP resets:
   Use *tcp.flags.reset == 1* to identify abrupt session terminations.
   If multiple failed login attempts are identified, implement security measures such as locking the affected account, banning the IP address, or enforcing more robust password policies. Wireshark's ability to pinpoint the attack's origin allows quick response and mitigation.

Spotting data exfiltration

Data exfiltration occurs when sensitive data is transferred out of a secure network, usually by an attacker or malware. The exfiltration may be disguised as normal traffic using legitimate protocols such as HTTP, HTTPS, or DNS. Wireshark can detect patterns in network traffic that may indicate data is being stolen.

Problem: Detecting large data transfers

Scenario: You suspect an insider is attempting to steal sensitive data by transferring it to an external server. The transfer occurs over HTTPS, making it difficult to detect using standard monitoring tools.

Step-by-step solution using Wireshark:

1. **Capture HTTPS traffic**
   Start capturing traffic on the network segment where the insider is located. Use the filter to capture only HTTPS traffic (Figure 8.2):
   ssl

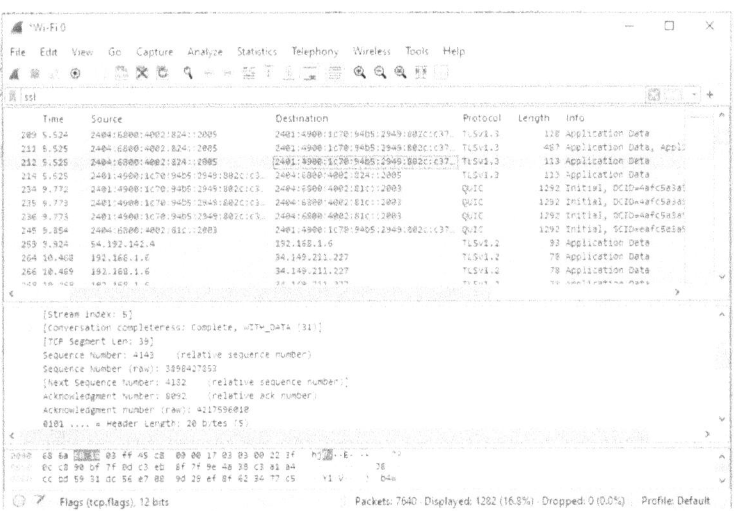

Figure 8.2 Wireshark showing SSL/TLS traffic with TCP stream analysis.

2. **Check for unusual large outbound data transfers**
   Go to **Statistics -> Conversations** and check for sessions that involve large amounts of data being transferred to external IPs. Look for excessive outbound data compared to typical usage (Figure 8.3).

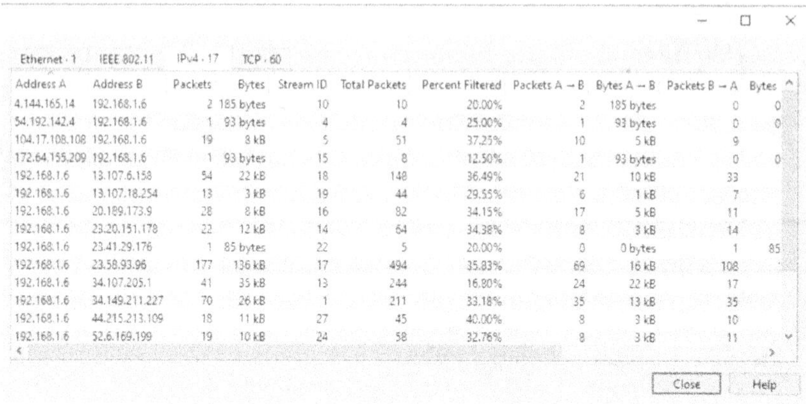

Ethernet · 1 IEEE 802.11 IPv4 · 17 TCP · 60

Address A	Address B	Packets	Bytes	Stream ID	Total Packets	Percent Filtered	Packets A → B	Bytes A → B	Packets B → A	Bytes
4.144.165.14	192.168.1.6	2	185 bytes	10	10	20.00%	2	185 bytes	0	0
54.192.142.4	192.168.1.6	1	93 bytes	4	4	25.00%	1	93 bytes	0	0
104.17.108.108	192.168.1.6	19	8 kB	5	51	37.25%	10	5 kB	9	
172.64.155.209	192.168.1.6	1	93 bytes	15	8	12.50%	1	93 bytes	0	0
192.168.1.6	13.107.6.158	54	22 kB	18	148	36.49%	21	10 kB	33	
192.168.1.6	13.107.18.254	13	3 kB	19	44	29.55%	6	1 kB	7	
192.168.1.6	20.189.173.9	28	8 kB	16	82	34.15%	17	5 kB	11	
192.168.1.6	23.20.151.178	22	12 kB	14	64	34.38%	8	3 kB	14	
192.168.1.6	23.41.29.176	1	85 bytes	22	5	20.00%	0	0 bytes	1	85
192.168.1.6	23.58.93.96	177	136 kB	17	494	35.83%	69	16 kB	108	
192.168.1.6	34.107.205.1	41	35 kB	13	244	16.80%	24	22 kB	17	
192.168.1.6	34.149.211.227	70	26 kB	1	211	33.18%	35	13 kB	35	
192.168.1.6	44.215.213.109	18	11 kB	27	45	40.00%	8	3 kB	10	
192.168.1.6	52.6.169.199	19	10 kB	24	58	32.76%	8	3 kB	11	

Close Help

Figure 8.3 Wireshark's Conversations tab with network statistics for Ethernet, IPv4, and TCP.

Here, you can see High-Volume Conversations. The conversation between **192.168.1.6** (local machine) and **23.58.93.96** stands out with:

- 177 packets exchanged.
- 136 kB of data transferred.
- A significant portion of data (16 kB) is transferred from Address B to Address A (likely download activity).

3. **Look for suspicious destinations**
   Identify if the large data transfers are going to unfamiliar or suspicious external IP addresses. These could be indicative of data being exfiltrated.
4. **Monitor DNS and protocols**
   Use DNS queries and SNI fields in TLS handshakes to see where the data is being sent.

General solution

If large data transfers to unknown destinations are detected, take immediate action to block the connection, isolate the device, and investigate further. Wireshark can provide vital information on the size, timing, and destination of the exfiltrated data.

Monitoring suspicious network behavior

Suspicious network behavior may include unusually high traffic, frequent connections to unknown IP addresses, or unexpected protocol usage. Detecting such behavior early can prevent a network breach or help identify ongoing attacks (see Figure 8.4).

Problem: Detecting a compromised device communicating with a command-and-control server (Figure 8.4a):

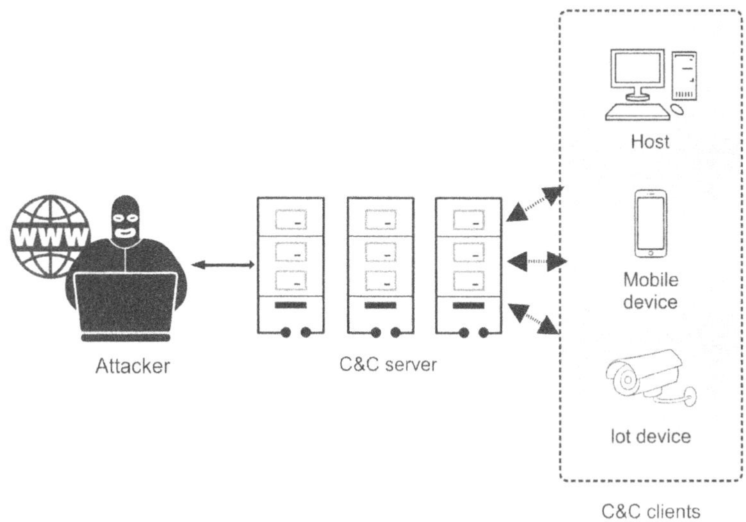

Figure 8.4 Command and Control (C&C) infrastructure in a Botnet attack.

Scenario: An internal device shows unusual traffic patterns, and you suspect it has been compromised and is communicating with an external Command-and-Control (C&C) server.

Step-by-step solution using Wireshark

1. **Capture traffic from the compromised device**
   Capture traffic using the IP address of the device in question:
   ip.addr == <compromised_device_IP>
2. **Look for suspicious IPs and domains**
   Check for connections to external IP addresses or domains not part of normal business operations. Filter for uncommon ports or protocols used for communication:
   tcp.port == 4444 (common C&C port)
1. **Analyze beaconing behavior**
   Attackers often use periodic "beaconing" to communicate with C&C servers. Use **Statistics -> I/O Graphs** to see if traffic to specific IP addresses follows a regular pattern.
2. **Monitor for suspicious data flows**
   Investigate whether the device sends more data than it receives, especially if communicating with unknown IPs.

General solution

If suspicious communications are detected, block the external IPs and isolate the compromised device. Further analysis of the captured traffic helps determine the full extent of the compromise and prevent further data leakage.

DETECTING LATERAL MOVEMENT IN THE NETWORK

Lateral movement is a technique attackers use to move from one compromised device to another within a network. After gaining an initial foothold, attackers perform reconnaissance to find valuable targets and then attempt to access those targets by exploiting vulnerabilities or brute-forcing credentials. Lateral movement is common in advanced persistent threats (APTs) and insider attacks.

Problem: Internal Reconnaissance and Lateral Movement

Scenario: You notice suspicious internal network traffic as attackers attempt to move laterally through the network, probing devices and services for vulnerabilities.

Step-by-step solution using Wireshark:

1. **Capture internal traffic**
   Use Wireshark to capture all internal traffic, especially on key servers and devices:
   ip.addr == <internal_network_subnet>
2. **Monitor for port scanning**
   Use a filter to capture multiple connection attempts to different ports on the same target, indicative of a port scan:
   tcp.flags.syn == 1 && tcp.flags.ack == 0
3. **Check for unusual SMB/Windows authentication traffic**
   Look for unusual SMB or Windows authentication attempts, as attackers may try to brute-force credentials:
   smb || kerberos || ntlmssp
   - SMB (Server Message Block) is a network file-sharing protocol used primarily in Windows to allow applications and users to access shared files, printers, and other network resources. It enables communication between devices within a local network, allowing file and printer sharing, remote access, and inter-process communication.
   - Kerberos is a widely used network authentication protocol designed to provide secure authentication over insecure networks like the Internet.
   - NTLMSSP stands for NT LAN Manager Security Support Provider, a part of the NTLM (NT LAN Manager) authentication protocol suite developed by Microsoft. NTLMSSP is a mechanism that securely facilitates challenge-response authentication and is commonly used in Microsoft-based networks.

General solution

If you detect port scanning or unauthorized access attempts, block the suspicious device's access and investigate the lateral movement path. Additionally, implement network segmentation to restrict lateral movement within your network.

Spotting rogue DHCP servers

A rogue DHCP server is an unauthorized server on the network that hands out incorrect IP addresses to clients. This can disrupt network operations by assigning incorrect IP configurations, causing connectivity issues. Attackers often use rogue DHCP servers to launch MITM attacks or redirect traffic to malicious endpoints.

Problem: Rogue DHCP server causing network disruptions

Scenario: Devices are getting assigned incorrect IP addresses, causing network disconnections. You suspect a rogue DHCP server has been introduced into the network, potentially by an attacker trying to intercept traffic.

Step-by-step solution using Wireshark:

1. **Capture DHCP traffic**
   Use Wireshark to capture DHCP traffic on the network:
   bootp || dhcp

Note: BOOTP (Bootstrap Protocol) and DHCP (Dynamic Host Configuration Protocol) are protocols used to assign IP addresses and other network configuration settings to devices in a network. While they serve similar purposes, DHCP is an evolution of BOOTP with added features and greater flexibility.

2. **Check for multiple DHCP servers**
   Examine the DHCP Offer and ACK packets and check for multiple servers responding with different IP address ranges:
   bootp.option.dhcp == 2
3. **Identify rogue servers**
   Analyse the MAC addresses of the DHCP servers offering IP addresses and identify any unauthorized devices not part of the legitimate network infrastructure.

General solution

Isolate the rogue DHCP server by blocking its MAC address and removing it from the network. Ensure that the network's DHCP server settings are correctly configured to avoid future rogue devices.

DETECTING DENIAL-OF-SERVICE (DOS) ATTACK

A Denial-of-Service (DoS) attack is an attempt by an attacker to make a network resource unavailable by overwhelming it with traffic. This can be accomplished by sending large volumes of requests, consuming all available bandwidth, or exploiting vulnerabilities in network services. DoS attacks can cripple services, affect network performance, and lead to downtime.

Problem: Unusual traffic flooding

Scenario: The network becomes unresponsive or experiences severe slowdowns. You suspect that a **Denial-of-Service (DoS)** attack is in progress, where the attacker is flooding the network with traffic to overload services.

Step-by-step solution using Wireshark:

1. **Capture high-volume traffic**
   - Use Wireshark to capture traffic on the affected network interface.
   - Apply a filter to focus on high-volume traffic (such as SYN floods):

   tcp.flags.syn == 1 && tcp.flags.ack == 0

   This image demonstrates that the captured traffic does not indicate a **SYN flooding DDoS attack**, as all connections have completed the three-way handshake and successfully exchanged data. The *filter tcp .flags.syn == 1 && tcp.flags.ack == 0* is being used to focus on the initial SYN packets, and the annotation confirms the absence of malicious activity (Figure 8.5).

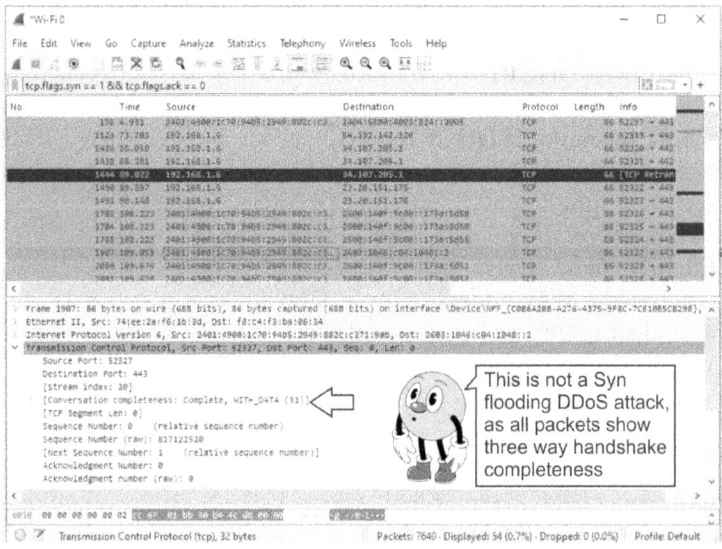

Figure 8.5 Wireshark highlighting TCP SYN packets used in connection establishment.

2. **Check for unusually high packet rates**
   Go to *Statistics -> I/O Graphs* to visualize the packet rate and spot sudden spikes, which may indicate a DoS attack (Figure 8.6).

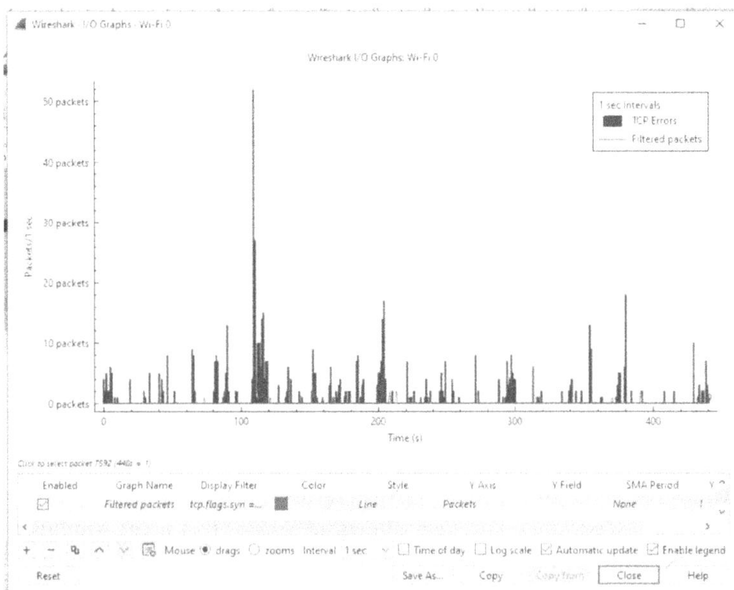

Figure 8.6 Wireshark I/O Graph depicting TCP errors and packet trends over time.

   The I/O graph highlights the number of SYN packets (*tcp.flags.syn == 1 && tcp.flags.ack == 0*) over time, showing a significant spike at around 100 seconds, which might indicate abnormal activity. Further analysis of source and destination IPs, as well as SYN-ACK responses, is necessary to determine if this is legitimate traffic or malicious behavior like a SYN flood attack
3. **Analyse top talkers**
   Use **Statistics -> Conversations** to identify the top IP addresses sending the most traffic. If a single source is flooding the network, it is likely the attacker.

General solution

Block the attacking IP address at the firewall level to mitigate the DoS attack. Additionally, rate limiting or an intrusion detection system (IDS) should be implemented to prevent future attacks.

DETECTING DNS TUNNELING FOR DATA EXFILTRATION

DNS tunneling is a technique attackers use to exfiltrate data or establish covert communication channels. By embedding malicious data in DNS queries or responses, attackers can bypass security controls like firewalls or intrusion detection systems. This technique is often used because DNS traffic is typically allowed in most networks, making it helpful in sneaking data out of the network.

Problem: Unusual DNS traffic Indicating DNS tunneling

Scenario: You suspect an attacker is using DNS tunneling to exfiltrate sensitive data from the network. DNS tunneling involves encoding data in DNS queries to bypass security controls.

Step-by-step solution using Wireshark:

1. **Capture DNS traffic**
   Apply a filter to capture all DNS traffic:
   dns
2. **Look for large or frequent DNS queries**
   Go to *Statistics -> Conversations -> DNS* and look for huge DNS query packets or a high frequency of queries, which may indicate DNS tunneling.
3. **Inspect unusual domains or subdomains**
   Analyse the DNS queries and check for unusual domain names or excessive use of subdomains, as DNS tunneling often involves encoding data in the subdomains.

General solution

If DNS tunneling is detected, block the suspicious domains or IP addresses at the DNS server or firewall. Investigate further to determine if sensitive data has already been exfiltrated and take preventive measures to secure DNS traffic.

Detecting unencrypted sensitive information

Sensitive data, such as usernames, passwords, and personal information, should always be transmitted over encrypted protocols like HTTPS, FTPS, or SSH. If this data is sent over unencrypted channels like HTTP or FTP, it is exposed to interception by attackers. Detecting unencrypted sensitive information in network traffic can help prevent data breaches.

Problem: Sensitive information sent in plaintext

Scenario: A routine security audit reveals that sensitive information (e.g., usernames, passwords, credit card numbers) is being transmitted over the network without encryption. This could expose the organization to significant security risks. First, we enter data into a form of an unencrypted website (http) (Figure 8.7).

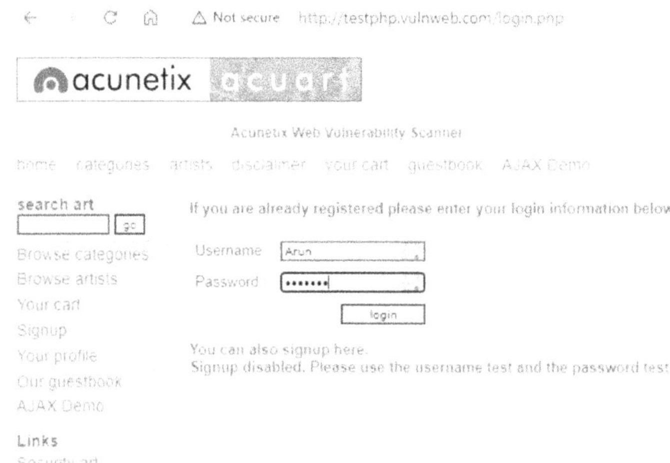

Figure 8.7 A web login page with plaintext credential submission, demonstrating an insecure setup.

Step-by-step solution using Wireshark:

1. **Capture all HTTP traffic**
   Use Wireshark to capture traffic on the network and filter for **unencrypted HTTP** traffic: Use the following display filter
   http.request.method == "POST"

Note: In the context of HTTP, the **POST** method is used to send data to a server to create or update a resource.

2. **Look for plaintext credentials or sensitive data**
   Analyse the packet content and look for sensitive information, such as login credentials being transmitted in plaintext over HTTP (Figure 8.8).

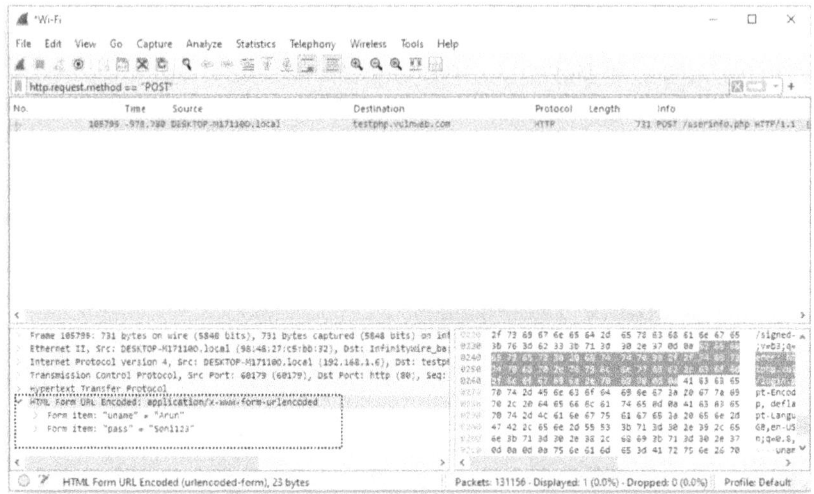

Figure 8.8 Wireshark capture of an insecure HTTP POST request exposing plaintext login credentials.

3. **Check for unencrypted protocols**
   Filter for other unencrypted protocols (e.g., FTP, Telnet) to check if sensitive data is being transmitted insecurely:
   ftp || telnet

General solution

If sensitive information is found in plaintext, enforce secure transmission protocols (e.g., HTTPS, FTPS, SSH) to protect the data. Also, ensure that encryption mechanisms are in place throughout the network.

TRACKING UNAUTHORIZED NETWORK SCANS

Network scanning is a reconnaissance technique attackers use to identify open ports, running services, and potential vulnerabilities in a network. Tools such as Nmap or Masscan are often used to probe devices to gather information systematically. While network scans are a normal part of network management, unauthorized network scans from external or internal sources can signal the early stages of a network attack. Scanning activity is typically a precursor to more targeted attacks like exploiting vulnerabilities, brute-force attempts, or lateral movement within the network.

Attackers scan networks for open ports and services to identify weak points they can exploit. Tracking and identifying these scans is crucial for proactively defending against attacks, as it allows administrators to block or isolate malicious sources before damage can occur.

Problem: To detect unauthorized scans

Scenario: You suspect an attacker is scanning the network to find open ports and vulnerabilities and gather information for future attacks.

Step-by-step solution using Wireshark:

1. **Capture Network traffic across multiple devices**
   Use Wireshark to monitor traffic on the network and capture packets between the attacker and any potential targets:
   ip.addr == <network_subnet>
2. **Look for TCP SYN scans**
   Apply a filter to detect TCP SYN scans, where an attacker rapidly sends SYN packets to various ports:
   tcp.flags.syn == 1 && tcp.flags.ack == 0
3. **Detect ICMP Echo Scans**
   Use a filter to detect ICMP ping sweeps, where an attacker attempts to map the network by sending ICMP Echo Requests to multiple IP addresses:
   icmp.type == 8

Note: ICMP Echo Scans are a type of network reconnaissance technique used to discover active hosts or devices within a network. In Wireshark, the filter icmp.type == 8 represents an ICMP Echo Request message. This type of ping request is sent from one device to another to check if the target device is online and reachable. If the target is active and configured to respond, it sends back an ICMP Echo Reply (with *icmp.type == 0*).

General solution

If unauthorized network scanning is detected, block the attacker's IP address and review network logs to determine if the attacker identified any vulnerabilities. Harden network defenses by closing unused ports and limiting ICMP traffic.

Detecting botnet activity

A **botnet** is a network of compromised devices, often controlled remotely by an attacker (the botmaster), which can be used to perform coordinated malicious activities, such as distributed denial-of-service (DDoS) attacks, data theft, or sending spam. Devices in a botnet (often called bots or zombies) communicate with a Command-and-Control (C&C) server to receive instructions from the attacker. Detecting botnet activity is critical because infected devices can cause significant harm to network infrastructure or be used to attack external systems.

Botnets often operate stealthily, communicating with C&C servers using protocols like HTTP, HTTPS, or IRC. The communication may appear legitimate, making it difficult to detect. Identifying the patterns of periodic communication (beaconing), large outbound data transfers, or communication with known malicious IPs can help detect botnets before they cause severe damage.

Problem: Infected devices communicating with botnet C&C servers

Scenario: Several devices on your network are behaving unusually, generating unexpected traffic. You suspect the devices have been compromised and are part of a botnet, communicating with a Command-and-Control (C&C) server.

Step-by-step solution using Wireshark:

1. **Capture traffic from the compromised devices**
   Capture traffic from the suspected devices and apply a general filter to monitor all outgoing communication:
   ip.addr == <compromised_device_IP>

2a. **Look for command-and-control traffic**
   Botnets often communicate with their C&C servers over obscure ports or encrypted channels. Apply filters for standard C&C communication ports:
   tcp.port == 6667 (IRC-based botnet)

2b. **Check for uncommon ports**
   Botnets may use uncommon ports for communication. The display filter for unusual port numbers (Figure 8.9):
   tcp.srcport > 1024 && tcp.dstport > 1024

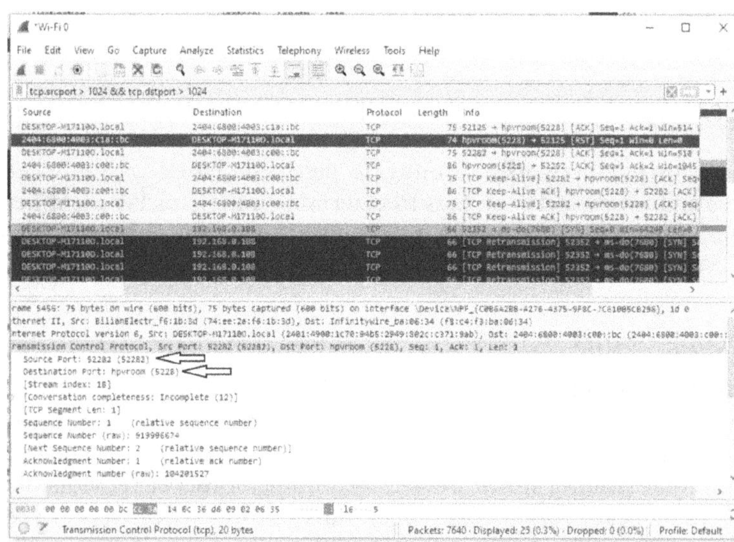

Figure 8.9 Wireshark displaying TCP communication on high-numbered ports, highlighting possible unusual port activity (Src: 52228, Dst: 5228).

ANALYZE TRAFFIC PATTERNS

Check for regular intervals of communication (beaconing) or large outbound data transfers, which are characteristic of botnet activity. This filter isolates outbound TCP packets from the IP address 192.168.1.6 that have a frame length greater than 1000 bytes. This helps identify potential data exfiltration activity (Figure 8.10).

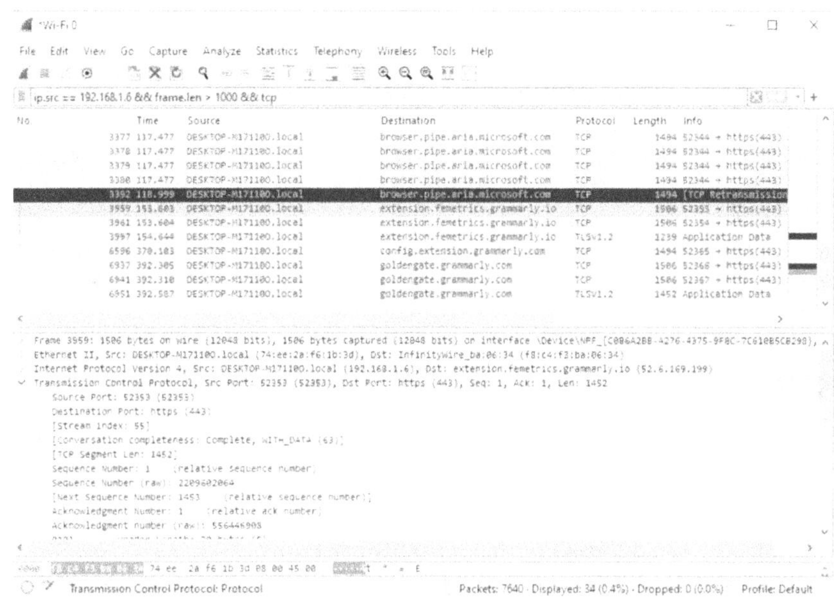

Figure 8.10 Wireshark displaying large TCP packets over HTTPS connections with application data and retransmissions.

ip.src == 192.168.1.6 && frame.len > 1000 && tcp

The screenshot shows outbound TCP packets from 192.168.1.6 to external servers, such as extension.fennetrics.grammarly.io, with frame lengths exceeding 1000 bytes, indicating potentially large data transfers over HTTPS (port 443). While large packets and successful data transmission could suggest data exfiltration, this cannot be confirmed without further investigation. The use of HTTPS makes the content of these transfers encrypted and more challenging to inspect. To confirm potential exfiltration, the external domains should be verified for legitimacy using tools like VirusTotal, traffic patterns should be analyzed for repetitive or unusual behavior, and the entire session can be reviewed using "Follow TCP Stream."

General solution

If botnet traffic is detected, disconnect the compromised devices from the network and block the external IP addresses of the C&C servers. Conduct a deeper forensic investigation and disinfect the affected devices.

CONCLUSION

Wireshark is an invaluable tool in the arsenal of network security professionals, providing granular insights into network traffic that are essential for detecting and mitigating security threats. Whether identifying malware communication, analyzing unauthorized access attempts, or spotting data exfiltration, or stopping attacks like DNS tunneling and botnet activity, Wireshark's packet-level visibility allows for proactive security measures and rapid incident response. By continuously monitoring network traffic and applying the appropriate filters, Wireshark can help prevent security breaches and protect the integrity of network systems.

MULTIPLE CHOICE QUESTIONS (MCQs)

1. What does the *tls.handshake.extensions_server_name* filter in Wireshark help identify?
   a) HTTP requests to malicious domains
   b) The IP addresses of devices on the network
   c) The hostname a client is trying to connect to during a TLS handshake
   d) The DNS server being used by the client

Answer: c)

2. Which Wireshark filter can be used to detect brute-force login attempts on SSH or RDP?
   a) tcp.port == 22 || tcp.port == 3389
   b) dns.time > 5
   c) ip.src == <device_IP>
   d) http.request.method == "POST"

Answer: a)

3. What is a common sign of DNS tunneling in network traffic?
   a) Repeated failed login attempts
   b) Large or frequent DNS queries with unusual domain names
   c) Excessive SYN packets without corresponding ACK responses
   d) Encrypted communication on port 443

Answer: b)

4. How can Wireshark help detect data exfiltration over HTTPS?
   a) By applying the filter http.request.method == "POST"
   b) By checking ssl or tls traffic for unusually large outbound data transfers
   c) By monitoring tcp.analysis.retransmission for failed data transmission
   d) By capturing broadcast traffic using eth.dst == ff:ff:ff:ff:ff:ff

Answer: b)

5. Which Wireshark filter helps detect TCP SYN scans during a potential reconnaissance attack?
   a) tcp.analysis.out_of_order
   b) tcp.flags.syn == 1 && tcp.flags.ack == 0
   c) icmp.type == 8
   d) tcp.port == 6667

Answer: b)

GLOSSARY

1. **Beaconing:** Regular, automated communications from a compromised device to a Command-and-Control (C&C) server, typically signaling an active botnet connection.
2. **Botnet:** A network of private computers infected with malicious software and controlled as a group without the owners' knowledge, e.g., to send spam or launch attacks.
3. **Brute-Force Attack:** A cyberattack method where attackers attempt to enter numerous passwords or passphrases with the hope of eventually guessing correctly.
4. **Command-and-Control (C&C) Server:** A computer that is controlled by a cybercriminal used to send commands to systems compromised by malware and to receive stolen data from a target network.
5. **Data Exfiltration:** Unauthorized transfer of data from a computer or server to an outside destination, typically used in cyber espionage or stealing sensitive information.
6. **DNS Tunneling:** Technique used to send data over DNS that is not meant for DNS, which can include transmitting malware or exfiltrating data in a way that appears as normal DNS queries and responses.
7. **ICMP Echo Scans:** A network reconnaissance technique that involves sending ICMP echo request packets to multiple hosts to determine which ones are active.
8. **Lateral Movement:** Techniques cyberattackers use to move through a network in search of key data and assets after gaining initial access through a breach.

9. **Port Scanning:** The act of systematically checking a server for open ports and services to find insecure services to exploit in further attacks.
10. **Rogue DHCP Server:** An unauthorized DHCP server on a network which provides incorrect IP addresses to clients, potentially directing them to malicious endpoints.
11. **SYN Scans:** A technique used to quickly determine if ports are open or closed by sending SYN packets and monitoring the responses without completing the TCP handshake.
12. **TCP Reset (RST) Flags:** A flag in the TCP header used to terminate a connection abruptly. It is also used in various network attacks to disrupt ongoing connections.

Chapter 9

Wireshark for port security

INTRODUCTION

Port security is critical to network defense, focusing on controlling access to specific network ports to prevent unauthorized access and mitigate potential threats. Ports serve as entry and exit points for data in network communication, and securing them is essential to maintain the integrity and confidentiality of sensitive information. Attackers can exploit misconfigured or vulnerable ports to gain unauthorized access, launch malware, or conduct denial-of-service (DoS) attacks.

Wireshark, a potent packet analysis tool, is crucial in enhancing port security by providing detailed insights into network traffic. It allows administrators to monitor open ports, detect unauthorized access attempts, and identify suspicious activities such as port scans or brute-force attacks. By leveraging Wireshark's filters, statistics, and visualization tools, network professionals can analyze traffic patterns, pinpoint vulnerabilities, and implement targeted security measures to safeguard their systems.

This chapter delves into how Wireshark can be effectively utilized for port security, covering techniques for monitoring traffic, detecting anomalies, and addressing common port-related threats. With practical examples and step-by-step guidance, it empowers readers to strengthen their network defenses and ensure the secure operation of their environments.

WHAT IS A PORT?

For the beginners, the word "port" can be confusing. So, let us understand it with the help of a simple example.

A **port** in networking is like a door that allows different types of data to enter and leave a device, such as a computer or a server, over the internet or a local network. Just like a house has multiple doors for different purposes (front door, back door, garage door), devices use different ports to manage various types of communication.

DOI: 10.1201/9781003539261-9

Simple example: Imagine your computer as a house; each port is a door for different visitors (data types). For example:

- **Port** 80 is used for web browsing (HTTP).
- **Port** 25 is used for email (SMTP).
- **Port** 22 is used for secure remote access (SSH).

When you visit a website, your computer sends a request through **port** 80 (for HTTP traffic) or **port 443** (for HTTPS, a secure version of HTTP). The website sends its response back to your computer through the same port, allowing you to view the site in your browser.

Note: In summary, ports manage specific types of network traffic, helping your device communicate with different services on the internet. Without them, your computer wouldn't know where to send or receive data.

UNDERSTANDING PORT SECURITY

Port security is a fundamental component of network security. Ports are communication endpoints that can be exploited if left unprotected. In port security, the primary goal is to monitor and control traffic flow through these network ports to prevent unauthorized access or malicious attacks.

Why port security is critical

Each open port represents a potential attack surface. For instance, leaving port 3389 (Remote Desktop Protocol) open can provide attackers access to your network if not properly secured. Attackers use techniques like port scanning to discover open or weakly protected ports.

Scenario: In 2020, a major ransomware attack exploited the RDP port (3389) to gain access to an organization's network. The attackers performed a brute-force attack on the port, eventually compromising the system.

Solution: Wireshark can be configured to monitor traffic on port 3389. By analyzing unusual patterns, such as multiple failed login attempts, administrators can detect and respond to brute-force attacks before they escalate.

ABOUT RDP

RDP (Remote Desktop Protocol) is a protocol developed by Microsoft that allows users to connect and control another computer or server remotely over a network. Using RDP, you can access a desktop environment on a remote machine as if sitting in front of it, even if it's located in another city or country.

How RDP works

When you use an RDP client (such as the **Remote Desktop** application in Windows), it opens a secure channel to the remote computer.

- This connection lets you see the remote desktop, interact with files, run applications, and manage the system, just like you would on your own computer.
- RDP can be a target for cyberattacks, especially **brute-force** attacks, if not adequately secured. Best practices include using strong passwords, enabling two-factor authentication, and limiting access through firewalls or VPNs.

For example, imagine working from home and needing to access your office computer. Instead of physically being at the office, you can use RDP to remotely log in to your office computer, access all the files and applications you need, and work as if you're in the office.

- **Your computer** (**Client**): Initiates the RDP connection.
- **Office computer** (**Server**): The machine you're connecting to.

In short, RDP is a handy tool for remote access. Still, proper security measures are needed to ensure it's not misused.

SETTING UP WIRESHARK FOR PORT SECURITY

To effectively use Wireshark for port security, it is important to configure it properly to capture relevant data. Wireshark offers filters that allow you to focus on specific traffic to/from certain ports.

Capture filters can significantly narrow down the traffic you want to monitor. For example, if you're investigating traffic on port 80 (HTTP), you can use the following capture filter:

tcp port 80

Scenario: An organization suspects that its web server on port 80 is being targeted by a denial-of-service (DoS) attack. By setting up a capture filter for port 80, network administrators can monitor traffic for abnormal spikes in incoming requests, indicating the onset of a DoS attack.

Solution: Use Wireshark to detect and block malicious IP addresses that contribute to traffic overload. The organization could then set up a firewall rule to block the offending IPs.

ANALYZING TRAFFIC FOR PORT SECURITY

Wireshark enables you to capture and analyze network traffic flowing through specific ports. This analysis is crucial for detecting anomalies, securing open ports, and preventing unauthorized access.

Identifying open ports and vulnerabilities

One of the first steps in securing a network is identifying open ports. Wireshark can reveal which ports are actively receiving traffic, potentially exposing vulnerabilities.

Scenario: An IT administrator discovers that port 23 (Telnet) is open on a server, which could expose the system to attacks since Telnet transmits data in plaintext.

Solution: After identifying Telnet traffic using the filter *tcp.port == 23*, the administrator advises disabling Telnet or replacing it with a secure alternative like SSH (port 22). This action reduces the likelihood of a man-in-the-middle attack.

DETECTING PORT SCANNING ATTEMPTS

Port scanning is a common reconnaissance technique used by attackers to find open or vulnerable ports. Wireshark can help detect these attempts by capturing traffic patterns that match typical port scanning behavior.

Scenario: A company's network starts experiencing random connection attempts across multiple ports. Using Wireshark, the security team detects multiple SYN packets without corresponding ACK responses, indicating a possible port scan.

Solution: If you suspect a specific device is being scanned, follow the steps given for that specific device.

1. **Apply a filter to isolate SYN packets**
   Use the following filter to display SYN packets:
   tcp.flags.syn == 1 and tcp.flags.ack == 0

This filter captures TCP packets with the SYN flag set and excludes those with the ACK flag, which are the initial connection attempts. Look for multiple SYN packets from a single source IP to various destination ports (Figure 9.1).

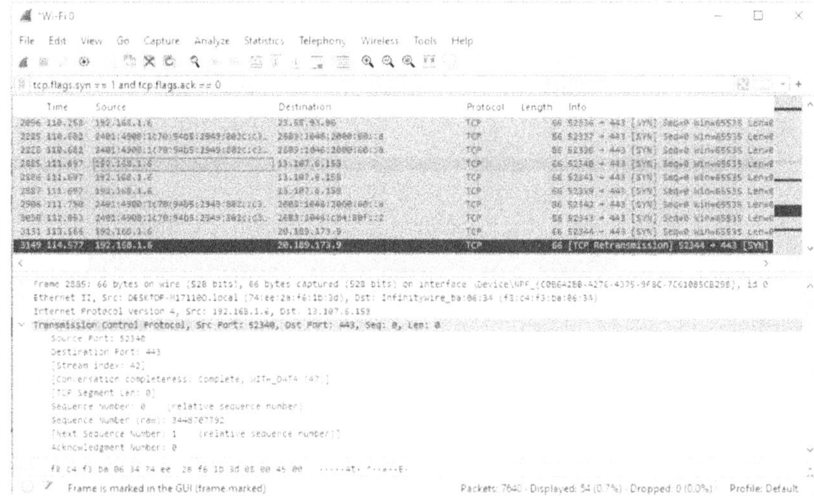

Figure 9.1 Wireshark screenshot displaying TCP SYN packets during connection establishment with applied filter, showing source/destination IPs and TCP details.

Saving packets in Step 1 is necessary when you want to focus solely on SYN packets for further analysis, especially in high-traffic networks or when creating a clean dataset for offline investigation. By saving only the filtered SYN packets, you ensure a manageable dataset for subsequent steps, such as checking for missing SYN-ACK responses, without needing to reapply filters on the entire capture. However, for quick real-time analysis, you can directly apply the necessary filters (e.g., SYN packets and then SYN-ACK packets) sequentially without saving. You can also highlight the filtered packets (Ctrl+A) and mark them using *Right-click → **Mark Packet*** or press **Ctrl+M**. This way, after applying the filter in step 3, the comparison becomes easy to make.

Note: You can also save packets to open in a notepad++ using *File → Export Packet Dissections → As Plain Text* to save SYN packet details.

2. **Identify suspicious patterns**
   Examine the Source IP and Destination Ports:
   - Suppose a single source IP is attempting to connect to many different destination ports. In that case, this is a strong indicator of a horizontal port scan.
   - Multiple source IPs targeting the same port could indicate a vertical scan or a distributed attack.
3. **Check for missing SYN-ACK responses**
   To confirm the lack of SYN-ACK responses, use this filter:
   tcp.flags.syn == 1 and tcp.flags.ack == 1

Suppose the original SYN packets do not have corresponding SYN-ACK responses. In that case, it indicates that the connection attempts are incomplete and likely malicious.

4. **Analyze conversations**
   Go to *Statistics → Conversations → TCP tab*:
   Look for:
   - Connections with only **1 or 2 packets** (indicating incomplete handshakes) and high-frequency connection attempts from a single source IP.
   - Sort the table by packet count or bytes to identify suspicious traffic patterns.
5. **Look for retransmissions**
   Use the filter:
   tcp.analysis.retransmission
   Repeated SYN packets from the same source indicate retries, often during a SYN flood or port scan.
6. **Export and save the capture**
   Save the relevant packets for documentation or further analysis:
   File → Save As → [filename].pcapng
7. **Use threat intelligence tools**
   Investigate the source IP using online threat intelligence platforms like virusTotal to determine if it is associated with known malicious activity.
8. **Mitigate the threat**
   - Block the source IP on the firewall.
   - Monitor for similar behavior across other devices in the network.

Monitoring specific ports for suspicious activity

Certain ports are more vulnerable to attacks than others. Monitoring critical ports, such as 21 (FTP), 22 (SSH), and 3389 (RDP), helps detect suspicious activity and prevent exploitation.

Scenario: An FTP server on port 21 shows unusual traffic patterns. Wireshark monitors all traffic on this port with the filter *tcp.port == 21.*

Solution: The analysis reveals that a large number of failed login attempts are occurring, signaling a potential brute-force attack. The administrator immediately blocks access to the FTP server from unrecognized IP addresses and configures the server to require two-factor authentication (2FA) for access.

DETECTING AND PREVENTING MALWARE ACTIVITY

Wireshark can also be used to detect malicious payloads being transmitted through network ports. For example, suppose malware is trying to communicate with an external command-and-control server. In that case, Wireshark can capture and analyze the packets.

Scenario: A network workstation communicates with an external IP address on port 4444, commonly associated with malicious Command-and-Control (C&C) traffic, raising concerns about potential malware activity or unauthorized data exchange.

Solution: The security team uses the following display filter

tcp.port == 4444

This filter shows all packets where the source or destination port is 4444.

1. Identify the external IP Address
- Check the Source IP and Destination IP columns in the capture.
- Look for the suspicious external IP involved in communication with the workstation.
- To focus on traffic involving this IP, use an additional filter:

  ip.addr == <suspicious_IP>
  Note: Replace <suspicious_IP> with the actual external IP address.
2. Analyze the traffic
- Inspect packet contents:
  - Click on packets involving the external IP and port 4444.
  - Examine the packet details pane (middle pane) for:
    - Protocol information (e.g., TCP payloads, potential shell commands, or suspicious patterns).
    - Application-layer details, if unencrypted.
- Follow the TCP stream:
  - Right-click on a packet and select *Follow → TCP Stream* to reconstruct the full conversation between the workstation and the external IP.

BLOCKING MALICIOUS IPS BASED ON PORT ACTIVITY

Wireshark can also help create firewall rules to block malicious traffic. By analyzing traffic to specific ports, administrators can block IP addresses that are engaging in suspicious behavior.

Scenario: Wireshark detects unusual traffic on port 25 (SMTP), likely indicating a spam or phishing attack originating from a specific IP address.

Solution: After identifying the malicious IP, the administrator adds a firewall rule to block all traffic from that address, preventing further abuse of the SMTP service.

CASE STUDY: PREVENTING A RANSOMWARE ATTACK VIA RDP

A ransomware group targeted a healthcare organization that exploited the RDP port (3389). The attackers used a brute-force technique to gain access to the system. Fortunately, the security team had Wireshark running and noticed repeated failed login attempts.

Solution: The team could identify the attack in real time by using Wireshark's display filter *tcp.port == 3389*. They immediately blocked the attacker's IP and disabled RDP access from external networks. In addition, they enforced multi-factor authentication (MFA) for all future RDP connections, preventing similar attacks.

CONCLUSION

Wireshark is a powerful tool for securing network ports by enabling in-depth traffic analysis, detecting suspicious activity, and identifying vulnerabilities. Administrators can proactively use Wireshark to monitor port activity, secure open ports, detect port scanning attempts, and prevent unauthorized access. Through real-time monitoring and packet analysis, Wireshark enhances port security, protecting networks from a wide range of threats.

MULTIPLE CHOICE QUESTIONS (MCQs)

1. What is the primary purpose of port security?
   A) To increase data transfer speeds
   B) To monitor and control traffic flow through network ports
   C) To ensure ports are always open for faster communication
   D) To reduce network latency

Answer: B)

2. Which Wireshark filter would you use to capture traffic on port 80?
   A) tcp.flags.syn == 1
   B) tcp.port == 80
   C) udp.port == 80
   D) ip.addr == 80.0.0.1

Answer: B)

3. What does the presence of multiple SYN packets without corresponding ACK responses indicate?
   A) Normal network behaviour
   B) A successful TCP connection

C) A potential port scan or SYN flood attack
D) An error in the network capture
Answer: c)

4. Which port is commonly associated with FTP traffic?
   A) 22
   B) 23
   C) 21
   D) 3389
Answer: C)

5. What is the recommended Wireshark display filter to identify suspicious activity on port 4444?
   A) udp.port == 4444
   B) tcp.port == 4444
   C) ip.addr == 4444
   D) tcp.analysis.retransmission && port 4444
Answer: B)

GLOSSARY

1. **Brute-force attack: It is a** method of guessing passwords, encryption keys, or IDs by trying many possibilities, like trying every word in a dictionary.
2. **Denial-of-Service (DoS) Attack:** An attack intended to shut down a machine or network, making it inaccessible to its intended users by overwhelming it with traffic from multiple sources.
3. **FTP (File Transfer Protocol):** A standard network protocol used to transfer computer files between a client and server on a computer network.
4. **Malware:**Malicious software designed to perform unauthorized processes that compromise data integrity, confidentiality, or availability.
5. **Man-in-the-Middle Attack:** An attack where the attacker secretly relays and possibly alters the communication between two parties who believe they are directly communicating.
6. **Port:**A virtual point where network connections start and end. Ports are software-based and managed by a computer's operating system.
7. **Port Scanning:** Systematically scanning a computer's ports to find vulnerabilities.
8. **RDP (Remote Desktop Protocol):** A proprietary protocol developed by Microsoft which provides a user with a graphical interface to connect to another computer over a network connection.
9. **SMTP (Simple Mail Transfer Protocol):** A protocol for sending email messages between servers. Most email systems that send mail over the Internet use SMTP to send messages from one server to another.

10. **SSH (Secure Shell):** A cryptographic network protocol for operating network services securely over an unsecured network. Typical applications include remote command-line login and remote command execution.
11. **SYN Packet:** A packet using the SYN flag is part of the TCP protocol used during the handshake process to establish a connection between two network devices.

Chapter 10

Detecting and analyzing MITM attacks

INTRODUCTION

A Man-in-the-Middle (MITM) attack is a cyberattack in which an attacker secretly intercepts, relays, and possibly alters communication between two parties who believe they are directly communicating with each other (Figure 10.1).

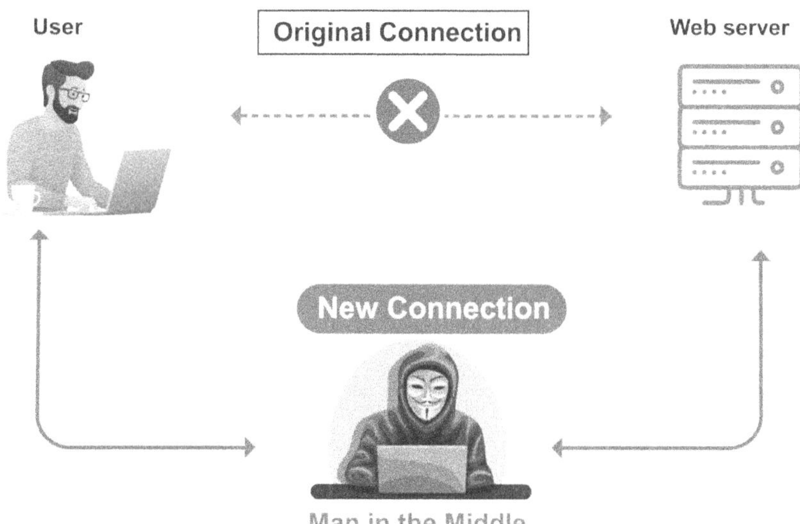

Figure 10.1 Illustration of a Man-in-the-Middle attack, showing a user, a web server, and an attacker intercepting the connection.

This attack can expose sensitive data, such as login credentials, personal messages, and financial details. Understanding the types of MITM attacks and their detection is crucial for preventing these sophisticated cyber intrusions. This chapter will explore various MITM attacks, provide real-life examples, and discuss detection and prevention methods using Wireshark.

DOI: 10.1201/9781003539261-10

UNDERSTANDING MAN-IN-THE-MIDDLE ATTACKS

In an MITM attack, the attacker aims to eavesdrop on communication or manipulate the data transmitted between two parties. This is usually achieved by positioning themselves between the two devices or intercepting their network communication. MITM attacks are often used in combination with techniques like phishing or malware infections to compromise user security.

Key components of an MITM attack

Interception: The attacker intercepts data transmitted between two devices (a user and a website).

Decryption/relaying: The attacker may decrypt the data (if it's encrypted) or alter the communication to steal information or inject malicious content.

Impersonation: The attacker may impersonate one party to manipulate the other, gaining access to sensitive data.

MITM attacks can take many forms depending on the attacker's objective and the vulnerabilities being exploited. Below, we outline some of the most common types of MITM attacks, provide real-world examples, and suggest solutions.

ARP spoofing (address resolution protocol spoofing)

ARP spoofing is a type of MITM attack where the attacker sends false ARP messages over a local network, associating their own MAC address with the IP address of a legitimate device. This allows the attacker to intercept traffic intended for the legitimate device, gaining access to sensitive data or furthering their attack by redirecting traffic to malicious websites. But for beginners, let us learn about ARP first.

About ARP table

An **ARP table** (also known as an **ARP cache**) is a data structure used by devices on a network to store mappings of **IP addresses** to **MAC addresses.** This table helps devices efficiently route traffic within a local area network (LAN) by avoiding the need to repeatedly perform ARP requests to resolve MAC addresses for known IP addresses. This cache is periodically updated.

Table 10.1 provides an example of how a simple **ARP table** might look on a network device.

Table 10.1 IP address, MAC address, and interface table

IP address	*MAC address*	*Interface*
192.168.1.1	00:14:22:01:23:45	Ethernet
192.168.1.2	00:16:17:01:45:67	Ethernet
192.168.1.3	00:18:C2:3E:67:89	Wi-Fi
192.168.1.4	00:1D:A2:34:89:12	Ethernet
192.168.1.5	00:13:F2:45:AB	Ethernet

How ARP works

ARP (Address Resolution Protocol) is a network protocol used to map an IP address (Internet Protocol address) to a MAC address (Media Access Control address) within a local network. This mapping is essential because, while devices on a network communicate with each other using IP addresses at the network layer, the actual data transfer at the physical layer (Ethernet) requires the MAC address. This is how ARP Works:

1. *Request*: When a device (let's call it Device A) wants to communicate with another device (Device B) on the same local network, it first checks if it knows the MAC address associated with Device B's IP address. If Device A doesn't know the MAC address, it sends out an **ARP request** to all devices on the network, asking, "Who has this IP address?"
2. *Response*: Device B, which owns the IP address, responds with an **ARP reply**, providing its MAC address. Device A can now use this MAC address to send data directly to Device B.

For example, suppose a computer with the IP address 192.168.1.10 wants to send data to another computer with the IP address 192.168.1.20. In that case, it first uses ARP (Address Resolution Protocol) to discover the MAC address associated with 192.168.1.20. Once it has the MAC address, it can send the data to the data link layer (like Ethernet and Wi-Fi).

Viewing the ARP table

- On **Windows**, you can view the ARP table (Figure 10.2) using the command:
  arp –a
- On **Linux** or **macOS**, use:
  arp -n

```
C:\Users\admin>arp -a

Interface: 192.168.1.6 --- 0x10
  Internet Address      Physical Address      Type
  192.168.1.1           f8-c4-f3-ba-06-34     dynamic
  192.168.1.3           fa-f1-ee-d2-63-14     dynamic
  192.168.1.5           00-6f-64-b8-df-ef     dynamic
  192.168.1.255         ff-ff-ff-ff-ff-ff     static
  224.0.0.2             01-00-5e-00-00-02     static
  224.0.0.22            01-00-5e-00-00-16     static
  224.0.0.251           01-00-5e-00-00-fb     static
  224.0.0.252           01-00-5e-00-00-fc     static
  239.192.152.143       01-00-5e-40-98-8f     static
  239.255.255.250       01-00-5e-7f-ff-fa     static
  255.255.255.255       ff-ff-ff-ff-ff-ff     static
```

Figure 10.2 A command prompt window displaying the output of the "arp -a" command, showing a list of IP addresses and their corresponding MAC addresses.

This ARP table helps your device quickly look up the MAC addresses of other devices on the same network, reducing the need for ARP requests and improving network performance.

Scenario: In a corporate office, an attacker within the same local network as employees uses ARP spoofing to intercept traffic between the company's gateway and employees' devices. The attacker captures login credentials for internal systems, gaining unauthorized access to critical data.

Solution:

Detection: Wireshark detects ARP spoofing by applying the display filter *arp.duplicate-address-frame*. It highlights duplicate ARP responses, which indicate ARP spoofing.

Prevention:

- **Use static ARP entries:** This method can limit the success of ARP spoofing by binding MAC addresses to specific IPs.
- **Enable port security on switches:** This can help limit which devices can send ARP requests and responses.
- **Use ARP inspection tools:** Dynamic ARP Inspection (DAI) on switches can prevent ARP spoofing by validating ARP packets.

DNS SPOOFING (DNS CACHE POISONING)

DNS spoofing, also known as DNS cache poisoning, occurs when an attacker corrupts the DNS cache of a device or network to redirect traffic intended for legitimate websites to malicious websites. Once users are redirected, the attacker can steal login credentials and financial information or infect their device with malware (see Figure 10.3).

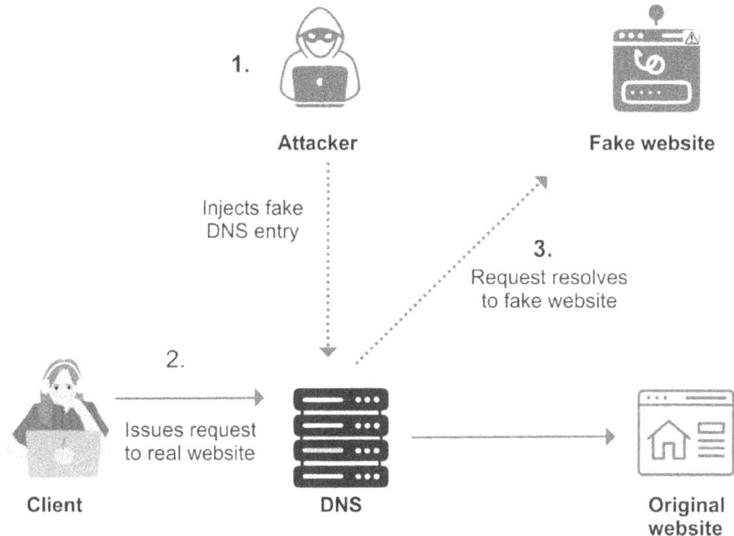

Figure 10.3 A diagram depicting a DNS spoofing attack, showing an attacker injecting a fake DNS entry and redirecting a client to a fake website.

Scenario: A user attempts to access their bank's website. But, due to DNS spoofing, they are redirected to a fake website that looks identical to the legitimate one. The user enters their login credentials, unknowingly giving the attacker access to their bank account.

Solution:

Detection: The *dns.flags.rcode != 0* filter helps detect DNS spoofing by identifying error responses that deviate from normal behavior. DNS spoofing attacks may generate errors like "Name Error" (Rcode 3) or "Refused" (Rcode 5) to block legitimate domains or redirect users to malicious sites. By analyzing these unexpected DNS error patterns, especially in response to valid queries, this filter enables you to spot potential manipulation in DNS traffic and investigate the possible spoofing activity, aiding in quicker threat detection and response. Also, check if the DNS response comes from unexpected or suspicious servers.

If there is no capture, you can perform two critical steps: detect multiple responses for the same query and check for anomalous IP addresses. First, monitor DNS traffic for duplicate responses with the same Transaction ID but different answer sections (in the middle pane, under the Domain Name System layer), as this often indicates an attacker attempting to spoof the response before the legitimate one arrives. Use filters like *dns.id* to identify these duplicates. Second, inspect DNS responses for unexpected or suspicious IP addresses. By focusing on the *dns.flags.response == 1* filter, you can analyze resolved IPs and verify whether they align with trusted destinations. These two steps are practical and efficient for identifying spoofed DNS traffic (Figure 10.4).

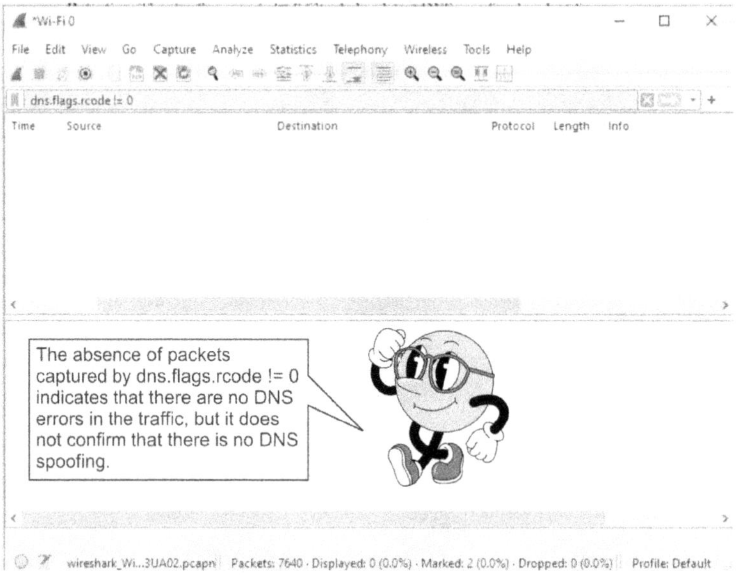

Figure 10.4 Wireshark screen showing absence of traffic.

Prevention:

- *Use DNSSEC*: DNS Security Extensions (DNSSEC) ensure that DNS responses are signed, making it harder for attackers to forge DNS responses.
- *Configure firewall rules*: Restrict which DNS servers can be accessed by users.
- *Regularly clear DNS cache*: This reduces the risk of a poisoned cache persisting on devices.

Note: For a regular user, using DNSSEC involves configuring your device or router to use a DNS resolver that supports DNSSEC validation, such as Google Public DNS (8.8.8.8 and 8.8.4.4), Cloudflare (1.1.1.1 and 1.0.0.1), or Quad9 (9.9.9.9). This ensures your DNS queries are authenticated and protected from tampering.

SSL STRIPPING

SSL stripping is an MITM attack where the attacker downgrades a secure HTTPS connection to an unencrypted HTTP connection. The attacker intercepts the initial request for an HTTPS site, relays it to the legitimate server, and then serves the HTTP version of the site to the user. This lets the attacker capture sensitive information like login credentials in plain text (see Figure 10.5).

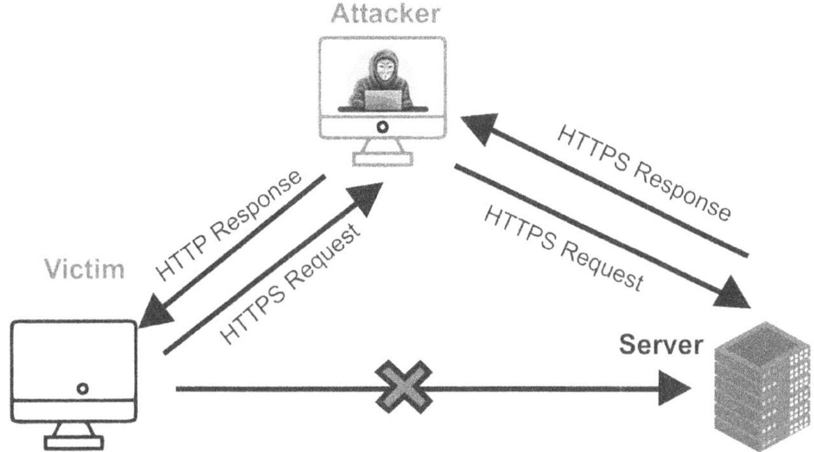

Figure 10.5 A diagram showing an SSL stripping attack where the attacker downgrades an HTTPS connection to HTTP to intercept data.

Scenario: A user tries to log in to a shopping website, but an attacker intercepts the HTTPS connection and downgrades it to HTTP. The user unknowingly submits their login information over an unencrypted connection, allowing the attacker to steal their credentials.

Solution

Detection: The two most important filters to detect SSL stripping in Wireshark are:

1. **Look for HTTP after HTTPS ClientHello:**
   Display Filter: *http && tcp.port == 80*
   This filter shows HTTP traffic (port 80) that may follow an HTTPS ClientHello (port 443), which could indicate SSL stripping if the traffic is downgraded from HTTPS to HTTP.
2 **Filter for HTTP Redirection (301/302):**
   Use the display filter: *http.response.code == 301* || *http.response.code == 302*
   This filter identifies HTTP redirects commonly used in SSL stripping to force a switch from HTTPS to HTTP. Or there could be no capture (Figure 10.6).

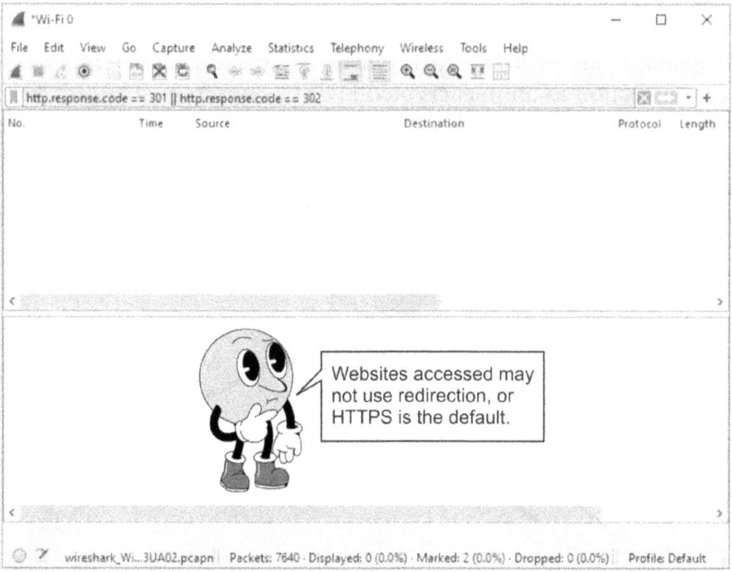

Figure 10.6 Wireshark's interface with a filter applied for HTTP response codes 301 or 302, indicating no packets matching the filter criteria.

- **http.response.code == 301**: Captures HTTP responses with the status code 301 (Moved Permanently).
- **http.response.code == 302**: Captures HTTP responses with the status code 302 (Found or Temporarily Moved).

PREVENTION

- **HSTS (HTTP Strict Transport Security)**: Websites can implement HSTS headers, which force browsers to connect only via HTTPS and prevent downgrading to HTTP.
- **Use a VPN**: A VPN can encrypt all traffic between a user and the internet, preventing MITM attacks.
- **Educate users**: Users should always check for the padlock symbol in their browser's address bar, indicating a secure HTTPS connection.

WI-FI EAVESDROPPING

Wi-Fi eavesdropping occurs when an attacker sets up a fake Wi-Fi network or infiltrates an existing one to intercept and monitor the communications of users connected to the network. In public places like cafes or airports, attackers can create fake Wi-Fi hotspots with names that resemble legitimate networks.

Scenario: An attacker sets up a Wi-Fi network named "CoffeeShop_FreeWiFi" in a popular cafe. Unsuspecting customers connect to the network, and the attacker intercepts their browsing data, including login credentials, emails, and personal messages (Figure 10.7).

Figure 10.7 A person working on a laptop at a coffee shop.

Solution:

Detection: You can use the following filters for the following mentioned purposes.

Filter for HTTP traffic (http): Displays unencrypted HTTP traffic (port 80), which is vulnerable to eavesdropping.

Filter for WEP handshakes (*wlan.fc.type_subtype == 0x08*): Identifies WEP traffic, which is weakly encrypted and easily intercepted.

Filter for WPA tandshakes (*eapol*): Captures WPA handshake packets, which can be analyzed for potential vulnerabilities in encryption.

Filter for open networks (*wlan.fc.type_subtype == 0x00*): Detects open, unencrypted Wi-Fi networks highly susceptible to eavesdropping. The info column displays something like Authentication Request (Open System). This indicates that the device is attempting to authenticate, and the authentication type is "Open System" (typically used for open, unsecured networks).

Filter for probe requests (*wlan.fc.type_subtype == 0x04*): Identifies probe requests, often sent by eavesdroppers to discover available Wi-Fi networks.

Filter for rogue access point (fake Wi-Fi network) (*wlan.ssid == "CoffeeShop_FreeWiFi")*: Suppose a rogue access point is set up with an SSID that mimics a legitimate network, like "CoffeeShop_FreeWiFi" in your example. In that case, you can identify it using SSID filters. Eavesdropping attackers often create these fake networks to lure users in.

Prevention:

- *Use VPNs on public Wi-Fi*: Always connect through a VPN when using public Wi-Fi to encrypt your traffic.
- *Avoid public Wi-Fi for sensitive activities*: Users should avoid accessing banking sites or online purchases on public Wi-Fi.
- *Verify legitimate networks*: Before connecting, verify the name and legitimacy of the public Wi-Fi network with the business or venue.
    - *Disable automatic Wi-Fi connections*: This prevents your device from automatically connecting to rogue networks without your consent, reducing the risk of future incidents.

SESSION HIJACKING

Session hijacking occurs when an attacker steals or predicts a valid session token, which allows them to impersonate the legitimate user in an active session. This typically happens in web applications where session cookies authenticate users (see Figure 10.8).

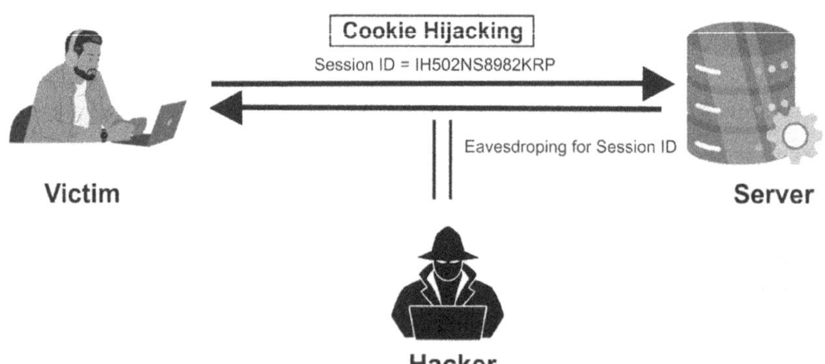

Figure 10.8 A diagram illustrating cookie hijacking, with a session ID being eavesdropped by an attacker between a victim and a server.

About session token

A session token is a unique identifier generated by a server and assigned to a user for the duration of a session, typically after the user has successfully authenticated. It is used to maintain the user's state across multiple requests to the server, enabling the server to recognize the user and manage their session without requiring them to log in repeatedly.

Scenario: An attacker on the same Wi-Fi network as the victim captures their session cookie for a social media site. The attacker then uses the session cookie to log in as the victim, gaining access to their account without needing their password.

Solution:

Detection: In Wireshark, use the following filters to protect from session hijacking.

- *http.cookie*: Detect HTTP traffic containing session cookies that could be vulnerable to interception.
- *http*: Identify unencrypted HTTP traffic, which could expose session information to attackers.
- *http.cookie contains "JSESSIONID"*: Look for specific session IDs in cookies that might be targeted in session hijacking or fixation. Suppose the JSESSIONID is set in the HTTP response (i.e., from the server to the client). In that case, the **Info** column indicates the HTTP response status (e.g., HTTP/1.1 200 OK) and may show Set-Cookie in the response header. In the Packet Details section (middle pane in Wireshark), expand the **HTTP** section and look for the **Cookie** field in the **request** or the **Set-Cookie** field in **response** to see the actual **JSESSIONID** value.
- *tcp.port == 80 or tcp.port == 443*: Monitor all HTTP and HTTPS traffic for any suspicious session data or potential hijacking attempts.
- *ssl.handshake*: Detect SSL/TLS handshakes and ensure the connection remains encrypted, helping to prevent SSL stripping.

Note: The JSESSIONID cookie maintains the session state between the client (browser) and the server. It ensures that requests from the same client are associated with the correct server-side session.

Prevention

- *Use HTTPS for all sessions*: Ensure that session cookies are always transmitted over an encrypted connection (HTTPS).
- *Implement Secure and HttpOnly flags on cookies*: This reduces the risk of stolen session cookies via cross-site scripting (XSS) attacks.
- *Session expiration*: Use short session expiration times and require reauthentication for sensitive actions.

GENERAL SOLUTIONS FOR MITM ATTACKS

The following are general solutions for MITM attacks.

Use encryption

Always use encrypted communication channels, such as SSL/TLS for web traffic and SSH for remote connections. When accessing sensitive accounts or websites, switch to mobile data or use a trusted VPN to encrypt your connection. Encryption makes it difficult for attackers to decipher the data they intercept.

Enable two-factor authentication (2FA)

Implement 2FA for all critical services to add a layer of security. Even if attackers intercept login credentials, they won't be able to access the account without the second authentication factor.

Employ intrusion detection systems (IDS)

Deploy an IDS or Intrusion Prevention System (IPS) to monitor network traffic for suspicious activity and flag potential MITM attacks.

Educate users

Train users to recognize signs of MITM attacks, such as certificate warnings or unexpected website behavior. Encouraging security best practices like checking for HTTPS and avoiding unsecured Wi-Fi can prevent many MITM attacks. They should learn to clear cookies in their browser settings to remove session cookies that might persist.

CONCLUSION

Man-in-the-Middle (MITM) attacks are among the most dangerous threats to network security, targeting sensitive communication between devices. This chapter explored various MITM attack techniques, such as ARP spoofing, DNS spoofing, SSL stripping, Wi-Fi eavesdropping, and session hijacking. Using tools like Wireshark, security professionals can detect these attacks in real time by analyzing anomalies in network traffic and applying targeted filters.

Organizations can mitigate the risk of MITM attacks by implementing robust security measures, such as encryption, two-factor authentication, and intrusion detection systems. Proactive education and tools like Wireshark ensure that professionals and users are better equipped to recognize and respond to potential threats. By combining technical expertise with preventive measures, MITM attacks can be effectively identified and neutralized, safeguarding critical data and communication.

MULTIPLE CHOICE QUESTIONS (MCQs)

1. AWhat is the primary purpose of an ARP table in a network?
   A) To manage session tokens between devices
   B) To store IP-to-MAC address mappings for efficient communication
   C) To detect DNS spoofing attempts in real time
   D) To log HTTP traffic details for analysis

   Answer: B)

2. Which Wireshark filter is most helpful in detecting ARP spoofing?
   A) tcp.port == 443
   B) arp.duplicate-address-frame
   C) dns.flags.rcode != 0
   D) http.cookie

   Answer: b)

3. What does the http.response.code == 301 || http.response.code == 302 filter detect in Wireshark?
   A) DNS tunneling attempts
   B) ARP spoofing attacks
   C) SSL stripping using HTTP redirects
   D) Session hijacking

   Answer: c)

4. How can Wireshark detect DNS spoofing attempts?
   A) By filtering for http.cookie traffic
   B) By analyzing dns.flags.rcode != 0 for errors in DNS responses
   C) By checking tcp.flags.syn == 1
   D) By monitoring ip.src == <device_IP>

   Answer: B)

5. Which prevention technique is most effective against session hijacking?
   A) Using unencrypted HTTP connections
   B) Implementing Secure and HttpOnly flags on cookies
   C) Disabling ARP table updates
   D) Increasing DNS cache size

   Answer: B)

GLOSSARY

1. **ARP Spoofing:** A type of MITM attack where the attacker sends false ARP (Address Resolution Protocol) messages over a local area network. This links the attacker's MAC address with the IP address of another host, such as the default gateway, causing any traffic meant for that IP address to be sent to the attacker instead.
2. **ARP Table (ARP Cache):** A table computers use to store IP addresses and their resolved MAC addresses. The table correlates each machine's IP address and its corresponding MAC address.
3. **DNS Spoofing (DNS Cache Poisoning):** A technique used by attackers to alter DNS records and mislead users into visiting fraudulent sites or intercepting email communications.
4. **HSTS (HTTP Strict Transport Security):** A web security policy mechanism that helps to protect websites against man-in-the-middle attacks such as protocol downgrade attacks and cookie hijacking.
5. **IDS (Intrusion Detection System):** A device or software application that monitors a network or systems for malicious activity or policy violations.
6. **IPSec (Internet Protocol Security):** A protocol suite for securing Internet Protocol (IP) communications by authenticating and encrypting each IP packet of a communication session
7. **MITM Attack (Man-in-the-Middle Attack):** A cyberattack where the attacker secretly intercepts and possibly alters the communication between two parties who believe they are directly communicating with each other.
8. **Session Hijacking:** An attack where the user session is taken over by the attacker, typically by obtaining or predicting the session token used to authenticate within a web session
9. **SSL Stripping:** A security exploit where an attacker intercepts and alters communications between a client and a server, downgrading the connection's security from HTTPS (secure) to HTTP (non-secure) to intercept data that should otherwise be encrypted.
10. **TLS Handshake:** The process that initiates a communication session in a TLS-secured connection. It ensures that the client and server agree on the encryption standards and keys before exchanging data.
11. **VPN (Virtual Private Network):** A service that extends a private network across a public network, enabling users to send and receive data across shared or public networks as if their computing devices were directly connected to the private network.

Chapter 11

Solving DNS-related issues

INTRODUCTION

The Domain Name System (DNS) is a foundational technology of the internet, serving as the protocol that translates human-friendly domain names into IP addresses, allowing users to navigate the web effortlessly. However, DNS can be a source of various issues that affect connectivity, security, and overall network performance. This chapter delves into troubleshooting DNS problems using Wireshark, providing solutions for various issues, from misconfigurations to security threats like DNS poisoning attacks.

UNDERSTANDING DNS

Before delving into troubleshooting, it's essential to understand how DNS operates:

Querying a DNS server

A user types a domain name in a browser. The local DNS resolver queries a DNS server to resolve this domain name into an IP address.

Example: When a user types "www.example.com" into their browser, their device sends a DNS query to the configured DNS server (e.g., 8.8.8.8) asking for the IP address associated with "www.example.com".

Wireshark Filter: Use the filter *dns && dns.qry.name == "www.example.com"* to capture only the DNS queries for this domain.

Recursive lookup

Suppose the DNS server does not have the IP address cached. In that case, it performs a recursive query, contacting other DNS servers until the IP is resolved.

Example: If the DNS server receives a request for "www.example.com" but doesn't have the answer in its cache, it will query the root DNS servers, then

DOI: 10.1201/9781003539261-11

the TLD (Top-Level Domain) servers for ".com", and finally the authoritative DNS server for "example.com" to find the correct IP address (Figure 11.1).

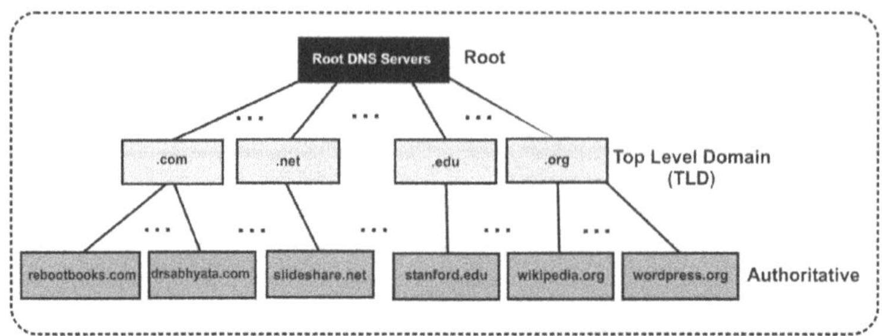

Figure 11.1 A hierarchy of DNS servers, including root DNS servers, top-level domains (TLDs), and authoritative domains like rebootbooks.com and wikipedia.org.

Wireshark filter: Use *dns.flags.recdesired* == *1* to filter for DNS recursive queries.

Returning the result

The resolved IP address is returned to the local resolver, allowing the user's device to connect to the target server.

Example: Once the DNS server resolves "www.example.com" to its IP address (e.g., 93.184.216.34), it returns this information to the user's device, which can now connect to the website.

Wireshark filter: Use *dns.flags.response* == *1* to filter for successful DNS responses (Figure 11.2).

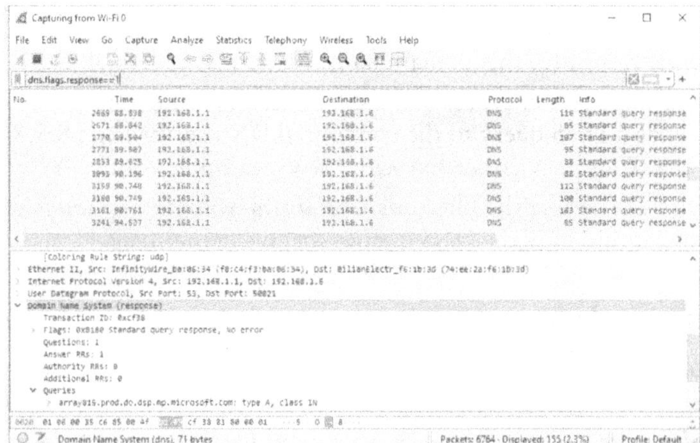

Figure 11.2 A Wireshark capture of DNS traffic, displaying standard query responses between a source (192.168.1.1) and destination (192.168.1.6).

Note: A filter such as *dns.flags.response == 1* may hide DNS query packets, showing only the responses. Using a broader filter like *dns* can display both queries and responses.

DNS ZONE

A DNS zone is a segment of the Domain Name System (DNS) namespace managed by a specific entity, such as an organization or administrator. It contains records that map domain names to IP addresses and other related information, like mail server details or name server (NS) delegations. DNS zones help divide the DNS hierarchy into smaller, more manageable parts to distribute control and ensure efficient resolution of domain names.

Each DNS zone has resource records (RRs), such as A records (for IPv4 addresses), AAAA records (for IPv6), MX records (for mail exchange), and CNAME records (for aliases). DNS zones can be primary (authoritative), where changes are made, or secondary, which act as backups with read-only copies of the primary zone. Additionally, DNS zones can be categorized as forward zones (for name-to-IP lookups) or reverse zones (for IP-to-name lookups). Efficient management of DNS zones ensures faster domain resolution and plays a critical role in the functioning of the internet.

DNS zone file

A DNS zone file is a text file that contains mappings between domain names and IP addresses along with other DNS records for a specific domain. It is critical to manage how DNS queries are handled for that domain. In Table 11.1 you can see the record type and its mapping to various parameters.

Table 11.1 Zone file for example.com

Record type	*Host*	*Value*	*TTL (Time-to-Live)*	*Description*
SOA	example.com.	ns1.example.com. admin .example.com. 1 3600 1800 604800 86400	86400	Start of Authority (Primary DNS and contact info)
NS	example.com.	ns1.example.com.	86400	Nameserver for the domain
NS	example.com.	ns2.example.com.	86400	Secondary nameserver
A	example.com.	192.0.2.1	3600	Maps domain name to IPv4 address
AAAA	example.com.	2001:db8::1	3600	Maps domain name to IPv6 address
CNAME	www.example .com.	example.com.	3600	Alias for example.com
MX	example.com.	mail.example.com. (Priority: 10)	3600	Mail server for the domain
TXT	example.com.	"v=spf1 ip4:192.0.2.1 -all"	3600	SPF record for email authentication

In this example:

- The SOA record specifies the start of authority for the domain.
- The NS record defines the name of the server responsible for the domain.
- The A record maps the domain to its IP address.
- The CNAME record maps "www.example.com" to "example.com".

Note: A DNS zone is the logical part of the DNS namespace managed by an organization or DNS server, while a DNS zone file is the physical configuration file that contains the records defining that zone. Essentially, the zone is the concept, and the zone file is the implementation.

COMMON DNS ISSUES

Here are some common DNS issues that can cause trouble in a network.

Misconfiguration

Misconfigurations can occur on client machines or DNS servers. Common issues include:

- *Incorrect DNS Server IP*: If a client uses an unreachable or incorrect DNS server, domain name resolution fails.
- *Zone File Errors*: Errors in DNS zone files can misroute traffic.

Problem: Incorrect DNS Server

Scenario: Imagine a scenario where users in a corporate environment report that they cannot access any external websites.

Step 1: Capture DNS requests

The network administrator needs to capture and analyze DNS traffic to identify any issues with the DNS configuration.

The administrator suspects a DNS issue.

Using Wireshark:

1. The administrator starts Wireshark on the network interface connected to the internal network.
2. To focus only on DNS packets, the administrator applies the following filter:

   dns

3. The administrator begins capturing packets while users attempt to access various websites.

The capture should show DNS queries sent to a DNS server from client machines.

Step 2: Identifying misconfiguration

After capturing DNS traffic, the administrator reviews the queries. They notice that all DNS requests are being sent to an IP address not belonging to the company's DNS server.

Analysis steps:

1. The administrator looks at the captured packets' source and destination IP addresses.
2. They see that the DNS queries are going to an outdated IP address (e.g., 192.168.1.5), which might have been used in a previous network setup but is no longer valid.
   The administrator can sort the captured packets by destination IP to quickly identify the DNS server IP. This can be done using the filter:

dns && ip.dst == 192.168.1.5

This filter lets the administrator see all DNS queries sent to that specific (incorrect) IP address (e.g., 192.168.1.5).

Step 3: Resolution steps

After identifying the outdated DNS server IP, the administrator consults the network documentation and finds the correct DNS server IP address (e.g., 192.168.1.10).

1. The administrator remotely accesses the DHCP server configuration or individual client machines to update the DNS settings.
2. If DHCP is used, the administrator changes the DNS server entry to the correct IP (192.168.1.10) and ensures all new leases point to this updated DNS server.
3. The administrator instructs users to manually update their DNS settings to point to the new IP for static IP configurations.

Testing the Resolution: After making changes, the administrator uses Wireshark again to capture DNS traffic. They apply the same filter:

dns

This is to check if DNS queries are now being sent to the correct DNS server IP.

Expected Outcome: The captured DNS packets should show queries being sent to the correct IP address (192.168.1.10), and users should regain access to external websites.

DNS lookup failures

Failures in DNS lookups can result from server unavailability or network issues. Common symptoms include timeout errors.

Problem: Server unavailability

Scenario: A user complains that they cannot access a specific website. The steps for the solution are as follows:

Step 1: Analyze DNS traffic

The administrator captures DNS packets using Wireshark and notices repeated requests without responses.

Use *dns && dns.qry.name == "www.specificwebsite.com"* to isolate DNS queries for the unresponsive website.

Step 2: Troubleshooting steps

1. By pinging the DNS server, the administrator finds it unresponsive, leading them to check the server's resource usage.
2. **Solution:** After restarting the DNS server, functionality is restored, allowing users to reaccess the website.

DNS poisoning attacks

DNS Poisoning, also known as DNS Spoofing, is a malicious attack in which incorrect DNS records are inserted into the cache of a DNS resolver. This can redirect users attempting to access a legitimate domain to a fraudulent website, potentially leading to phishing attacks, data theft, or malware infections.

How DNS poisoning happens?

DNS poisoning typically occurs through various methods, including:

1. *Cache poisoning*: This is the most common form of DNS poisoning. An attacker exploits the DNS cache of a resolver by injecting false information. This can happen if the attacker can respond to DNS queries faster than the legitimate DNS server.

   Scenario: Suppose a user wants to visit "www.bank.com". The attacker sends a fake DNS response to the resolver, claiming that "www.bank.com" points to their malicious IP address. If the resolver accepts this false response, it will cache it and direct all subsequent users trying to access "www.bank.com" to the attacker's server instead of the legitimate bank.

2. *Man-in-the-middle attacks*: In a Man-in-the-Middle (MitM) attack, an attacker intercepts communications between the client and the DNS server. The attacker can modify the DNS responses on the fly.

   Scenario: While a user is querying a DNS server, the attacker intercepts the request and responds with a fake DNS record, redirecting the user to a phishing site without them realizing it.

3. *Malicious DNS servers*: An attacker can set up a rogue DNS server that provides incorrect DNS resolutions. This can occur if a user's device is configured to use a malicious DNS server through manual configuration or malware.

   Scenario: If malware alters a user's DNS settings to point to an attacker-controlled DNS server, any DNS queries return malicious IP addresses, redirecting users to fraudulent sites.

4. *DNS server vulnerabilities*: Exploiting vulnerabilities in DNS server software can also lead to DNS poisoning. Attackers can exploit weaknesses to gain access and modify DNS records if a DNS server is not adequately secured.

   Scenario: An attacker could exploit a vulnerability in an outdated DNS server to modify its zone files directly, inserting malicious entries.

Consequences of DNS poisoning

There is not one, but many consequences of DNS poisoning

- Phishing attacks: Users are redirected to counterfeit sites that mimic legitimate services, allowing attackers to steal login credentials and personal information.
- Malware distribution: Users may unknowingly download malicious software from compromised sites.
- Service disruption: Legitimate services may become inaccessible if users are consistently directed to incorrect IP addresses.

5. *Phishing websites*: In a DNS poisoning attack, the attacker alters the DNS records to redirect users to malicious websites instead of the legitimate ones they intended to visit. For example, even if you type in the correct URL for your bank's website, a poisoned DNS might lead you to a fraudulent website that looks identical to your bank's real website.

   Scenario: The employees in a company report being redirected to phishing sites when accessing a legitimate banking website. The following steps can detect the problem.

Steps to detect DNS poisoning with the filter:

1. Capture DNS traffic
   Use Wireshark to capture DNS traffic on your network.Apply the filter *dns.flags.rcode == 0 && dns.a* to capture all successful DNS responses that return **A** records (which resolves a domain name to an IP address) .
2. Analyze the results
   Look for suspicious or unexpected IP addresses returned in the A records. For example:
   - Suppose you see a legitimate domain (e.g., example.com) resolving to an IP address that is not expected (e.g., a foreign or unfamiliar IP address). In that case, this might indicate a DNS poisoning attempt.
   - The attacker may have poisoned the DNS cache by inserting their own IP address for a common domain, leading users to a malicious website.
3. Compare with legitimate data
   Compare the suspicious IP addresses with known, legitimate IP addresses for the domain. If the IP does not match the legitimate record (e.g., example.com resolves to a different IP address), it could indicate DNS poisoning.

Note: Regularly monitoring DNS traffic for unusual patterns can help detect potential poisoning attempts. Logs should be maintained to identify and analyze suspicious activities

DNS QUERY FLOODING

DNS query flooding is a denial-of-service (DoS) attack where an attacker overwhelms a DNS server with excessive queries, rendering it unresponsive.

Problem: Detecting query flooding

Scenario: An organization notices a significant slowdown in internet performance and frequent service interruptions.

1. Traffic analysis
   Using Wireshark, the administrator captures DNS traffic and filters for excessive queries from specific IP addresses. Use DNS and sort by source IP to identify IP addresses that generate excessive DNS queries. Use the following display filter:
   udp.port == 53 && dns.flags.response == 0
   This filter captures DNS query packets (where *dns.flags.response == 0* indicates a query, not a response) (Figure 11.3).

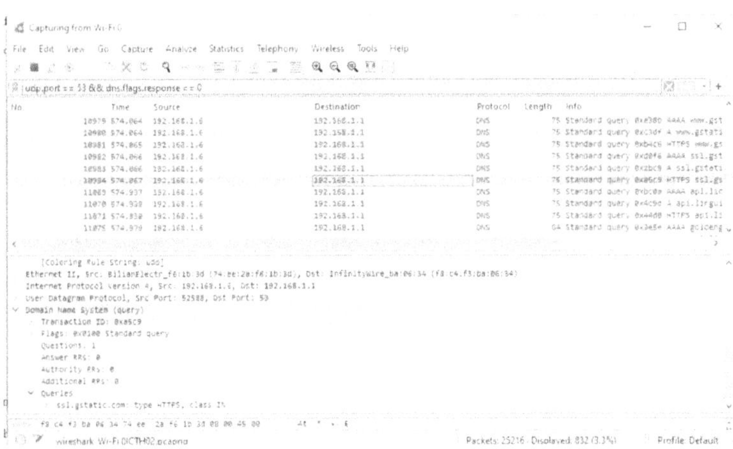

Figure 11.3 Wireshark displaying DNS query traffic, highlighting potential DNS query flooding behavior.

2. Identifying attack patterns
   The analysis shows a high volume of queries from a single IP address, indicating a flooding attack.

3. Response
   The administrator can implement rate limiting on the DNS server and block the offending IP address, mitigating the attack's impact.

Reason for showing only the IP address of your router

If the filter *udp.port == 53 && dns.flags.response == 0* shows only your router's IP address, which is likely because you're filtering DNS **queries** originating from your local device to your router or DNS server, which is expected. This means the filter captures the DNS queries that your device sends to resolve domain names.

To detect **DNS query flooding** (or excessive DNS queries), you'll need to focus on the volume of queries and the sources of those queries or even capture DNS queries from multiple sources if you suspect distributed query flooding.

Steps to refine the filter for query flooding

1. **Detect queries from external sources**
   Suppose you want to capture DNS queries from external sources (such as an attacker or other devices on the network). In that case, you can filter out your router's IP by specifying the source IP address you're interested in or simply by filtering for all DNS queries across the network.
   For example, to capture DNS queries that are not coming from your router (assuming your router IP is 192.168.1.1):
   udp.port == 53 && dns.flags.response == 0 && ip.src != 192.168.1.1
   This filters DNS queries where the source IP is not your router's IP address.
2. **Detect queries from multiple sources (Flooding)**
   Suppose you want to monitor DNS query flooding from multiple sources. In that case, you can use *Statistics > Conversations or Statistics > Endpoints* in Wireshark to better understand which IPs are generating the most DNS queries.
   Here's how you can use *Statistics > Conversations*:
   - After applying the filter *udp.port == 53 && dns.flags.response == 0*, go to Statistics --> Conversations.
   - In the **Conversations** window, look at the **IPv4** tab to see a list of source and destination IPs.
   - This will show which devices are sending the most DNS queries. **Anomalies** in the number of queries (e.g., an unusually high volume from a single source IP) may indicate query flooding.

3. **Use I/O graphs to detect flooding**
   You can also use **I/O Graphs** to visualize traffic patterns and detect any spikes in DNS queries:
   - Go to *Statistics --> I/O Graphs.*
   - Set the Display Filter to *udp.port == 53 && dns.flags.response == 0.*
   - Look for spikes or unusually high query rates over time.
4. **Capture DNS queries from specific IPs**
   If you suspect that a particular device on the network is flooding with DNS queries, filter for DNS queries from that IP address. For example: *udp.port == 53 && dns.flags.response == 0 && ip.src == 192.168.1.100*
   This shows DNS queries coming specifically from 192.168.1.100.

DNS TIMEOUT ISSUES

DNS timeouts sometimes occur due to server misconfigurations or network connectivity problems, resulting in prolonged delays in loading web pages.

Problem: User Complaints of Slow Internet

Scenario: Employees report slow internet access, particularly when accessing specific domains.

1. **DNS Traffic Analysis:** The administrator uses Wireshark to monitor DNS response times, identifying unusually long response delays.

Use *dns && dns.flags.response == 1* and analyze the response times to identify latency issues.

Expected Latency Ranges:

Low latency: <50 ms

Moderate latency: 50–100 ms

High latency: >100 ms

you can add a column in Wireshark to display the **latency** (time difference) between the DNS query and response packets. Wireshark does not directly have a "latency" field. Still, you can calculate the **time delta** between packets, representing the latency. You can add a column (Edit → Preferences), and the **field name** for the time delta is *frame.time_delta_displayed* (Figure 11.4).

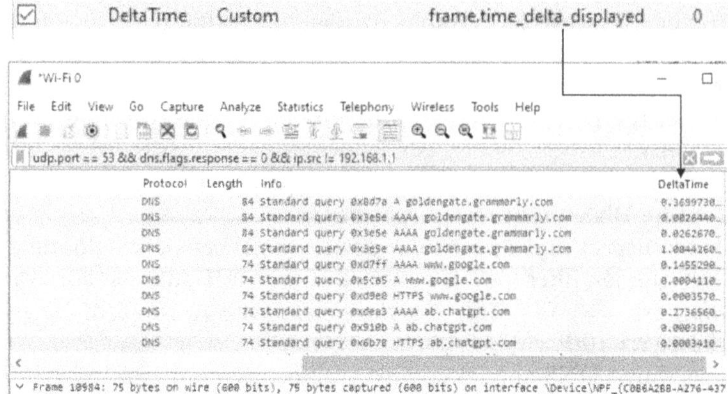

Figure 11.4 A Wireshark capture of DNS queries with custom DeltaTime filtering, displaying queries for domains like goldengate.grammarly.com and www.google .com, along with time intervals.

2. **Identifying the Bottleneck:** They discovered that one of the upstream DNS servers is experiencing high latency.
3. **Resolution:** By changing the DNS settings to a more reliable server, the administrator significantly reduces DNS lookup times, improving overall network performance.

Adding more field names

Table 11.2 shows the power of adding more DNS-related field names to resolve issues and build security.

Table 11.2 DNS field names and their uses

Field Name	*Purpose*	*Usage Example*
dns.time	Shows the response time for DNS queries	Helps identify delays in DNS resolution
dns.time.response	Indicates the time taken for the DNS server to respond	Used to measure server performance for individual queries
dns.time.request	Captures the timestamp of the DNS request	Used to calculate the total query time when paired with the response
dns.qry.name	Displays the domain name being queried	Used to see what domain names are being requested
dns.flags.response	Indicates whether the packet is a query or a response	Used to distinguish between DNS requests and replies
dns.flags.rcode	Shows the response code from the DNS server	Helps troubleshoot issues like NXDOMAIN or SERVFAIL
dns.a	Displays the resolved IPv4 address in the DNS response	Used to verify if a domain resolves to the correct IP
dns.ns	Displays the nameserver in the DNS response	Used to identify authoritative nameservers
dns.srv	Displays the service record (SRV) details	Used to troubleshoot service-specific DNS queries
dns.resp.ttl	Indicates the time-to-live (TTL) for a DNS response	Used to understand caching behavior and expiration times
dns.response_in	Shows the ID of the matching DNS response for a query	Used to track which query a response corresponds to
dns.request_in	Indicates the ID of the matching DNS request for a response	Used to track which response matches a query

Best practices for DNS security

Following are some best practices which can be adopted for DNS Security

1. Implement DNSSEC
   DNS Security Extensions (DNSSEC) add a layer of security by digitally signing DNS records, helping to prevent spoofing and cache poisoning attacks.
2. Use secure DNS resolvers
   Most routers provide basic DNS forwarding services, allowing devices on the network to resolve domain names by forwarding queries to external DNS servers. These are typically managed via the router's firmware rather than dedicated DNS software. Encourage using trusted and secure DNS resolvers, such as those provided by Google

(8.8.8.8) or Cloudflare (1.1.1.1), which offer enhanced security features and reliability.
3. Regularly update DNS software
Keeping DNS server software updated helps protect against vulnerabilities and exploits. Regular updates also ensure that new features and improvements are implemented. To extend your knowledge, for enterprise DNS management, **Microsoft DNS** (for Windows Server) and **Infoblox** (available for both Windows and Linux) are commonly used on **Windows**-based systems, offering integration with Active Directory and advanced features like dynamic updates and IP address management. On **Unix/Linux** systems, **BIND** and **PowerDNS** are widely deployed for authoritative and recursive DNS roles, supporting extensive configurations, DNSSEC, and scalability.
4. Monitor DNS traffic
Regularly monitoring DNS traffic can help identify unusual patterns indicating security threats. Tools like Wireshark can aid in this analysis.
5. Configure rate limiting
Implementing rate limiting on DNS servers can help mitigate the impact of query flooding attacks by restricting the number of requests a single IP address can make within a specified timeframe.
Note: For routers, firmware updates often include DNS software updates, while for enterprise software like BIND or Microsoft DNS, administrators must check for updates from the vendor's website and apply them manually or through automated tools.

CONCLUSION

This chapter explored various DNS-related issues, focusing on effective troubleshooting techniques using Wireshark to maintain network security and efficiency. Administrators can proactively address these challenges by understanding the fundamental operations of DNS and recognizing common problems such as DNS misconfigurations, DNS poisoning, and query flooding. Employing tools like Wireshark for detailed traffic analysis allows for precise diagnosis and swift resolution of DNS issues. Implementing best practices like DNSSEC, using secure DNS resolvers, and regularly monitoring DNS traffic are critical steps in enhancing DNS security. As threats evolve, continuous education on DNS security remains indispensable for maintaining the integrity of network operations.

MULTIPLE CHOICE QUESTIONS (MCQs)

1. What is DNS Poisoning?
   A) Incorrectly configuring DNS records
   B) Malicious redirection of DNS queries to fraudulent sites
   C) A standard method for speeding up DNS queries
   D) A type of legal DNS operation

Answer: B)

2. Which Wireshark filter would you use to capture only DNS recursive queries?
   A) dns.flags.response == 1
   B) dns && dns.qry.name == "www.example.com"
   C) dns.flags.recdesired == 1
   D) udp.port == 53

Answer: C)

3. Which DNS record is essential for mail services?
   A) A Record
   B) NS Record
   C) SOA Record
   D) MX Record

Answer: D)

4. What is the purpose of DNSSEC?
   A) To speed up DNS queries
   B) To sign DNS records digitally to prevent spoofing
   C) To cache DNS queries
   D) To record DNS queries

Answer: B)

5. What would be a potential sign of DNS query flooding?
   A) Low network traffic
   B) Decreased number of DNS queries
   C) High volume of queries from a single IP address
   D) Fewer DNS responses

Answer: C)

GLOSSARY

1. **A Record (Address Record):** Links a domain to the physical IP address of a computer where the domain is hosted.
2. **Cache Poisoning:** A type of DNS poisoning where false information is inserted into the DNS cache of a resolver, causing the resolver to return an incorrect IP address, redirecting someone to a malicious site.

3. **CNAME Record (Canonical Name):** A type of DNS record that maps an alias name to a true or canonical domain name.
4. **DNS (Domain Name System):** A system that translates human-friendly domain names like "www.example.com" into numerical IP addresses necessary for locating and identifying computer services and devices on the internet.
5. **DNS Poisoning (or DNS Spoofing):** A technique that tricks a DNS server into believing it has received authentic information when, in fact, it has not. This can redirect users to malicious websites.
6. **DNS Query:** A request made by a device to a DNS server asking for the IP address associated with a specific domain name.
7. **DNS Resolver:** A type of server that resolves, or translates, domain names into IP addresses. When a device makes a DNS query, it is sent to the DNS resolver which processes the query and returns the IP address.
8. **DNS Server:** A server that contains a database of public IP addresses and their associated hostnames and is responsible for answering queries from your computer about the IP address of a specific domain name.
9. **DNS Zone File:** A text file that contains mappings between domain names and IP addresses as well as other DNS records for a specific domain, critical for managing how DNS queries are handled.
10. **DNSSEC (DNS Security Extensions):** A suite of extensions that add security to the DNS protocol by enabling DNS responses to be validated. It is designed to protect against DNS attacks like cache poisoning.
11. **Man-in-the-Middle Attack (MiTM):** A cyberattack where the attacker secretly intercepts and possibly alters the communication between two parties who believe they are directly communicating with each other.
12. **NS Record (Name Server):** A record that lists the DNS servers responsible for a specific domain, helping to direct traffic to the correct locations where domain information is stored.
13. **Recursive Lookup:** A method used by DNS servers to resolve a domain name by making a series of requests to other DNS servers until the IP address is found.
14. **SOA Record (Start of Authority):** A type of DNS record in the zone file that specifies authoritative information about the domain, including the primary DNS server, email of the domain administrator, domain serial number, and timers.

Chapter 12

Identifying DDoS attacks

INTRODUCTION

Distributed Denial-of-Service (DDoS) attacks are among the most prevalent and damaging threats organizations face today. These attacks aim to disrupt the normal functioning of targeted servers, services, or networks by overwhelming them with a flood of internet traffic. Understanding how to identify DDoS attacks is critical for network administrators and cybersecurity professionals, enabling them to respond swiftly to mitigate potential damage (Figure 12.1).

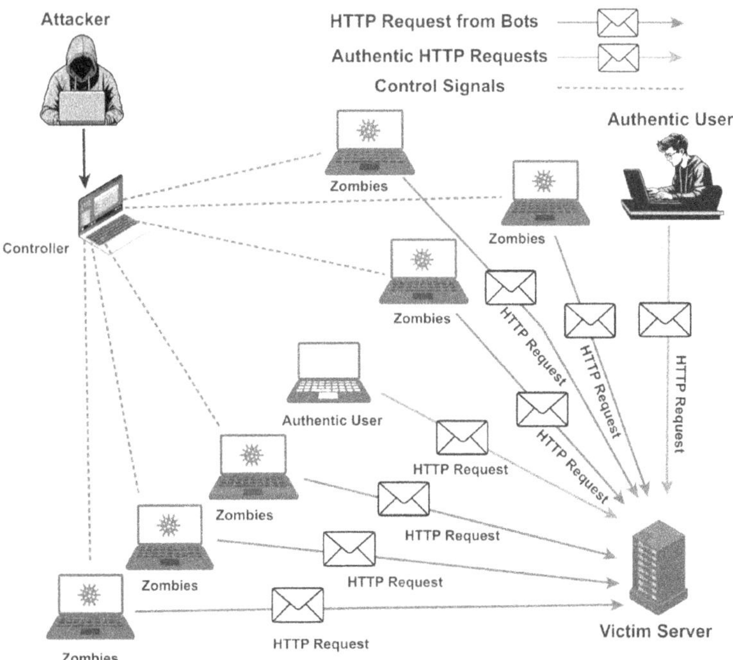

Figure 12.1 A botnet attack diagram showing an attacker controlling infected computers (zombies) to send HTTP requests to a victim server.

DOI: 10.1201/9781003539261-12

DDOS ATTACK LIFE CYCLE

Understanding the life cycle of a Distributed Denial-of-Service (DDoS) attack is essential for effective detection and mitigation. Here's a brief overview of each phase:

1. **Preparation phase**
   a) *Reconnaissance*: Attackers gather information about the target, including IP addresses, services, and vulnerabilities.
   b) *Identifying targets*: They choose specific services or applications to attack.
   c) *Building a botnet*: Attackers infect devices with malware to create a network of compromised machines (botnet) for launching the attack.

2. **Execution phase**
   a) *Launching the attack*: The botnet floods the target with traffic, employing various attack types (e.g., SYN flood, UDP flood).
   b) *Utilizing multiple vectors*: Attackers may combine different attack methods to enhance the impact.

3. **Amplification phase**
   a) *Exploiting protocols*: In amplification attacks, attackers send small requests to public servers with the target's IP address, leading to larger responses that overwhelm the target.
   b) *Example*: DNS amplification, where a small query produces a much larger response directed at the target.

4. **Mitigation phase**
   a) *Traffic monitoring*: Administrators monitor network traffic for anomalies indicative of an attack
   b) *Implementing mitigation strategies:* These include rate limiting, filtering traffic, and using DDoS protection services. These absorb and filter malicious traffic.

5. **Aftermath phase**
   a) *Post-attack analysis*: Security teams analyze logs and traffic data to understand the attack's impact.
   b) assessment: Organizations evaluate the effects on services and potential financial losses
   c) Improving security posture: Based on analysis, organizations strengthen security measures, update incident response plans, and communicate with users about the incident

Note: The DDoS attack life cycle outlines the critical phases that attackers follow. By understanding these phases, organizations can enhance their preparedness and response strategies against DDoS threats.

FAMOUS DDOS ATTACK CASE STUDIES

Here are four of the most famous DDoS attack case studies that had significant impacts on the affected organizations and the broader internet landscape:

1. **Dyn DDoS attack (October 2016)**

The Dyn attack was one of history's most significant and disruptive DDoS attacks, affecting numerous high-profile websites.

What happened: The attack targeted Dyn, a major DNS provider, using a massive botnet composed of compromised IoT devices, including cameras and DVRs.

Impact: The attack peaked at around 1.2 Tbps, causing widespread outages for popular services like Twitter, Netflix, Reddit, and CNN for several hours.

Lessons learned: This incident highlighted vulnerabilities in DNS infrastructure and the need for better security measures, such as DNS redundancy and securing IoT devices against exploitation.

2. **GitHub DDoS attack (February 2018)**

GitHub experienced one of the most significant recorded DDoS attacks at the time, peaking at 1.35 Tbps.

What happened: The attack utilized a technique known as Memcached amplification, which exploited misconfigured Memcached servers. Attackers sent small queries to these servers, which responded with much larger packets directed at GitHub.

Impact: The attack briefly took down GitHub's services but was mitigated within minutes due to GitHub's robust DDoS protection infrastructure.

Lessons learned: This incident emphasized the importance of securing services that can be exploited to amplify attacks and showcased the effectiveness of DDoS mitigation technologies.

4. **Cloudflare DDoS attack (June 2020)**

Cloudflare, a major web performance and security company, reported a significant DDoS attack targeting one of its customers.

What happened: The attack peaked at 1.1 Tbps and targeted a customer in the cryptocurrency sector. It used a combination of application layer attacks and volumetric attacks.

Impact: Cloudflare's network successfully mitigated the attack, ensuring minimal customer downtime. The attack showcased the evolving nature of DDoS tactics, with attackers employing sophisticated methods to overwhelm targets.

Lessons learned: This incident demonstrated the effectiveness of modern DDoS mitigation techniques and the importance of robust security measures, especially for organizations in high-risk sectors like cryptocurrency.

5. **Reddit DDoS attack (April 2024)**

In April 2024, Reddit experienced a significant DDoS attack that temporarily disrupted its services.

What happened: The attack involved a massive flood of traffic targeting Reddit's web services to overwhelm its infrastructure. Attackers utilized a mix of botnets and amplification techniques, causing users to experience slow load times and service outages.

Impact: Many users could not access Reddit, leading to frustrations and discussions on alternative platforms about the attack. Reddit's engineering team worked quickly to implement mitigation strategies, rerouting traffic and leveraging DDoS protection services.

Lessons learned: The incident highlighted the ongoing threat of DDoS attacks on popular online platforms. It reinforced the importance of continuous monitoring, robust incident response plans, and investment in advanced DDoS protection solutions to safeguard against future attacks.

DDOS ATTACK TYPES

A DDoS attack involves multiple compromised computers (often part of a botnet) that are used to send a large volume of traffic to a target, overwhelming its resources. DDoS attacks can vary in method and intensity, but they generally fall into three categories:

Volume-based attacks:

- UDP flood
- ICMP (Ping) flood
- Amplification attacks (e.g., DNS amplification, NTP amplification, memcached amplification)

Protocol-based attacks:

- SYN flood
- ACK flood
- Ping of death
- Smurf attack

Application layer attacks:

- HTTP flood
- Slowloris
- DNS query flood
- SQL query flood

We discuss some of these attacks here.

VOLUME-BASED ATTACKS

These attacks aim to overwhelm the target with massive traffic, typically measured in bits per second (bps). Common types include ICMP floods, UDP floods, and DNS amplification attacks.

Example: UDP flood attack

What happens:

a) The attacker sends a large number of User Datagram Protocol (UDP) packets to random ports on the target server.
b) Upon receiving these packets, the server checks for an application listening on the specified port. It responds with an ICMP "Destination Unreachable" packet if none is found.
c) This creates additional traffic back to the source, and since the attacker typically spoofs their IP address, the server's resources are consumed by processing these unnecessary packets.
d) As a result, the target becomes overwhelmed, leading to legitimate users experiencing slow response times or complete service outages.

Example: ICMP flood attack

An ICMP Flood Attack is a Denial-of-Service (DoS) attack where the attacker overwhelms a target with a large volume of ICMP Echo Request (ping) packets, exhausting network bandwidth and system resources. As the target tries to respond to each ping, it becomes overloaded, causing network slowdown or unavailability.

What happens:

a) In an ICMP flood attack, the attacker sends a barrage of ICMP Echo Request (ping) packets to the target.
b) Upon receiving these requests, the target system attempts to respond to each one with an ICMP Echo Reply.
c) Excessive requests can saturate the target's bandwidth and consume its processing power, causing it to become unresponsive to legitimate traffic.

Note: ICMP stands for Internet Control Message Protocol. It is a network layer protocol used for diagnostic and control purposes in Internet Protocol (IP) networks. ICMP sends error messages and operational information related to IP processing back to the packet's source.

Example: DNS amplification attack

A DNS amplification attack is a Distributed Denial-of-Service (DDoS) attack that leverages misconfigured DNS servers to flood a target with large amounts of traffic. The attacker sends small DNS queries with a spoofed IP (the victim's), and the DNS servers respond with amplified data, overwhelming the victim's network.

What happens:

a) The attacker sends small DNS queries to publicly accessible DNS servers, spoofing the source IP address of the victim's server.
b) The DNS server responds to the victim's IP address with a much larger DNS response, amplifying the volume of traffic sent to the target.
c) This method can significantly increase the volume of traffic directed at the target, overwhelming its resources (Figure 12.2).

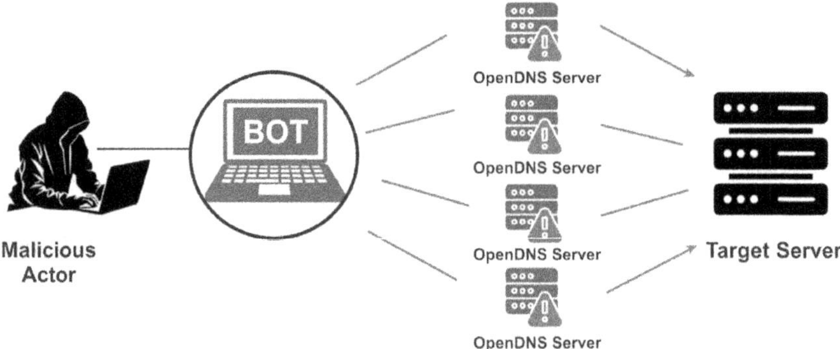

Figure 12.2 A DNS amplification attack diagram where a bot sends spoofed requests to OpenDNS servers, amplifying traffic to a target server.

Note: In a DNS amplification attack, an attacker exploits open DNS resolvers—DNS servers configured to respond to queries from any client without authentication, such as Google's public DNS server (8.8.8.8) or poorly configured private DNS resolvers, receives the query, it processes it and sends a response containing all records, which can be significantly larger (e.g., 3000 bytes for a 60-byte query).

About close DNS resolvers

Closed DNS resolvers prioritize security and control, ensuring DNS services are accessible only to legitimate users within a specific scope. The following example will make concepts more clear.

A company configures its internal DNS server to resolve names only for devices within its corporate LAN. Employees working remotely must connect via a VPN to access the resolver. Attempts from external IP addresses to query the DNS server are denied by default.

Protocol attacks

These attacks exploit weaknesses in network protocols, often targeting specific protocol behaviors or characteristics. Examples include SYN floods, fragmented packet attacks, and Ping of Death.

Example: SYN flood attack

What happens:

a) In a SYN flood attack, the attacker sends a high volume of SYN (synchronize) packets to the target server to initiate TCP connections.
b) The server responds to each SYN packet with a SYN-ACK (synchronize-acknowledge) packet and waits for the client's final ACK (acknowledge) packet to establish the connection.
c) The attacker, however, never sends the final ACK packet, leaving the server with half-open connections, consuming its resources and potentially leading to a denial-of-service as it cannot accept legitimate connections (Figure 12.3).

Figure 12.3 A SYN flood attack diagram showing a bot sending spoofed SYN packets to a victim, overwhelming the system with incomplete connections.

Example: Ping of death

A Ping of Death (PoD) attack is a type of Denial-of-Service (DoS) attack where an attacker sends malformed or oversized ICMP packets (exceeding the allowed 65,535 bytes) to the target system. When the target attempts to reassemble these packets, it can cause a buffer overflow, leading to system crashes or network disruptions.

What happens:

a) The attacker sends malformed or oversized ICMP packets to the target system.
b) These packets exceed the maximum allowable size for ICMP packets, causing the target system to crash or become unstable when it attempts to process them.
c) The result can be system reboots, application crashes, or a complete denial-of-service.

Example: Fragmented packet attack

A Fragmented Packet Attack is a Denial-of-Service (DoS) attack where the attacker sends maliciously fragmented network packets that the target system struggles to reassemble. Suppose the reassembly process consumes excessive resources or encounters malformed fragments. In that case, it can crash the system or make the network unavailable.

What happens:

a) In a fragmented packet attack, the attacker sends TCP packets that are deliberately fragmented into smaller pieces.
b) The target system must then reassemble these packets, which consume processing resources.
c) Suppose the attacker sends a large volume of these fragmented packets. In that case, the target can become overwhelmed trying to reassemble them, leading to performance degradation or unavailability.

APPLICATION LAYER ATTACKS

These attacks target specific applications or services with the goal of exhausting resources and causing service disruptions. Examples include HTTP floods and slowloris attacks.

Example: HTTP flood attack

An HTTP Flood Attack is a type of Distributed Denial-of-Service (DDoS) attack where the attacker sends many legitimate-looking HTTP requests (e.g., GET or POST) to overwhelm a web server. Since the requests mimic regular traffic, they can exhaust server resources, making it difficult to differentiate between malicious and genuine users and making the website slow or inaccessible (Figure 12.4).

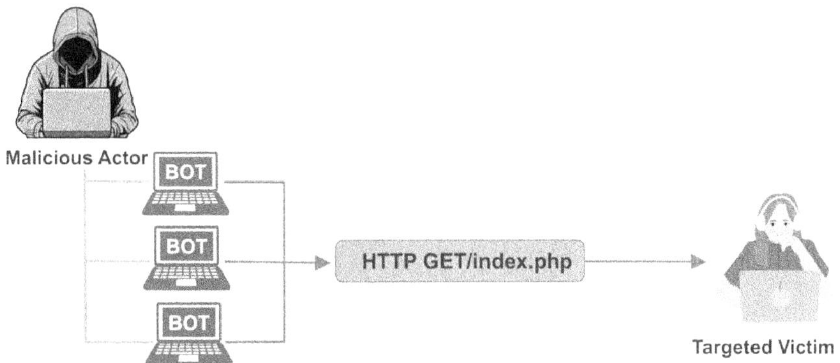

Figure 12.4 An HTTP GET flood attack diagram illustrating multiple bots sending HTTP GET requests to overload a victim's server.

What happens:

a) In an HTTP flood attack, the attacker sends a large number of HTTP requests to the target web server, often targeting specific URLs to exhaust server resources.
b) Each request consumes server resources as the server processes them, establishes connections, and prepares responses.
c) Suppose the volume of requests is high enough. In that case, it can lead to the server becoming slow or unresponsive, effectively denying service to legitimate users.

Example: Slowloris attack

A Slowloris attack is a Denial-of-Service (DoS) attack that aims to overwhelm a web server by sending partial HTTP requests and simultaneously keeping many connections open. Unlike traditional DoS attacks that flood the target with traffic, Slowloris consumes minimal bandwidth, making it difficult for the server to detect and mitigate.

Note: Slowloris attack is a type of Application Layer (Layer 7) DDoS attack. It targets the web server by exploiting how it handles concurrent connections, aiming to exhaust its resources and make it unavailable to legitimate users.

What happens:

a) The Slowloris attack involves sending partial HTTP requests to the target server and keeping connections open for as long as possible without completing them.
b) The attacker sends multiple requests, but instead of sending complete headers, it only sends a few bytes and waits.
c) This keeps the connections open, and the server allocates resources to maintain them. If enough connections are held open, the server can exhaust its available connections, leading to denial-of-service for legitimate users.

Example: RUDY attack (R-U-Dead-Yet)

A RUDY (R-U-Dead-Yet) attack is a Denial-of-Service (DoS) attack that targets web servers by sending slow POST requests with long content-length headers. The attacker sends the data extremely slowly, keeping the connection open for as long as possible, which exhausts server resources and prevents legitimate users from accessing the service.

What happens:

a) In a RUDY attack, the attacker sends very slow POST requests to the target application. When a user fills out a form on a website (e.g., registration, login, contact forms), the data is typically sent to the server using a POST request.
b) The attack targets web forms or applications that require longer response times, effectively tying up server resources and connections.
c) By keeping connections open and sending data slowly, the attacker can exhaust the server's available connections, resulting in denial-of-service for genuine users.

Note: Each type of DDoS attack utilizes different techniques and methods to disrupt services, highlighting the importance of understanding the nature of these threats.

Real-life scenarios of DDoS attacks

Following are some real-life scenarios of DDoS attacks and observing how Wireshark was used to detect them. Some scenarios have detailed steps; others follow similar Wireshark filters to detect the attack.

Scenario 1: DDoS attack on a financial institution

Incident: A large bank experiences a sudden spike in traffic, making its online banking services inaccessible to customers.

Detection: Network administrators notice a significant increase in incoming traffic directed toward the bank's web servers from a particular IP.

Wireshark analysis:

- **Filter used:** *ip.src == [attacker_ip]* to isolate packets from a suspected attacker's IP.
- **Findings:** The analysis reveals that a single IP address sends an unusually high volume of SYN packets, indicating a potential SYN flood attack.

Steps used to Analyze the surge in traffic

1. **Start capturing traffic**
   Open Wireshark and select the appropriate network interface (e.g., Ethernet or Wi-Fi) to monitor incoming traffic to the web server.
2. **Filter for All traffic to the website:**
   - Use the following filter to isolate traffic targeting your server:
     ip.dst == <website_IP>
3. **Identify high-traffic source IPs:**
   - Use **Statistics → Conversations → IPv4 tab** to identify source IPs generating excessive traffic.
   - Apply the filter to investigate specific sources:
     ip.src == <suspicious_IP>
4. **Analyze HTTP/HTTPS requests:**
   - For HTTP traffic, use:
     http
   - For HTTPS traffic, use:
     tls
   - If specific pages are being repeatedly targeted, filter for POST or GET requests:
     http.request.method == "GET" or http.request.method == "POST"
5. **Detect SYN flooding:**
   - If you suspect incomplete TCP handshakes, use the filter:
     tcp.flags.syn == 1 and tcp.flags.ack == 0
6. **Detect UDP flooding:**
   - If UDP traffic is suspected, use:
     udp and ip.dst == <website_IP>
7. **Check for unusual protocols or ports:**
   - If the attack targets a specific service, filter traffic based on the port:
     tcp.port == <target_port> or *udp.port == <target_port>*
8. **Save and export data for further analysis**
   - Export filtered traffic for reporting or deeper analysis:
     File → Export Specified Packets → Save As [filename].pcapng.

Response: The security team implements rate limiting on the affected server and blocks the attacking IP address, restoring access for legitimate users. Rate limiting is a technique that controls the number of requests a client can make to a server within a specified time frame, preventing abuse or overloading. Deploying a Content Delivery Network (CDN) or DDoS protection service, such as Cloudflare or AWS Shield, can help absorb malicious traffic and prevent server overload. Implementing a Web Application Firewall (WAF) filters malicious HTTP/HTTPS requests and distinguishes legitimate users from attackers.

Note: A Content Delivery Network (CDN) is a distributed network of servers strategically located across the globe to deliver web content, such as websites, applications, videos, and other digital assets, to users more efficiently and reliably. CDNs help improve performance, reduce latency, and mitigate security risks like Distributed Denial-of-Service (DDoS) attacks.

Scenario 2: DDoS attack during a major event

Incident: A streaming service experiences a DDoS attack during a popular sports event, leading to significant interruptions in service.

Detection: The operations team observed an increase in traffic 10 times the average volume.

Wireshark analysis:

- **Filter used:** *tcp.port == 80* to focus on HTTP traffic.
- **Findings:** Anomalous patterns emerge, such as numerous repeated requests from various IP addresses, suggesting a distributed attack.

Response: The streaming service provider deploys a web application firewall (WAF) to filter out malicious traffic and maintain service availability for legitimate users.

Scenario 3: DNS amplification attack

Incident: A gaming company's DNS servers are targeted by a DDoS attack that leverages DNS amplification.

Detection: Players report high latency and disconnection issues while accessing the game servers.

Wireshark analysis:

- **Filter used:** *dns && udp* to capture DNS queries and responses.
- **Findings:** The administrator discovers that the attacker sends a DNS query with a spoofed source IP (the victim's IP, which could be the

gamer's IP), causing a DNS resolver (often an open DNS server) to send a large DNS response back to the victim. This results in the gamer's network being flooded with amplified traffic, leading to network congestion, timeouts, and potential disconnections from the game. Although the DNS responses do not directly impact the game server, the gamer experiences significant disruptions to their gameplay, such as lag, increased latency, or complete service unavailability.

Response: The company implements response rate limiting on its DNS servers and works with its ISP to filter the incoming traffic. Finally, anti-DDoS services can help absorb large traffic volumes and protect the gamer's network, even though the attack targets the player's IP address. When applied together, these strategies can effectively reduce the impact of DNS amplification attacks.

Scenario 4: Application Layer DDoS Attack

Incident: A non-profit organization's website experiences a sudden surge in traffic, causing it to crash during a fundraising campaign.

Detection: The website becomes unresponsive, and users report being unable to access it.

Wireshark analysis:

- **Filter used:** *http.request* to analyze HTTP traffic.
- **Findings:** The analysis reveals thousands of requests per second targeting a specific URL associated with the donation page, indicative of an HTTP flood attack.

Response: The organization utilizes a content delivery network (CDN) to absorb the excess traffic and employs application-layer security measures to distinguish between legitimate users and attackers.

Scenario 5: IoT device-based DDoS attack

Incident: A smart home device manufacturer experiences an attack where compromised IoT devices flood their servers.

Detection: The manufacturer notices erratic server performance and spikes in resource usage.

Wireshark analysis:

- **Filter used:** *tcp* to analyze all TCP traffic to the web servers.
- **Findings:** Many TCP SYN packets originate from various IP addresses associated with compromised IoT devices, forming a botnet.

Steps with filters for detecting IoT-based DDoS attack

1. Filter for excessive traffic from specific IP ranges (IoT Devices)
   ip.src == <IoT_device_IP_range>
2. Filter for traffic to the targeted server
   ip.dst == <server_IP>
3. Filter for specific protocols
   - For TCP-based attacks:
     tcp and ip.dst == <server_IP>
   - For UDP-based attacks:
     udp and ip.dst == <server_IP>
   - For ICMP flooding:
   icmp and ip.dst == <server_IP>
4. Filter for SYN flood (TCP SYN packets)
   tcp.flags.syn == 1 and tcp.flags.ack == 0 and ip.dst == <server_IP>
5. ilter for unusually large packets (Amplification Attacks)
   ip.len > 1000 and ip.dst == <server_IP>
6. Filter for traffic to specific ports
   - For HTTP traffic:
     tcp.port == 80 or tcp.port == 443 and ip.dst == <server_IP>
   - For custom IoT protocols:
     tcp.port == <custom_port> and ip.dst == <server_IP>

Response: Start by capturing all traffic to identify the high-level patterns. Apply the filters sequentially to narrow down suspicious traffic targeting your server. Use the results to identify the attack's characteristics, including source IPs, protocols, and traffic volumes. The manufacturer implements more robust authentication protocols for IoT devices and collaborates with law enforcement to address the botnet.

GENERAL STEPS AND FILTERS TO IDENTIFY DDOS ATTACK

Wireshark is an essential tool for identifying DDoS attacks. Here are some practical steps and filters that can be utilized during analysis:

1. **Capture traffic**
   To identify a potential DDoS attack, begin by capturing network traffic during periods of suspected attack.
   Filter: Use *ip* or *tcp* to capture all IP or TCP packets.
2. **Analyze traffic volume**

High traffic volume can indicate a DDoS attack. Use Wireshark to monitor incoming and outgoing traffic patterns.
Filter: *ip.src == [suspected_ip]* to focus on traffic from a particular IP address or use *tcp* to examine TCP traffic.

3. **Monitor specific protocols**
   Different types of DDoS attacks utilize various protocols. Monitor the traffic for specific signs of attacks.
   - **SYN floods:** Use *tcp.flags.syn == 1 && tcp.flags.ack == 0* to filter for SYN packets.
   - **UDP floods:** Use the *udp* filter to capture all UDP packets.
   - **ICMP floods:** Use *the icmp* filter to monitor ICMP traffic.
4. **Examine response patterns**
   Look for response patterns to identify amplification attacks or misconfigured servers.
   Filter: *dns && udp* to capture DNS-related traffic, particularly useful for identifying DNS amplification attacks.
5. **Identify anomalous patterns**
   Analyzing traffic for unusual patterns can help identify the type of DDoS attack.
   Filter: Use *http.request* to analyze HTTP requests and detect patterns such as a high number of requests to a single endpoint.

CONCLUSION

Identifying DDoS attacks is crucial for maintaining the availability and reliability of services. Network administrators can quickly detect anomalies and take appropriate actions to mitigate potential impacts by understanding the different types of DDoS attacks and utilizing tools like Wireshark. Real-life scenarios demonstrate the diverse nature of DDoS attacks and the importance of implementing robust security measures and monitoring practices.

It is recommended that enterprises bake in a mitigation plan while designing networks. Deploying distributed and redundant networks to minimize impact and having a service contract with DDoS mitigation vendors should be considered. For example, if DNS is a critical part of your infrastructure, consider distributing your DNS services among two or more DNS providers.

With proactive strategies and effective network analysis tools, organizations can protect themselves against the ever-evolving threat landscape of DDoS attacks.

MULTIPLE CHOICE QUESTIONS (MCQs)

1. What type of DDoS attack exploits publicly accessible DNS servers to overwhelm a target system with DNS response traffic?
   A) SYN Flood
   B) UDP Flood
   C) DNS Amplification
   D) ICMP Flood

Answer: C

2. In the context of Wireshark analysis, which filter would you use to detect potential SYN flood attacks by monitoring SYN packets?
   A) tcp.flags.syn == 1 && tcp.flags.ack == 0
   B) tcp.flags.reset == 1
   C) udp
   D) icmp

Answer: A

3. Which Wireshark filter most effectively identifies a UDP flood attack during a suspected DDoS incident?
   A) tcp.flags.syn == 1
   B) udp
   C) icmp
   D) dns && udp

Answer: B

4. During a DDoS attack, which phase involves using botnets to launch the attack, and may various attack methods be employed for more significant impact?
   A) Preparation Phase
   B) Execution Phase
   C) Amplification Phase
   D) Mitigation Phase

Answer: B

5. What Wireshark filter would be appropriate for analyzing HTTP flood attacks targeting web servers?
   A) http.request.method == "GET" or http.request.method == "POST"
   B) tcp.port == 80 or tcp.port == 443
   C) tcp.flags.syn == 1
   D) ip.dst == [target_ip]

Answer: A

GLOSSARY

1. **Botnet:** A network of private computers infected with malicious software and controlled as a group without the owners' knowledge, e.g., to send spam messages or launch DDoS attacks.
2. **DDoS (Distributed Denial-of-Service) Attack:** A type of cyberattack that attempts to make a machine or network resource unavailable to its intended users by overwhelming the target or its surrounding infrastructure with a flood of Internet traffic
3. **DNS Amplification:** A DDoS attack exploits publicly accessible DNS servers to overwhelm a target system with DNS response traffic.
4. **ICMP (Internet Control Message Protocol):** A network protocol used by network devices, like routers, to send error messages indicating, for instance, that a requested service is not available or that a host or router could not be reached
5. **IoT (Internet of Things) Devices:** Physical devices that connect with other web-enabled devices and systems over the Internet
6. **Memcached Server:** A high-performance distributed memory caching system typically used to speed up dynamic database-driven websites by caching data and objects in RAM to reduce the number of times an external data source must be read.
7. **RUDY (R-U-Dead-Yet?) Attack:** A DDoS attack that targets web application servers by sending a complete but extremely slow HTTP POST request.
8. **Slowloris:** A DDoS attack that opens multiple connections to the targeted web server and keeps them open as long as possible. It does this by continuously sending partial HTTP headers but never completing a request.
9. **SYN Flood:** A denial-of-service attack in which an attacker sends a succession of SYN requests to a target's system to consume enough server resources to make the system unresponsive to legitimate traffic.
10. **UDP Flood:** A type of DDoS attack in which the attacker floods random ports on a remote host with IP packets containing UDP datagrams.

Chapter 13

Deep packet analysis with advanced functionalities

INTRODUCTION

Deep Packet Analysis (DPA) is a vital tool in network security, allowing for detailed inspection of packet headers and payloads. This chapter explores advanced techniques in DPA, including graphical tools for data visualization and the utilization of OS fingerprinting to enhance network analysis and security (Figure 13.1).

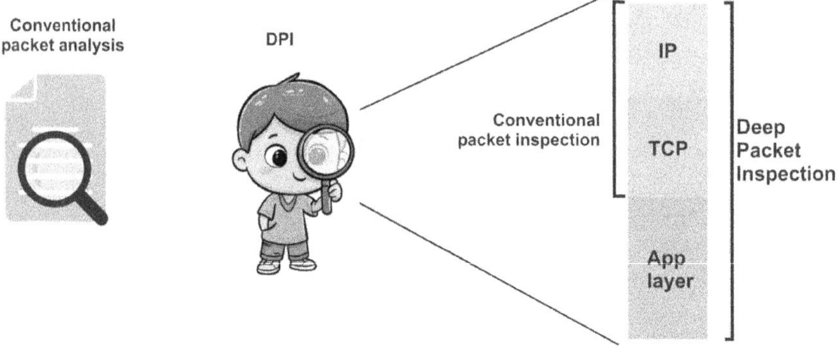

Figure 13.1 A diagram comparing conventional packet inspection (focusing on IP and TCP layers) with deep packet inspection (DPI), which extends analysis to the application layer.

Deep Packet Analysis (DPA) aims to gain a detailed view of network traffic to identify patterns, abnormalities, and potential security threats like malware. Here's a breakdown of what you typically look for and how **malware** can be identified through this process:

 DOI: 10.1201/9781003539261-13

KEY ELEMENTS TO LOOK FOR IN DPA

Packet structure and headers

- **IP headers:** Inspecting source and destination IPs, Time-To-Live (TTL) values, and other metadata to detect unusual routing or IP addresses that don't align with expected network patterns.
- **TCP/UDP headers:** Review flags, sequence numbers, and port numbers for anomalies, like unusual or out-of-range port numbers commonly used by malware.

Payload inspection

- Examining the payload (actual data sent in the packet) reveals the application-layer data being transmitted.
- Malware often communicates with external command-and-control (C2) servers, and inspecting the payload may reveal suspicious patterns, like base64-encoded data or compressed files, which are used to hide malicious activity.

Protocol anomalies

- Some malware exploits vulnerabilities in specific protocols or uses non-standard ports and protocols for communication. Looking for unexpected or abnormal use of protocols (like HTTP, DNS, or SMTP) is crucial.
- **DNS Tunneling:** Malware may hide data in DNS queries to bypass network security filters. Analyzing DNS traffic and its payload can reveal this type of attack.

Traffic patterns

- **Unusual traffic volume:** Malware, especially botnets or DDoS attacks, can generate large traffic volumes. Monitoring packet or byte count spikes over time can help detect malicious activity.
- **Repeated patterns:** Identifying repetitive traffic patterns could indicate automated malware communication (e.g., continuous pings and odd intervals of data packets)

Payload decoding

- **Base64 encoding:** Malware often uses base64 encoding to hide the real data within packets. By decoding the payload, you can reveal hidden malicious files or instructions.

- **Executable files:** A packet's payload may contain executable code, such as shellcode or binary files transferred over the network. This could be an indicator of a malware infection.
- **Encrypted payloads:** Malicious traffic often uses encryption (e.g., SSL/TLS) to hide its contents. While encrypted, it can still be flagged by unusual behavior, like frequent encryption or abnormal connections.

Command and control (C2) communication

- **Beaconing:** Malware often communicates with its C2 server regularly (beaconing). Monitoring for periodic packets sent to the same external IP address, often at fixed times, can reveal this type of activity.
- **Exfiltration:** Malware may attempt to send sensitive data to an external server. In DPA, you look for unusual outbound traffic to unfamiliar external servers or unusual data types sent out.

File transfers

- Many malware variants download or upload files as part of their operation. You can identify suspicious file downloads that may indicate malware payloads by inspecting TCP or UDP streams for file transfers (e.g., HTTP, FTP, or SMB traffic).

IDENTIFYING MALWARE

The following methods can be used to identify malware.

Suspicious domains or IPs

- Malware frequently communicates with known bad IP addresses or domains. DPA can help identify whether traffic is sent to suspicious or previously identified malicious endpoints. A lookup against threat intelligence feeds can confirm if an IP is associated with known malware C2 servers.

Unusual port activity

- Malware may use uncommon ports to avoid detection by firewalls or intrusion detection systems. Anomalous traffic on ports not typically used in normal operations could indicate malicious activity.

Protocol and payload anomalies

- Malware may unintentionally manipulate certain protocols, such as sending unusually large DNS queries (DNS tunneling), using unusual HTTP headers, or embedding suspicious data in the HTTP body.

Malformed packets

- Malware can sometimes use malformed or non-standard packets to exploit vulnerabilities. Identifying oddities in the packet structure—such as invalid checksums or out-of-order packets—can indicate potential exploitation attempts or traffic generated by malicious tools.

Suspicious communication patterns

- **Outbound Traffic to Foreign Servers:** Malware often sends exfiltrated data to external servers. By analyzing the destination IP addresses, a sudden spike in traffic going to foreign or unusual locations can raise a red flag.
- **Unusual Traffic Spikes:** Bots or malware often generate large traffic bursts. You can detect botnets or DDoS attacks by looking for spikes in packet rates, especially over short periods.

Payload analysis

- **File Transfers:** If a large binary or executable file is being transferred in a packet, it can be analyzed for malware. Executable files might be disguised as legitimate or compressed into archives (e.g., ZIP, RAR).
- **Payload Size and Encoding:** Malware authors may use techniques like data obfuscation, encoding (e.g., base64), or compression to hide the true nature of the payload. Deep packet analysis can help reveal such obfuscation.

BEHAVIORAL INDICATORS

- Malware often exhibits specific behaviors, such as trying to connect to known malicious domains, sending periodic requests (like pings), or establishing connections to command-and-control servers.

EXAMPLE OF MALWARE IDENTIFICATION IN DPA

1. *Traffic Analysis*: A packet capture reveals a series of HTTP packets with odd user-agent strings (possibly crafted to avoid detection), followed by connections to an IP address flagged in a threat intelligence feed as a known C2 server.
2. *Suspicious Payload*: The payload of the HTTP packet contains a large base64-encoded string, which, when decoded, reveals a compressed executable file (malware payload).
3. *Beaconing Behavior*: The malware periodically "beacons" the C2 server every 5 minutes with minimal data—another indicator of botnet communication.

OS FINGERPRINTING AND ITS APPLICATION IN WIRESHARK

OS fingerprinting is a technique used in network security and management to identify the operating system running on a remote device based solely on characteristics evident in packets sent by the device across the network. This identification is based on variations in the network stack behavior, which varies from one OS to another due to differences in the default values for TCP window sizes, packet fragmentation handling, and specific idiosyncrasies in protocol implementation.

Importance of OS fingerprinting

Understanding the operating system of network devices helps administrators tailor security policies and understand potential vulnerabilities inherent to specific operating systems. It's also crucial for network design and traffic management, as different OS may respond differently under various network conditions.

Wireshark as a tool for OS fingerprinting

Wireshark, the world's foremost network protocol analyzer, offers tools to capture and analyze packets from any network connection. Given its comprehensive parsing and filtering capabilities, Wireshark can observe and record discrepancies and details in packet construction that hint at an OS's identity.

How Wireshark supports OS fingerprinting

1. *Capture and analysis capabilities*: Wireshark captures packets in real time and displays them in human-readable format. Users can inspect individual packets for characteristics unique to specific operating systems, such as TCP window size, TTL (time-to-live) values, and the presence or absence of specific TCP options.
2. *TCP/IP stack behaviors*: By examining how a device's TCP/IP stack interacts with the network, Wireshark can help infer which operating system is in use. For example, different operating systems handle packet fragmentation, reassembly, and TCP connection teardown differently.
3. *Filters and plugins*: Wireshark allows users to set up filters to capture only the traffic likely to reveal OS-specific traits. It also supports plugins and scripts (like Lua) that can automate detecting and logging these traits, making OS fingerprinting more efficient.

STEP-BY-STEP GUIDE TO USING WIRESHARK FOR OS FINGERPRINTING

Here is a step-by-step guide for the same

Step 1: Configuring Wireshark

Configure Wireshark to capture traffic of interest. Depending on the network's scale and the fingerprinting exercise's goals, this might be traffic from a specific device or subnet.

Step 2: Analyzing TCP/IP stack behavior

Focus on details such as the SYN packets for TCP connections. Look for:

- *TCP window size*: Different OS have default settings that might be reflected in these values.
- *TCP options*: TCP options like selective acknowledgment (SACK), window scaling, and others can indicate an OS.
- *TTL values*: These can vary by OS, as different systems use different default values for TTL.

Note: If you can see the window size, you are likely in the TCP section. The TTL appear in the IP section, so focus on the correct protocol layer.

Step 3: Using filters to isolate relevant packets

Apply filters such as *tcp.flags.syn == 1* to capture only SYN packets sent at the start of a TCP connection and contain many of the identifiers necessary for OS fingerprinting as shown in Table 13.1. The same can be observed in Figure 13.2.

Table 13.1 Windows vs Linux: OS fingerprinting identifiers

Identifier	*Description*	*Windows (typical values)*	*Linux (typical values)*
TTL (time-to-live)	Default initial TTL value in IP packets	128	64
TCP Window size	Default TCP window size in bytes	65535	5840 (varies by distribution)
TCP options	Selective acknowledgment, window scaling, etc.	SACK Permitted, Window Scaling	SACK Permitted, Window Scaling
IP ID increment	Behavior of IP ID field incrementation	Incremental	Randomized
DF (Don't fragment) flag	Default setting for the DF flag in IP headers	Set	Set
ICMP echo reply	Structure of ICMP echo reply packets	Standard, with specific field padding	Standard, minimal padding (varies)
Packet retransmission timing	Interval between TCP retransmissions	200ms, exponential backoff	300ms, exponential backoff
Malformed packet handling	Response to malformed or invalid packets	Often sends RST or ICMP errors	Varies; typically sends ICMP error
DNS query behavior	Handling of DNS queries and responses	Standard response: supports EDNS	Standard response: supports EDNS

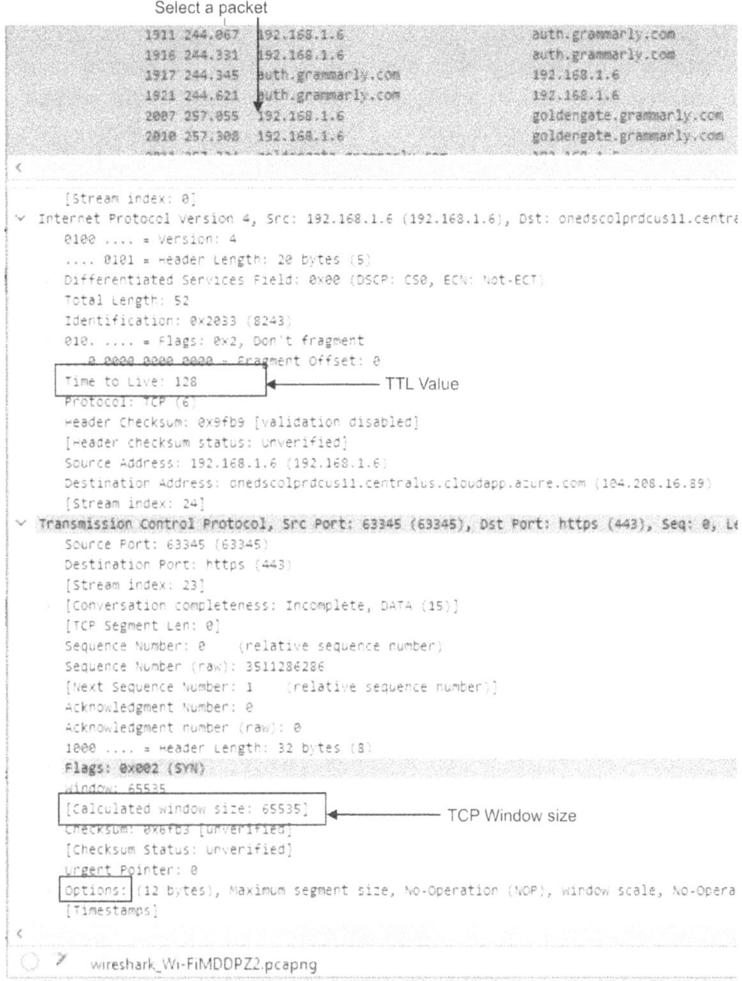

Figure 13.2 A Wireshark capture of TCP packets showing communication between 192.168.1.6 and auth.grammarly.com, with details about IP version, TCP flags, and sequence numbers.

Step 4: Comparing against known signatures

Use the information collected to compare against known OS fingerprints. This can be done manually or through automated scripts that match characteristics against a database of known values. Tools like **Nmap** or **p0f** automate the process. These tools capture packets, extract OS-related characteristics, and compare them to their internal databases to identify the operating system. For example, Nmap might output "Windows 10 or Server 2016" based on matching TCP/IP stack characteristics.

In summary, OS fingerprinting is a valuable aspect of DPA, as it helps identify the devices on the network and can also be used for security assessments, penetration testing, or network management. It complements deep packet analysis by providing insights into the OS behavior, which could reveal vulnerabilities specific to that OS.

LIMITATIONS AND CONSIDERATIONS

While effective, OS fingerprinting with Wireshark has its limitations. Network devices like routers and firewalls can alter packet headers, potentially obscuring or modifying indicators of the underlying OS. Additionally, with the increasing use of custom security configurations and hardened operating systems, the reliability of passive OS fingerprinting can be compromised.

Note: OS fingerprinting is a valuable technique in network administrators' and security professionals' toolkits. Wireshark provides a powerful platform for conducting such fingerprinting through detailed packet analysis. By understanding the capabilities and limitations of this approach, users can effectively enhance their network security and management strategies.

THE COMPLETE PACKET ANALYSIS

We have analyzed the above screenshot in terms of OS Fingerprinting. Let us decode it completely. As we can see, the two IP Layer and TCP layers are visible. Let us check all the elements.

1. **Internet protocol version 4 (IP layer)**
   This section describes the details of the IPv4 packet header.
   - Version: 4
     Indicates that the packet uses IPv4 (Internet Protocol version 4).
   - Header length: 20 bytes
     It specifies the length of the IP header in bytes. This is the standard size without any optional fields.
   - Differentiated services field: 0x00 (DSCP: CS0, ECN: Not-ECT)
     - **DSCP (Differentiated Services Code Point)**: Class Selector 0 (CS0) means no special QoS is requested.
     - **ECN (Explicit Congestion Notification)**: Not-ECT means no congestion notification is enabled.
   - Total length: 52
     The entire length of the IP packet (header + payload) in bytes

- Identification: 0x2033 (8243)
  A unique identifier for this packet is used for reassembling fragmented packets
- Flags: 0x02 (Don't Fragment)
  - Indicates that this packet should not be fragmented.
  - **Fragment offset: 0:** No fragmentation is present.
- Time-to-live (TTL): 128
  Specifies how many hops (routers) this packet can travel before being discarded. A TTL of 128 is typical for packets from Windows devices.
- Protocol: TCP (6)
  Indicates that the packet's payload is a TCP segment.
- Header checksum: 0x9fb9 (Validation disabled)
  The checksum of the IP header verifies the integrity of the header data. In this case, it's unverified during capture.
- Source address: 192.168.1.6 (192.168.1.6)
  The private IP address of the client device sending this packet.
- Destination address: onedscoldprdcu11.centralus.cloudapp.azure.com (104.208.16.89)
  The public IP address and domain of the server receiving this packet.

2. **Transmission control protocol (TCP layer)**
   This section describes the details of the TCP segment.
   - Source port: 63345
     This connection uses the ephemeral (temporary) port on the client device.
   - Destination port: 443
     The well-known port for HTTPS traffic
   - [Stream Index: 24]
     Indicates the TCP stream to which this packet belongs. Wireshark assigns unique numbers to streams for more straightforward analysis.
   - Sequence number: 0 (Relative sequence number)
     - The starting sequence number of this packet in the TCP connection.
     - Relative sequence numbers are used for more straightforward interpretation instead of raw sequence numbers.
   - Next Sequence number: 1 (Relative sequence number)
     This indicates the sequence number for the next packet in this connection.
   - Acknowledgment number: 0
     - No acknowledgment has been sent since this is an **SYN** packet initiating the connection.
   - Header length: 32 bytes
     The length of the TCP header (including options)

- Flags: 0x02 (SYN)
  - **SYN** flag: This packet is part of the TCP three-way handshake and is used to synchronize sequence numbers.
- Window: 65535
  The client device's receive window size indicates how much data it can buffer for this connection.
- [Calculated Window Size: 65535]
  Wireshark's calculation of the effective window size is based on the window field.
- Checksum: 0xfb73 (Unverified)
  It is a checksum to verify the integrity of the TCP header and data. This is unverified during capture.
- Urgent pointer: 0
  Not used in this packet (indicates no urgent data).
- Options (12 bytes)
  TCP options used in this connection:
  - **Maximum segment Size (MSS): 1460**
    Specifies the largest amount of data (in bytes) that can be sent in a single TCP segment.
  - **No-operation (NOP)**
    It is a placeholder used to align options to 4-byte boundaries
  - **Window scale: 0 (no window scaling)**
    No scaling is applied to the TCP window size.
  - **SACK permitted**
    Selective acknowledgment (SACK) is allowed, which enhances TCP performance during packet loss.

CONCLUSION OF THE ANALYSIS

This packet analysis highlights key aspects of a **TCP SYN packet** that is part of the initial handshake for establishing a secure HTTPS connection. Below are the main conclusions:

The packet appears normal and contains no indications of anomalies or issues, such as:

- Unexpected flags.
- Misconfigured TCP options.
- Suspicious data patterns.

Actionable insights

This analysis provides a foundation for understanding client-server communication over HTTPS. In more complex scenarios, deeper analysis could include:

- Inspecting subsequent packets in the handshake (e.g., SYN-ACK and ACK) for anomalies.
- Monitoring for signs of malicious activity, such as unusual flags or patterns.

GRAPHICAL TOOLS FOR IN-DEPTH ANALYSIS

IO Graphs in Wireshark are used to represent data graphically. Firstly, observe the elements of the I/O graph in Table 13.2.

Table 13.2 Elements of I/O graph in Wireshark

Element	*Description*	*Usage Example*
X-Axis (time)	Represents the time interval for captured traffic	Used to observe traffic patterns over a specific duration
Y-Axis (packets/ bytes)	Displays the number of packets or bytes per time interval	Used to analyze traffic volume trends
Filters	Allows display filters to be applied to focus on specific traffic types	Used to analyze HTTP traffic by applying "http" as a filter
Graph style	Defines the style of the graph, such as line or bar graphs.	Choose line style for continuous data analysis
Interval	Specifies the time interval for dividing the graph (e.g., I second)	Use smaller intervals to analyze finer traffic details
Color coding	Assign colors to different filters for better visualization	Assign red to "tcp" and blue to "udp" for easier differentiation
Units	Specifies units for measurement on the Y-axis (e.g., packets or bytes)	Switch between packets and bytes based on the analysis requirements
Graphing mode	Allows toggling between cumulative and non-cumulative views	Use cumulative mode to see total traffic trends over time

Using the IO graph

IO Graphs in Wireshark provide a graphical representation of data flow over time, which is instrumental in identifying trends, spikes, or anomalies.

Case scenario: Analyzing network throughput during a product launch to monitor traffic spikes and potential DDoS attacks.

- **Step 1:** Launch Wireshark and begin capturing packets on the network segment of interest.

- **Step 2:** Navigate to Statistics -> IO Graphs.
- **Step 3:** Set the graph to display packets or bytes per second on the Y-axis.
- **Step 4:** Use filters to isolate relevant traffic, such as requests to the product page or API.
- **Step 5:** Analyze the graph for sudden traffic increases, which may indicate a DDoS attack or other network issues (Figure 13.3).

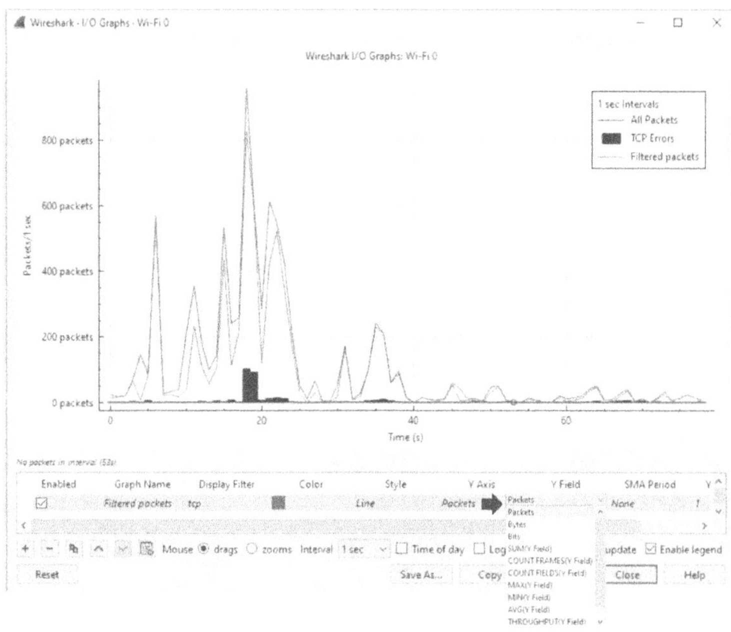

Figure 13.3 A Wireshark I/O graph displaying packet traffic over time on Wi-Fi 0, with filtered TCP packets represented as a line graph.

This is a **Wireshark I/O Graph** showing network traffic activity over time, plotting multiple graphs based on specific filters and configurations. Here's what it shows:

1. Key elements of the graph
    - **X-Axis (time):**
        - Represents time in seconds, divided into intervals (1-second intervals in this case)
    - **Y-Axis (packets/second):**
        - Represents the number of packets observed per second
    - **Legends (graph types):**
        - **All packets:**

    - The light-colored line (brownish) shows the total number of packets captured at each interval.
  - **TCP errors:**
    - The red bars represent TCP errors identified using the tcp .analysis.flags filter (e.g., retransmissions, duplicate ACKs).
  - **Filtered packets:**
    - The darker line corresponds to packets filtered with the tcp filter, isolating TCP traffic specifically.

2. Observations
   a. **Traffic peaks:** Significant peaks in total traffic (All Packets) occur around the 20-second mark, indicating bursts of activity. This could be due to legitimate traffic spikes or unusual network behavior.
   b. **TCP errors:** A visible red bar (TCP Errors) during the peak at around the 20-second mark suggests some TCP-related issues (e.g., retransmissions, duplicate ACKs) occurring during this high-traffic period.
   c. **Filtered packets:** The darker line showing TCP traffic matches the overall traffic trend, indicating that a significant proportion of the captured traffic is TCP-based.
3. Potential Causes
   a. **High traffic bursts:** This could indicate normal traffic behavior, such as file downloads or heavy user activity. Alternatively, it might suggest malicious activity, such as a burst of packets from a DDoS attack.
   b. **TCP errors:** Errors might occur due to:
      - Network congestion.
      - Packet loss or retransmissions.
      - Misconfigured devices or network instability
4. Next Steps for Analysis
   a. **Investigate TCP errors:** Use the filter tcp.analysis.flags to identify specific TCP issues like retransmissions or duplicate ACKs.
   b. **Analyze traffic source:** Apply filters to identify the source of the traffic peaks:
      ip.src == <specific_IP>
      Check if traffic is coming from unexpected or malicious sources.
   c. **Check protocol distribution:**
      Use filters to identify the protocols causing the traffic spike:
      - HTTP:
        http
      - UDP:
        udp

The graph shows a traffic surge around the 20-second mark with associated TCP errors, which may indicate network performance issues or potential malicious activity. Further analysis is needed to confirm the root cause by isolating the source and nature of the traffic. Let me know if you'd like to help apply filters or diagnose this further!

CONCLUSION

This chapter provides a comprehensive view of advanced deep packet analysis techniques using graphical analysis tools and OS fingerprinting in Wireshark. These methodologies empower network professionals to monitor, troubleshoot, and secure their networks more effectively.

MULTIPLE CHOICE QUESTIONS (MCQs)

1. What information is critical when using Wireshark to perform OS fingerprinting on a packet?
   A) The packet's data rate and frequency
   B) The source and destination MAC addresses
   C) TCP window size, TTL values, and TCP options
   D) The Wireshark version being used

Answer: C)

2. According to the screenshot, which TCP flag indicates that a packet is part of the three-way handshake to establish a TCP connection?
   A) ACK
   B) SYN
   C) FIN
   D) RST

Answer: B)

3. What can a TCP packet's "Window Size" indicate when performing DPA with Wireshark?
   A) The number of bytes the sender is willing to accept
   B) The packet transmission speed
   C) The packet's priority level in the network
   D) The encryption method used in the packet

Answer: A)

4. From the screenshot analysis, what does a "Stream Index" signify in Wireshark?
   A) The sequence number of the packet
   B) The unique identifier for a TCP session

C) The total number of packets in the capture file
D) The port number used for the communication

Answer: B)

5. What does a "Checksum" help determine in a packet when analyzed with Wireshark, as shown in the screenshot?
   A) The physical location of the server
   B) The integrity of the packet data
   C) The type of application transmitting the data
   D) The size of the data payload

Answer: B)

GLOSSARY

1. **Acknowledgment Number:** The sequence number of the next byte expected by the receiver used to acknowledge receipt of data.
2. **Checksum:** It is a value calculated to verify the integrity of a header or payload. If incorrect, the packet is considered corrupted.
3. **Cloud Server:** It is a remote server hosted in a cloud environment that provides services or resources over the Internet.
4. **Differentiated Services Code Point (DSCP):** A field in the IP header used for Quality of Service (QoS) to prioritize certain types of traffic.
5. **Destination Address:** The IP address of the device receiving the packet.
6. **Destination Port:** The port number on the server used to identify the service being accessed (e.g., port 443 for HTTPS)
7. **Explicit Congestion Notification (ECN):** A feature that allows routers to notify endpoints of network congestion without dropping packets.
8. **Ephemeral Port:** A temporary port used by a client device for establishing a connection with a server
9. **Flags:** Control bits in the TCP header. Common flags include SYN (used to initiate a connection), ACK (used to acknowledge received data), and FIN (used to terminate a connection).
10. **Fragment Offset:** Specifies the position of a fragmented packet relative to the original packet
11. **Fragmentation:** The process of breaking a large packet into smaller fragments to fit a network's maximum transmission unit (MTU)
12. **Header Length:** The size of the protocol header in bytes, which contains metadata about the packet
13. **HTTPS (Hypertext Transfer Protocol Secure):** A secure version of HTTP, using encryption to protect data during transmission over the Internet
14. **Identification:** A unique identifier for each packet used to reassemble fragmented packets

15. **Internet Protocol (IP):** A set of rules that governs how data is sent and received over the Internet. In this context, IPv4 (version 4) is used.
16. **Maximum Segment Size (MSS):** The largest segment of data (in bytes) that a device can receive in a single TCP packet
17. **No-Operation (NOP):** A placeholder in TCP options to align fields to 4-byte boundaries
18. **Payload:** The actual data carried by a packet, excluding the header.
19. **Protocol:** Specifies the transport layer protocol used (e.g., TCP, UDP)
20. **Quality of Service (QoS):** A mechanism to prioritize certain types of traffic over others to ensure better performance for critical applications
21. **Selective Acknowledgment (SACK):** An option allowing the receiver to acknowledge non-contiguous packets, improving performance during packet loss
22. **Source Address:** The IP address of the device sending the packet
23. **Source Port:** The temporary port number on the client device initiates the connection
24. **Stream Index:** A unique identifier for a TCP session (stream) in Wireshark used for analyzing specific connections.
25. **SYN (Synchronize) Packet:** A type of TCP packet used to initiate a connection by synchronizing sequence numbers between devices
26. **Three-Way Handshake:** A process in TCP used to establish a connection involving three steps: SYN, SYN-ACK, and ACK.
27. **Time-to-Live (TTL):** The maximum number of hops (routers) a packet can pass through before being discarded.
28. **Total Length:** The entire length of the IP packet, including the header and payload
29. **Transmission Control Protocol (TCP):** A transport layer protocol that ensures reliable communication between devices.
30. **Window Scaling:** An option in TCP to increase the maximum window size for high-speed networks
31. **Window Size:** The amount of data (in bytes) the receiver is willing to accept before sending an acknowledgment

Chapter 14

Real-world applications and case studies

In today's digital age, where technology permeates every aspect of our lives, cybersecurity has become a critical concern for individuals, organizations, and governments worldwide. The frequency and complexity of cyberattacks have escalated, targeting everything from personal data to critical infrastructure. This evolving threat landscape demands robust network security measures and sophisticated tools to detect, analyze, and mitigate potential threats. While it is not explicitly documented how Wireshark was used in each incident, one can speculate that this tool has proven indispensable in the arsenal of cybersecurity professionals (Figure 14.1).

Figure 14.1 A symbolic image of the world-wide protection from Cyber-attack.

Wireshark provides deep insights into network traffic and, through specific filters, could have played a crucial role in uncovering vulnerabilities,

DOI: 10.1201/9781003539261-14

tracking malicious activities, and enforcing security protocols effectively. Here, we explore 25 significant cyber incidents from 2017 to 2024, demonstrating the crucial role of network security and the potential impact of Wireshark in navigating these challenges. Remember, all uses of Wireshark are hypothetical and need deep packet analysis for investigation.

WANNACRY RANSOMWARE ATTACK (2017)

Incident details: Originating from North Korea, this global cyberattack targeted computers running the Microsoft Windows operating system by encrypting data and demanding ransom payments in Bitcoin. It exploited the SMB protocol, affecting over 200,000 computers in 150 countries.

Wireshark use: Could detect ransomware spread within networks by monitoring SMB traffic for anomalies and unusual external connections.

Potential Wireshark filter: *smb.cmd == 0x25* and *ip.dst != [List of Internal IPs]*

- *smb.cmd* refers to the SMB (Server Message Block) command field, which identifies the type of operation within the SMB protocol (used for operations like file sharing, network browsing, and printing.).

- *0x25* is the hexadecimal code for the Trans2_Secondary command in SMB. This command is part of a transaction-based operation within SMB. It is often used to extend a request initiated by a Trans2 command (like reading directory contents).

  Suppose you are filtering for *smb.cmd == 0x25*. In that case, you are specifically looking for SMB packets with Trans2 secondary commands—which could help troubleshoot file share operations or detect potential anomalies related to these extended operations.

- *ip.dst* refers to the destination IP address in the packet.

The filter explained: The Wireshark filter *smb.cmd == 0x25 and ip.dst != [List of Internal IPs]* captures SMB (Server Message Block) Trans2 Request packets—indicated by the command code 0x25—that are destined for external IPs, excluding those within a predefined list of internal IP addresses. This filter is beneficial for monitoring unauthorized data sharing or file access attempts over SMB, as it focuses on outbound requests that could indicate data leakage or malware activity (such as ransomware spreading through SMB). Excluding internal traffic highlights potentially malicious communication with external systems, helping network analysts detect and mitigate security breaches.

Note: The "Trans2" refers to a more advanced set of commands or requests beyond basic file access (such as reading or writing files). These packets are a specific type of network packet used in the Server Message Block (SMB) protocol, a network file-sharing protocol commonly used in Microsoft Windows systems for sharing files, printers, and other resources over a network.

What does the filter look like?

smb.cmd == 0x25 and !(ip.dst == 192.168.1.1 || ip.dst == 192.168.1.2 || ip .dst == 10.0.0.1 || ip.dst == 10.0.0.2)

This filter captures SMB Trans2 Request (0x25) packets where the destination IP is not one of the specified internal addresses: 192.168.1.1, 192.168.1.2, 10.0.0.1, or 10.0.0.2. It helps focus on SMB traffic potentially leaving the internal network, which is useful for detecting suspicious file access attempts or data exfiltration.

Note: Both *&&* and *and* can be used in Wireshark capture filters to perform logical AND operations. Their choice often comes from personal preference or familiarity with programming syntax. However, in display filters within Wireshark, only *and* (and *or*) are valid, while && is not accepted.

NOTPETYA ATTACK (2017)

Incident details: Initially targeting organizations in Ukraine, including government offices and financial institutions, NotPetya spread globally, affecting businesses worldwide. Unlike typical ransomware, NotPetya aimed primarily to disrupt systems by masquerading as ransomware.

Wireshark use: It helps trace the malware's propagation methods and identify movement within affected networks.

Potential Wireshark filter: *tcp.flags.syn == 1* and *ip.src == [Range of Affected IPs]*

The TCP flag SYN (Synchronize) plays a crucial role in setting up a TCP connection, specifically in the process known as the TCP three-way handshake. When the SYN flag is set to 1 (tcp.flags.syn == 1), it indicates that the packet is attempting to initiate a new TCP connection.

The filter explained: The filter *tcp.flags.syn == 1 and ip.src == [Range of Affected IPs]* is highly useful in network forensics and threat analysis. It helps detect abnormal connection attempts (such as SYN floods) or monitor specific devices for suspicious behavior, providing valuable insights into the initial stages of TCP communications or attacks.

EQUIFAX DATA BREACH (2017)

Incident details: In Atlanta, Georgia, USA, attackers exploited a vulnerability in Apache Struts on Equifax's servers to access the personal data of approximately 147 million people, leading to one of the most significant data breaches in history.

Wireshark use: Monitor and analyze network traffic for signs of unauthorized data access and exfiltration.

Potential Wireshark filter: *ip.dst == [Equifax Server IPs] and http.request .method == "POST"*

The filter explained: The filter *ip.dst == [Equifax Server IPs] and http .request.method == "POST"* captures HTTP POST requests explicitly sent to Equifax's servers. This is useful for identifying potential data exfiltration attempts. POST requests typically carry sensitive information in the request body, such as personal data, login credentials, or payment details.

SOLARWINDS ORION SOFTWARE HACK (2020)

Incident details: Originating from a Russian cyber espionage group, malicious code was covertly inserted into SolarWinds' Orion platform software updates, affecting thousands of private companies and government agencies worldwide.

Wireshark use: Could detect anomalies in network traffic to and from compromised Orion servers, aiding in identifying malicious activities.

Potential Wireshark filter: *ip.src == [Orion Server IP] and (tcp.port == 443 or tcp.port == 80)*

The filter explained: The *filter ip.src == [Orion Server IP] and (tcp.port == 443 or tcp.port == 80)* captures HTTP and HTTPS traffic originating from the Orion server. This helps monitor the server's web-related activity, detecting potential malicious communications or unauthorized data transmissions, as these protocols are often used for legitimate or stealthy data exchanges.

MICROSOFT EXCHANGE SERVER HACKS (2021)

Incident details: Vulnerabilities in Microsoft Exchange servers were exploited to access emails and install additional malware for long-term access to victims' environments across thousands of organizations globally, originating from China. Microsoft Exchange Server is a powerful email, calendaring, contact, scheduling, and collaboration platform developed by Microsoft.

Wireshark use: Useful in detecting unusual inbound and outbound traffic on Exchange servers to detect exploitation attempts.

Potential Wireshark filter: *tcp.port == 443 and ip.dst == [Exchange Server IP] and http.request.method == "POST"*

The filter explained: The filter *tcp.port == 443 and ip.dst == [Exchange Server IP] and http.request.method == "POST"* captures encrypted HTTP POST requests (HTTPS) sent to the Exchange server. This is useful for identifying potential data uploads or suspicious activities, such as email-related data exfiltration attempts or unauthorized transmissions to the server, since POST requests often contain sensitive information in their payloads.

COLONIAL PIPELINE RANSOMWARE ATTACK (2021)

Incident details: In the United States, a ransomware attack targeted Colonial Pipeline, leading to a shutdown of the major fuel pipeline supplying gasoline and jet fuel to the Eastern US, and the company paid about $5 million in ransom.

Wireshark use: Could identify ransomware communication with C2 servers before file encryption. C2 servers, or Command and Control servers, are computers or servers that cyberattackers or malware operators use to maintain communications with compromised systems(botnet) within a target network.

Potential Wireshark filter: *ip.dst == [Known C2 server IPs]*

The filter explained: The filter *ip.dst == [Known C2 server IPs]* captures network traffic directed toward Command and Control (C2) servers. This filter helps identify potential malware infections or botnet communications, as infected machines often communicate with C2 servers to receive instructions or send stolen data.

TWITCH DATA BREACH (2021)

Incident details: An extensive data leak at Twitch exposed source code, creator payout information, and internal security tools.

Wireshark use: Monitoring unexpected data exfiltration activities and unauthorized access.

Potential Wireshark filter: *ip.dst != [Twitch IPs] and tcp.length > 1000*

The filter explained: The filter ip.dst != [Twitch IPs] and tcp.length > 1000 captures TCP packets larger than 1000 bytes that are not destined for

Twitch servers. This is useful for focusing on large data transfers unrelated to Twitch streaming, helping identify suspicious file uploads, data exfiltration attempts, or unusually large network traffic that may indicate potential security threats.

LOG4SHELL VULNERABILITY EXPLOITATION (2021)

Incident details: A critical vulnerability in Apache Log4j, a popular Java logging library, allowed attackers to execute remote code on affected servers, impacting millions of devices worldwide.

Wireshark use: Track exploitation attempts and unusual server responses.

Potential Wireshark filter: *http contains "jndi:ldap"*, or *http contains "jndi:rmi"*

The filter explained: The filter *http contains "jndi:ldap" or http contains "jndi:rmi"* used in network analysis tools like Wireshark is designed to identify HTTP traffic that contains specific strings related to Java Naming and Directory Interface (JNDI) lookups for LDAP (Lightweight Directory Access Protocol) or RMI (Remote Method Invocation). This type of filter is particularly significant in the context of security, especially for detecting attempts to exploit vulnerabilities related to JNDI injections.

OPTUS DATA BREACH (2022)

Incident details: In Australia, telecom giant Optus experienced a data breach affecting 9.8 million users due to a vulnerability in an API, exposing personal data including driver's licenses and passport numbers.

Wireshark use: Monitor API traffic for unauthorized access attempts.

Potential Wireshark filter: *ip.dst == [Optus API Server IP] and http.request .method == "GET"*

The filter explained: The filter *ip.dst == [Optus API Server IP] and http .request.method == "GET"* captures HTTP GET requests sent to the Optus API server. This helps monitor data retrieval operations from the API, ensuring legitimate usage or detecting potential misuse, such as unauthorized data scraping or abnormal querying behavior.

Note: An API server is a server that handles Application Programming Interface (API) requests. APIs are sets of rules and protocols that allow different software applications to communicate with each other. An API server hosts and processes these requests, usually as part of a backend system, and responds with data or performs actions based on those requests.

Example use case

- **Web application:** A client-side web application might send a request to an API server to get a list of products. The API server handles this request, fetches the data from a database, and returns the product list in a structured format (like JSON).
- **Mobile app:** A mobile app can send a request to an API server to submit a user's login credentials. The server authenticates the user and returns a success message or error based on the login details.

OKTA DATA BREACH (2022)

Incident details: Okta, a significant identity and access management provider based in San Francisco, USA, was breached through a third-party customer support vendor, impacting clients globally.

Wireshark use: Analyze third-party connections to detect unusual activities

Potential Wireshark filter: ip.src == [Third-party IPs] and ssl.handshake.type == 1

API traffic refers to data flow between two or more software applications via their APIs (Application Programming Interfaces). APIs are sets of rules and protocols for building and interacting with software applications.

The filter explained: The filter ip.src == [Third-party IPs] and ssl.handshake.type == 1 captures SSL/TLS handshake packets (specifically Client Hello messages) originating from third-party IPs. This helps identify and analyze connection initiation attempts from external sources, which could be used to establish encrypted communication, potentially indicating legitimate services, malicious probes, or man-in-the-middle attack attempts.

UBER HACK (2022)

Incident details: An 18-year-old hacker gained extensive unauthorized access to Uber's internal systems by tricking an employee through social engineering, affecting operations globally from their headquarters in San Francisco, USA.

Wireshark use: It could have helped detect the initial compromise and subsequent lateral movement within the network.

Potential Wireshark filter: *tcp.flags* == *"SYN, ACK"* and *ip.src != [List of Known Uber IPs]*

The filter expression tcp.flags == "SYN, ACK" is used in Wireshark to filter for TCP packets where both the SYN (Synchronize) and ACK (Acknowledgment) flags are set. This filter is crucial for analyzing and troubleshooting network traffic, especially when studying the TCP three-way handshake process, which is essential for establishing a TCP connection.

The filter explained: The filter tcp.flags == "SYN, ACK" and ip.src != [List of Known Uber IPs] captures SYN-ACK packets from sources that are not Uber's known IPs. This is useful for monitoring unexpected or unauthorized network activity, as SYN-ACK packets indicate responses to incoming connection attempts, which could suggest port scanning, unauthorized access attempts, or network reconnaissance by unknown entities.

AIIMS DELHI CYBERATTACK (2022)

Incident details: The All India Institute of Medical Sciences (AIIMS) in Delhi was hit by a ransomware attack, crippling its digital infrastructure and affecting patient care across India.

Wireshark use: Could identify malicious network behavior and ransomware traffic patterns.

Potential Wireshark filter: *tcp.port == [File Sharing Ports] and ip.dst != [Whitelisted IPs]*

The filter explained: The filter *tcp.port == [File Sharing Ports] and ip.dst != [Whitelisted IPs]* captures file-sharing traffic (e.g., via ports like 445 for SMB or 21 for FTP) that is not directed to allowed or whitelisted IPs. This is useful for detecting unauthorized file transfers or potential data exfiltration attempts, ensuring that sensitive files are not shared with unapproved external systems.

NVIDIA DATA BREACH (2022)

Incident details: Nvidia experienced a ransomware attack where sensitive employee credentials and proprietary information were stolen, affecting its operations in Santa Clara, California, USA.

Wireshark use: Monitor for data exfiltration and unusual network activity associated with ransomware.

Potential Wireshark filter: *tcp.flags == "PSH, ACK"* and *ip.dst != [List of Nvidia IPs]*

The filter explained: The filter tcp.flags == "PSH, ACK" and ip.dst != [List of Nvidia IPs] captures TCP packets with the PSH (Push) and ACK (Acknowledgment) flags set that are not directed to Nvidia's servers. This is useful for identifying immediate data transmissions containing potentially significant payloads, which could indicate suspicious data exfiltration, malware communication, or unauthorized information transfers to non-approved destinations.

GLOBAL FINANCIAL EXCHANGE CYBERATTACK (2023)

Incident details: Cybercriminals targeted global financial exchanges, using spear-phishing to gain initial access, followed by network exploitation to disrupt trading algorithms.

Wireshark use: Analyze inbound and outbound traffic to identify anomalies or unauthorized data transfers in real time

Potential Wireshark filter: *ip.dst == [Trading System IPs]* and (*tcp.flags.syn == 1* and *tcp.flags.ack == 1*)

The filter explained: The filter *ip.dst == [Trading System IPs]* and (*tcp.flags.syn == 1* and *tcp.flags.ack == 1*) captures TCP packets with both SYN and ACK flags set, indicating the completion of the TCP three-way handshake, and are directed to the Trading System IPs. This is useful for monitoring established connections to trading systems, allowing analysts to track legitimate trading activities or detect potential unauthorized access attempts aimed at these critical systems.

SMART HOME DEVICE LEAK (2024)

Incident details: Several vulnerabilities in widely used smart home devices were exploited to gain unauthorized access to private home networks, leaking personal data and allowing remote control over the devices globally.

Wireshark use: Track unexpected inbound and outbound traffic from smart devices to identify malicious activity.

Potential Wireshark filter: *ip.src == [Smart Device IP Range]* and (*http contains "login"* or *http contains "token"*)

The filter explained: The filter ip.src == [Smart Device IP Range] and (http contains "login" or http contains "token") captures HTTP traffic originating from a specified range of smart device IPs that contains the keywords "login" or "token" in the request. This is useful for monitoring authentication attempts or token exchanges from smart devices, helping identify potential security vulnerabilities, unauthorized access attempts, or suspicious activity related to the devices within that range.

AUTOMOTIVE MANUFACTURER ESPIONAGE (2024)

Incident details: An automotive manufacturer in Detroit, Michigan, USA, experienced a breach where proprietary data related to autonomous vehicle technology was stolen.

Wireshark use: Monitor network segments handling sensitive R&D information for unauthorized access or anomaly traffic patterns.

Potential Wireshark filter: ip.src == [R&D Subnet] and tcp.len > 1000

The filter explained: The filter *ip.src == [R&D Subnet]* and *tcp.len > 1000* captures TCP packets originating from the R&D subnet larger than 1000 bytes. This is useful for monitoring large data transfers from the research and development department, which may indicate file uploads, data exfiltration, or significant internal communications, helping to identify any unusual activity that could pose a security risk.

MAJOR RETAIL CHAIN POS MALWARE INFECTION (2024)

Incident details: Point of Sale (PoS) systems at a major retail chain were infected with malware designed to skim credit card information during transactions, affecting stores across the USA.

Wireshark use: Inspect PoS network traffic for malware signatures and data leakage to external IPs.

Potential Wireshark filter: *ip.src == [PoS IPs]* and (tcp.payload contains "creditcard" or ip.dst != [Corporate Network IPs])

The filter explained: The filter ip.src == [PoS IPs] and (tcp.payload contains "creditcard" or ip.dst != [Corporate Network IPs]) captures traffic originating from Point of Sale (PoS) systems that either contains the term "creditcard" in the TCP payload or is directed to non-corporate network IPs. This is useful for identifying potentially sensitive transactions involving credit card information and detecting suspicious communications that could indicate data exfiltration or unauthorized transfers from PoS systems to external or unapproved destinations.

HEALTH SECTOR RANSOMWARE EPIDEMIC (2023)

Incident details: Throughout 2023, multiple healthcare providers across the globe were targeted with a new strain of ransomware exploiting vulnerabilities in Electronic Health Record (EHR) systems.

Wireshark use: Monitor EHR system traffic for signs of command and control (C2) communications and data exfiltration.

Potential Wireshark filter: *tcp.port == [EHR System Port]* and (*ip.dst == [C2 IPs]* or *tcp.flags.push == 1*)

The filter explained: The filter tcp.port == [EHR System Port] and (ip .dst == [C2 IPs] or tcp.flags.push == 1) captures traffic on the specified

EHR (Electronic Health Record) system port that is either directed toward Command and Control (C2) servers or has the PSH (Push) flag set. This is useful for monitoring potential malicious activity where EHR data might be sent to external C2 servers and identifying immediate data transmissions that could indicate unusual or unauthorized access to sensitive health information within the EHR system.

GLOBAL SUPPLY CHAIN CYBERATTACK (2023)

Incident details: A sophisticated cyberattack disrupted global supply chains by targeting logistics and shipping companies with ransomware originating from cybercriminal groups in Eastern Europe.

Wireshark use: Analyze traffic to detect ransomware propagation and C2 communications.

Potential Wireshark filter: (*tcp.port == 80* or *tcp.port == 443* or *tcp.port == 53*) and (*ip.dst == [Known C2 IPs] or tcp.len > 1000*) or (*http.request.uri contains "encrypt"* or *http.request.uri contains "ransom"* or *dns.qry.name contains "[known-malicious-domain]"*)

The filter explained: The filter (tcp.port == 80 or tcp.port == 443 or tcp.port == 53) and (ip.dst == [Known C2 IPs] or tcp.len > 1000) or (http.request.uri contains "encrypt" or http.request.uri contains "ransom" or dns.qry.name contains "[known-malicious-domain]") is designed to detect potential ransomware propagation and Command and Control (C2) communications within network traffic. It captures traffic on common ports (80 for HTTP, 443 for HTTPS, and 53 for DNS), monitoring for connections to known C2 server IPs or large data transfers indicative of exfiltration. Additionally, it checks HTTP request URIs for keywords like "encrypt" or "ransom," which suggest a malicious activity, and it filters DNS queries for known bad domains associated with ransomware. This comprehensive approach enhances the ability to identify suspicious behaviors that could signal ransomware attacks or unauthorized communications within the network.

HEALTHCARE RANSOMWARE CRISIS (2023)

Incident details: In early 2023, a widespread ransomware attack impacted over 100 healthcare facilities across the United States and Canada. The attackers exploited vulnerabilities in outdated operating systems and demanded substantial ransoms to decrypt affected systems.

Wireshark use: Wireshark could be utilized to analyze the ransomware's communication patterns with its command and control centers and identify the initial infection vector through traffic anomalies.

Potential Wireshark filter: tcp.port == 445 and ip.dst == [Known C2 IPs] to monitor SMB traffic, commonly used in ransomware attacks for lateral movement and control.

UNIVERSITY DATA BREACH (2023)

Incident details: A major university in Boston, Massachusetts, USA, experienced a data breach resulting from a phishing attack that compromised several administrative accounts.

Wireshark use: Wireshark could analyze SMTP and HTTP traffic to identify the origin of phishing emails and subsequent unauthorized access to sensitive data.

Potential Wireshark filter: smtp contains "login" or http.request.uri contains "credential"

The display filter smtp contains "login" or http.request.uri contains "credential" and focuses on identifying potentially sensitive information in network traffic. The first part, smtp, contains "login" and captures SMTP packets that contain the word "login" in their payload, which could indicate an authentication process over email (e.g., during plaintext logins or protocol exchanges). The second part is http.request.uri contains "credential" and filters HTTP requests where the URI contains the keyword "credential." This is useful for identifying web traffic involving login forms or credential transmission, helping network administrators detect insecure or suspicious transmissions that could pose security risks. These filters are particularly valuable for cybersecurity professionals monitoring potential breaches or data leaks.

GOVERNMENT AGENCY ESPIONAGE (2024)

Incident details: A sophisticated state-sponsored attack targeted government agencies in Washington, DC, aiming to steal classified information relating to national security.

Wireshark use: Monitoring SSL/TLS traffic for anomalies could help detect data exfiltration or unauthorized encrypted communications.

Potential Wireshark filter: ssl.handshake.type == 1 and ip.dst != [List of Government IPs]

The filter explained: The Wireshark filter ssl.handshake.type == 1 and ip.dst != [List of Government IPs] isolates **TLS/SSL Client Hello messages,** which initiate secure communication by presenting the client's supported cyphers and protocols. This filter focuses on identifying handshake attempts while excluding traffic destined for predefined government IPs, allowing network analysts to monitor non-governmental outbound connections. It is beneficial for detecting suspicious or unauthorized encrypted traffic, such as C2 (Command and Control) communication or data exfiltration attempts, ensuring that legitimate government-bound traffic does not clutter the analysis.

MAJOR TELECOMMUNICATIONS CYBER ESPIONAGE (2023)

Incident details: A telecommunications giant in Germany was hit by a cyber espionage campaign believed to be orchestrated by a rival nation-state. The attackers aimed to intercept communications and gather intelligence.

Wireshark use: Could analyze SIP (Session Initiation Protocol) and RTP (Real-time Transport Protocol) traffic for signs of tampering or rerouting.

Potential Wireshark filter: *sip.method == "INVITE" and ip.dst != [Telecom IPs]*

The filter explained: The Wireshark filter sip.method == "INVITE" and ip.dst != [Telecom IPs] captures *SIP INVITE messages*—used to initiate VoIP (Voice over IP) calls—while excluding traffic destined for a predefined list of telecom IPs. This helps network administrators focus on *non-telecom-related VoIP activity*, which could indicate unauthorized or rogue call attempts within the network. Such filtering is essential for fraud detection, preventing toll fraud, or identifying potential misuse of VoIP infrastructure by ensuring that only relevant traffic is analyzed and legitimate connections with telecom providers are ignored.

FINANCIAL SECTOR MALWARE SPREAD (2024)

Incident details: Banks across New York City were targeted with malware that infiltrated trading platforms designed to manipulate transactions and steal financial data.

Wireshark use: Monitoring network traffic for unusual patterns or anomalies in financial transaction protocols could identify malicious activities.

Potential Wireshark filter: tcp.port == [Financial Transaction Port] and (tcp .flags.fin == 1 or tcp.flags.reset == 1)

The filter explained: The Wireshark filter tcp.port == [Financial Transaction Port] and (tcp.flags.fin == 1 or tcp.flags.reset == 1) focuses on monitoring

TCP connections related to financial transactions. It captures packets where the specified port is used—commonly associated with payment gateways or secure transaction services—and identifies sessions that are being terminated. The filter flags connections with FIN (Finish), indicating an orderly shutdown, or RST (Reset), signaling an abrupt termination. This can help network analysts detect abnormal connection closures, such as disrupted transactions or potential attacks like session hijacking or man-in-the-middle (MITM) attempts, ensuring financial communication integrity.

INTERNATIONAL AIRPORT CYBERTERRORISM (2024)

Incident details: Cyber terrorists targeted international airport systems in Dubai, UAE, to disrupt flight operations and sow panic among travellers by tampering with flight data and display systems.

Wireshark use: Wireshark could be used to track the airport's internal network traffic for unauthorized access and unusual data requests to flight control systems.

Potential Wireshark filter: ip.src == [Public IP Ranges] and ip.dst == [Airport System IPs] and tcp.len > 500

The filter explained: The Wireshark filter ip.src == [Public IP Ranges] and ip.dst == [Airport System IPs] and tcp.len > 500 captures **TCP packets from public IP ranges directed toward airport systems**, with a payload length greater than 500 bytes. This filter helps monitor potentially large or suspicious data transmissions targeting airport infrastructure. Such filtering is valuable for identifying **anomalies** like **unauthorized access attempts**, **DDoS attacks**, or **data exfiltration**, ensuring that only relevant traffic with significant payloads is analyzed. This can assist in proactive security measures by focusing on unusual or large-scale communication between external sources and critical airport systems.

Note: Cyberattacks on critical infrastructure like airport systems can lead to cascading effects that disrupt global travel and logistics networks, highlighting the interconnected risks in our globalized world.

WHAT IF THERE ARE MANY IPS TO GIVE IN THE FILTER?

Suppose you have a large number of IP addresses that you want to address in a Wireshark filter. In that case, it can become unwieldy and lengthy. However, there are more efficient ways to handle this situation:

1. Using **IP Ranges**: If the IP addresses belong to certain ranges, you can use CIDR notation to simplify the filter. For example, if many addresses are within the 192.168.1.0/24 range, you can filter out that entire subnet with:
   smb.cmd == 0x25 and !(ip.dst >= 192.168.1.0 && ip.dst <= 192.168.1.255)
2. Using a **Subnet Mask**: You can use a subnet mask to cover multiple IPs. For instance:
   smb.cmd == 0x25 and !(ip.dst >= 10.0.0.0 && ip.dst <= 10.0.0.255)
3. Using a **Capture Filter**: In some cases, you can set up capture filters in Wireshark to exclude certain IP addresses before the capture begins. For example:
   not host 192.168.1.1 and not host 192.168.1.2 and not host 10.0.0.1 and not host 10.0.0.2
4. External **File or Lookup Table**: If you use a script or tool that interacts with Wireshark, consider storing the IP addresses in an external file and programmatically constructing your filter.

CONCLUSION

The 25 cyber incidents spanning from 2017 to 2024 underscore the critical role that network security plays in defending against a wide range of threats across various sectors, from financial services to critical infrastructure. Tools like Wireshark, a sophisticated network protocol analyzer, are indispensable in this landscape. Wireshark aids in detecting anomalies, troubleshooting, forensic analysis, and real-time response during active cyberattacks, providing granular insights into packet-level network traffic. This capability is crucial for identifying the sources and methods of attacks, validating security measures, and educating new cybersecurity professionals. By integrating tools like Wireshark into a comprehensive network security strategy, organizations can enhance their ability to safeguard sensitive information, ensuring the integrity and reliability of their operations in a world where digital threats are increasingly complex and impactful.

MULTIPLE CHOICE QUESTIONS (MCQs)

1. What Wireshark filter would you use to detect potential WannaCry ransomware propagation in a network?
   A) tcp.flags.syn == 1 and ip.src == [Range of Affected IPs]
   B) ip.dst == [Equifax Server IPs] and http.request.method == "POST"
   C) smb.cmd == 0x25 and ip.dst != [List of Internal IPs]
   D) ip.src == [Orion Server IP] and (tcp.port == 443 or tcp.port == 80)

Answer: C)

2. Which Wireshark filter is appropriate for tracing the NotPetya malware's propagation methods within an affected network?
   A) ip.dst == [Equifax Server IPs] and http.request.method == "POST"
   B) tcp.flags.syn == 1 and ip.src == [Range of Affected IPs]
   C) ip.src == [Orion Server IP] and (tcp.port == 443 or tcp.port == 80)
   D) smb.cmd == 0x25 and ip.dst != [List of Internal IPs]

Answer: B)

3. During the Equifax data breach analysis, which Wireshark filter would be most useful for monitoring signs of unauthorized data access?
   A) ip.src == [Orion Server IP] and (tcp.port == 443 or tcp.port == 80)
   B) tcp.flags.syn == 1 and ip.src == [Range of Affected IPs]
   C) ip.dst == [Equifax Server IPs] and http.request.method == "POST"
   D) smb.cmd == 0x25 and ip.dst != [List of Internal IPs]

Answer: C)

4. For monitoring traffic related to the SolarWinds Orion software hack, which filter would help detect anomalies in traffic to and from compromised servers?
   A) tcp.flags.syn == 1 and ip.src == [Range of Affected IPs]
   B) smb.cmd == 0x25 and ip.dst != [List of Internal IPs]
   C) ip.src == [Orion Server IP] and (tcp.port == 443 or tcp.port == 80)
   D) ip.dst == [Equifax Server IPs] and http.request.method == "POST"

Answer: C)

5. Which filter effectively identifies Microsoft Exchange Server hacks through unusual inbound and outbound traffic?
   A) smb.cmd == 0x25 and ip.dst != [List of Internal IPs]
   B) tcp.flags.syn == 1 and ip.src == [Range of Affected IPs]
   C) ip.dst == [Equifax Server IPs] and http.request.method == "POST"
   D) tcp.port == 443 and ip.dst == [Exchange Server IP] and http .request.method == "POST"

Answer: D)

GLOSSARY

1. **API (Application Programming Interface):** A set of rules and protocols for building and interacting with software applications, allowing different systems to communicate seamlessly.
2. **C2 (Command and Control) Servers:** Remote servers used to command and control a network of infected machines or botnets, often for malicious purposes.

3. **Cyber Espionage:** The act of using cyber techniques to gain illicit access to confidential information, typically for political, military, or economic advantage.
4. **Data Exfiltration:** unauthorized data transfer from a computer or other device to an external location.
5. **JNDI (Java Naming and Directory Interface):** A Java API that provides naming and directory functionality to applications developed in Java, facilitating the lookup and management of distributed resources.
6. **LDAP (Lightweight Directory Access Protocol):** A protocol used to access and maintain distributed directory information services over an Internet Protocol network.
7. **Phishing:** A cyberattack that uses disguised email as a weapon. The goal is to trick the email recipient into believing that the message is something they want or need—a request from their bank, for instance, or a note from someone in their company—and to click a link or download an attachment.
8. **Ransomware:** A type of malicious software designed to block access to a computer system until a sum of money is paid.
9. **Remote Code Execution (RCE):** A security vulnerability that allows an attacker to execute commands remotely on another computing device.
10. **SIP (Session Initiation Protocol):** A protocol used in signaling and managing multimedia communication sessions such as voice and video calls.
11. **SMB (Server Message Block):** A network file-sharing protocol that allows applications on a computer to read and write to files and to request services from server programs in a computer network.
12. **Spear-Phishing:**A more targeted version of phishing that involves hackers infiltrating an organization to steal sensitive information.
13. **TCP Three-Way Handshake:** The three-step process (SYN, SYN-ACK, ACK) used in a TCP/IP network to connect a client and a server.

Chapter 15

Lab time scenarios

INTRODUCTION

This chapter presents 25 real-life network security and troubleshooting problems. Each problem challenges your understanding and practical skills in managing, diagnosing, and securing network environments. For each scenario, a hint is provided to guide you toward finding a solution using network analysis tools, particularly Wireshark. Test Yourself

1. DNS hijacking detection
   Scenario: Users are redirected to malicious sites despite entering the correct URLs.
   Hint: Analyze DNS responses to ensure they match expected IP addresses for known domains.
   Filter ______________________________

2. DDoS attack mitigation
   Scenario: The corporate website is experiencing unusually high traffic, disrupting service.
   Hint: Monitor for excessive SYN packets and unusual IP addresses flooding the server.
   Filter ______________________________

3. MITM attack identification
   Scenario: There is suspicion of data being intercepted between clients and the server.
   Hint: Check ARP tables for discrepancies and monitor SSL/TLS handshakes for anomalies.
   Filter ______________________________

4. Unencrypted HTTP traffic
   Scenario: Sensitive data might be transmitted over unsecured HTTP on port 80.

DOI: 10.1201/9781003539261-15

Hint: Filter for HTTP traffic and inspect for sensitive data patterns like personal identifiers.
Filter ________________________________

5. TCP retransmission issues
   Scenario: Network performance issues are reported, possibly due to packet losses.
   Hint: Look for high rates of TCP retransmissions that might indicate line quality issues or congestion.
   Filter ________________________________

6. Data loss via email
   Scenario: Confidential data might be leaking through outgoing emails.
   Filter ________________________________
   Hint: Monitor SMTP traffic for attachments and keywords associated with sensitive information.

7. Insecure IoT device communications
   Scenario: IoT devices may be transmitting sensitive operational data insecurely.
   Hint: Examine IoT traffic for unencrypted data transmissions and enforce encryption protocols.
   Filter ________________________________

8. Rogue DHCP server detection
   Scenario: Unexpected network behavior and IP conflicts suggest a rogue DHCP server.
   Hint: Capture DHCP traffic to identify unauthorized servers issuing IP addresses.
   Filter ________________________________

9. VoIP eavesdropping
   Scenario: Suspected interception of VoIP calls within the organization
   Hint: Monitor for anomalies in VoIP traffic, such as unexpected RTP source IPs.
   Filter ________________________________

10. Cloud service misconfiguration
    Scenario: Misconfigurations in cloud services are causing data exposure.
    Hint: Track access logs and data transfers to and from cloud platforms to detect misconfigurations.
    Filter ________________________________

11. BYOD compliance check
    Scenario: Personal devices might be accessing restricted network resources.
    Hint: Analyze network traffic from non-registered devices and enforce BYOD policies.
    Filter ______________________________

12. Web application firewall bypass
    Scenario: A web application is receiving traffic that seems to bypass firewall rules.
    Hint: Inspect HTTP and HTTPS traffic to identify potentially malicious requests that circumvent firewall settings.
    Filter ______________________________

13. Unauthorized remote access
    Scenario: Reports of unauthorized users accessing internal systems remotely
    Hint: Filter for remote access protocols (e.g., RDP, SSH) and verify against authorized user lists.
    Filter ______________________________

14. Malware traffic detection
    Scenario: Network endpoints might be communicating with known malicious external IPs.
    Hint: Use threat intelligence feeds to block traffic to and from bad IPs and monitor for command and control traffic.
    Filter ______________________________

15. Network printer security issues
    Scenario: Network printers are receiving jobs from unauthorized users.
    Hint: Monitor printer network traffic and set up access controls based on device authentication.
    Filter ______________________________

16. P2P file sharing on corporate network
    Scenario: Unauthorized peer-to-peer file sharing is consuming significant bandwidth.
    Hint: Identify and block P2P traffic to preserve bandwidth and enforce network usage policies.
    Filter ______________________________

17. Social media data exfiltration
    Scenario: Sensitive information is being inadvertently shared via social media platforms.

Hint: Inspect traffic to popular social media sites for data patterns that match confidential information.
Filter ______________________________

18. SSL certificate misconfiguration
Scenario: Users experience certificate warnings when accessing internal applications.
Hint: Examine the SSL/TLS setup and validate certificate chains and expiration dates.
Filter ______________________________

19. Database injection attacks
Scenario: The database server receives SQL queries that appear as part of an injection attack.
Hint: Filter for SQL commands within application traffic and validate query structures.
Filter ______________________________

20. Wireless network eavesdropping
Scenario: Unauthorized access to wireless communications could be occurring.
Hint: Use encryption detection on Wi-Fi traffic to ensure data is securely transmitted.
Filter ______________________________

21. VPN tunnel hijacking
Scenario: Active VPN sessions are being hijacked by external attackers.
Hint: Monitor for sudden changes in VPN traffic patterns and check for session takeovers.
Filter ______________________________

22. Unauthorized API access
Scenario: External systems are making unauthorized requests to internal APIs.
Hint: Monitor and validate API traffic against access control policies.
Filter ______________________________

23. Legacy protocol vulnerabilities
Scenario: Older network protocols in use may be exposing the network to known vulnerabilities
Hint: Identify and phase out legacy protocols like FTP or Telnet in favor of more secure alternatives.
Filter ______________________________

24. Encrypted traffic monitoring
    Scenario: Monitoring the content of encrypted traffic to prevent data loss is necessary due to regulatory requirements.
    Hint: Implement decryption points and inspect SSL/TLS traffic for compliance.
    Filter ________________________________

25. Cross-site scripting (XSS) detection
    Scenario: Web applications are vulnerable to XSS attacks due to improper user input handling.
    Hint: Filter HTTP requests for patterns typical of XSS and review for proper input sanitization measures.
    Filter 

Here are the detailed Wireshark filters, including examples and explanations for each of the 25 scenarios based on the latest chapter document:

1. **DNS hijacking detection**
   Filter: dns.qry.name && ip.dst != [Trusted DNS Server IP]
   Example filter: dns.qry.name && ip.dst != 8.8.8.8
   Explanation: Filters DNS queries to ensure they only go to trusted DNS servers, helping detect redirection to malicious sites.

2. **DDoS attack mitigation**
   Filter: tcp.flags.syn == 1 && ip.dst == [Server IP]
   Example filter: tcp.flags.syn == 1 && ip.dst == 192.168.1.100
   Explanation: Captures SYN packets targeting a specific server, useful for identifying potential SYN flood attacks aimed at overwhelming the server.

3. **MITM attack identification**
   Filter: arp.isgratuitous == 1
   Example filter: arp.isgratuitous == 1
   Explanation: Detects gratuitous ARP messages which can indicate a MITM attack through ARP spoofing.

4. **Unencrypted HTTP traffic**
   Filter: http.request && tcp.port == 80
   Example filter: http.request && tcp.port == 80
   Explanation: Monitors all HTTP traffic on port 80, useful for detecting unencrypted transmission of sensitive data.

5. **TCP retransmission issues**
   Filter: tcp.analysis.retransmission
   Example filter: tcp.analysis.retransmission
   Explanation: Identifies TCP retransmissions, which can help diagnose network congestion or unstable network conditions.

6. **Data loss via email**
   Filter: smtp && (smtp.file_data contains "sensitive" || smtp.subject contains "confidential")
   Example filter: smtp && (smtp.file_data contains "sensitive" || smtp.subject contains "confidential")
   Explanation: Checks for email messages with potentially sensitive attachments or subject lines, helping prevent data leaks.

7. **Insecure IoT device communications**
   Filter: ip.addr == [IoT Device IP] && (tcp.port != 443 && udp.port != 443)
   Example filter: ip.addr == 192.168.1.150 && (tcp.port != 443 && udp.port != 443)
   Explanation: Monitors traffic from IoT devices that are not using encrypted channels, indicating potential security risks.

8. **Rogue DHCP server detection**
   Filter: dhcp && eth.src != [Authorized DHCP Server MAC]
   Example filter: dhcp && eth.src != 00:1A:2B:3C:4D:5E
   Explanation: Captures DHCP traffic originating from unauthorized sources, indicating a possible rogue DHCP server.

9. **VoIP eavesdropping**
   Filter: rtp && ip.src != [Trusted VoIP Server IP]
   Example filter: rtp && ip.src != 192.168.1.200

Explanation: Identifies RTP streams not originating from trusted VoIP servers, which could suggest eavesdropping or unauthorized access.

10. **Cloud service misconfiguration**
    Filter: tls && ip.dst == [Cloud Service IP] && tls.handshake.type == 1
    Example filter: tls && ip.dst == 192.0.2.1 && tls.handshake.type == 1
    Explanation: Monitors the SSL/TLS handshake to cloud services, which is useful for detecting misconfigured or insecure connections.

11. **BYOD compliance check**
    Filter: dhcp && not eth.src == [Authorized MAC List]
    Example filter: dhcp && not eth.src == {00:1D:2C:3B:4A:5B}
    Explanation: Filters DHCP requests from MAC addresses not on the authorized list, identifying non-compliant BYOD devices.

12. **Web application firewall bypass**
    Filter: http.request.uri contains "bypass"
    Example filter: http.request.uri contains "bypass"
    Explanation: It looks for HTTP requests containing keywords related to bypassing security measures, which could indicate attempts to circumvent a web application firewall.

13. **Unauthorized remote access**
    Filter: tcp.port == 22 || tcp.port == 3389 && ip.src != [Authorized IP Range]
    Example filter: tcp.port == 22 || tcp.port == 3389 && ip.src != 10.0.0.0/24
    Explanation: Monitors for SSH (port 22) and RDP (port 3389) traffic from unauthorized external IPs, indicating potential unauthorized remote access.

14. **Malware traffic detection**
    Filter: ip.dst == [Malicious IP List]
    Example filter: ip.dst == 203.0.113.10
    Explanation: It filters traffic to known malicious IPs, which helps identify active malware communication within the network.

15. **Network printer security issues**
    Filter: ipp || lpr && ip.src == [Unauthorized IP Range]
    Example flter: ipp || lpr && ip.src == 172.16.10.0/24
    Explanation: Monitors print job traffic from unauthorized IPs, helping safeguard against unauthorized printing and data leakage.

16. **P2P file sharing on corporate network**
    Filter: bittorrent
    Example filter: bittorrent
    Explanation: Identifies BitTorrent traffic, which is useful for enforcing policies against peer-to-peer file sharing on the corporate network.

17. **Social media data exfiltration**
    Filter: http.host contains "facebook.com" || http.host contains "twitter.com" && http.request.method == "POST"
    Example filter: http.host contains "facebook.com" || http.host contains "twitter.com" && http.request.method == "POST"
    Explanation: It tracks POST requests to social media sites, which could be used to exfiltrate data under the guise of normal social media usage.

18. **SSL certificate misconfiguration**
    Filter: tls.handshake.type == 11 && tls.alert_message.level == 2
    Example filter: tls.handshake.type == 11 && tls.alert_message.level == 2
    Explanation: Captures TLS handshake failures and alerts, indicating potential SSL certificate issues that could affect application access and security.

19. **Database injection attacks**
    Filter: mysql.query contains "select" && tcp.payload contains "drop"
    Example filter: mysql.query contains "select" && tcp.payload contains "drop"
    Explanation: It looks for SQL injection patterns, such as unauthorized "drop" commands in SQL queries, which could indicate an attack.

20. **Wireless network eavesdropping**
    Filter: wlan.fc.type_subtype == 0x20
    Example filter: wlan.fc.type_subtype == 0x20
    Explanation: Monitors for Wi-Fi management frames could be used in eavesdropping or man-in-the-middle attacks on wireless networks.

21. **VPN tunnel hijacking**
    Filter: ipsec && ip.addr != [VPN Server IP]
    Example filter: ipsec && ip.addr != 192.168.1.1
    Explanation: Detects IPSec traffic not associated with the official VPN server, potentially indicating hijacked VPN sessions.

22. **Unauthorized API access**
    Filter: http.request.full_uri contains "/api/" && ip.src != [Authorized API Consumers]

Example filter: http.request.full_uri contains "/api/" && ip.src != 10.1.2.0/24
Explanation: Filters API requests from unauthorized sources, helping prevent unauthorized access and potential data breaches.

23. **Legacy protocol vulnerabilities**
Filter: tcp.port == 21 || tcp.port == 23
Example filter: tcp.port == 21 || tcp.port == 23
Explanation: Captures traffic on legacy FTP (port 21) and Telnet (port 23) protocols, which are less secure and could expose the network to attacks.

24. **Encrypted traffic monitoring**
Filter: tls && ip.addr == [Sensitive Data Servers]
Example filter: tls && ip.addr == 192.168.50.5
Explanation: Monitors encrypted traffic to and from sensitive data servers, ensuring that encryption is implemented correctly and no unauthorized data is being transmitted.

25. **Cross-Site Scripting (XSS) detection**
Filter:http.request.full_uri contains "<script>"
Example filter: http.request.full_uri contains "<script>"
Explanation: Looks for patterns typical of XSS attacks within HTTP requests, helping to identify and mitigate these security threats.

Appendix

In addition to the valuable insights offered by the Wireshark book, the application includes several key menus—Analyze, Statistics, Wireless, and Tools—that extend beyond the scope of printed resources. These menus are essential for practical, hands-on network analysis, offering tools and features crucial for real-time data examination and troubleshooting. The important menu options discussed under each menu, discussed in additional sections beyond the book, represent the application's adaptive and detailed approach to network analysis, which is crucial for professionals navigating complex network environments.

ANALYZE MENU

These options under the "Analyze" menu enhance Wireshark's packet analysis capabilities, enabling more precise control over how you view, filter, and interpret network data.

On the next page, you will find an explanation of the important options under the "Analyze" menu in Wireshark (Figure A.1).

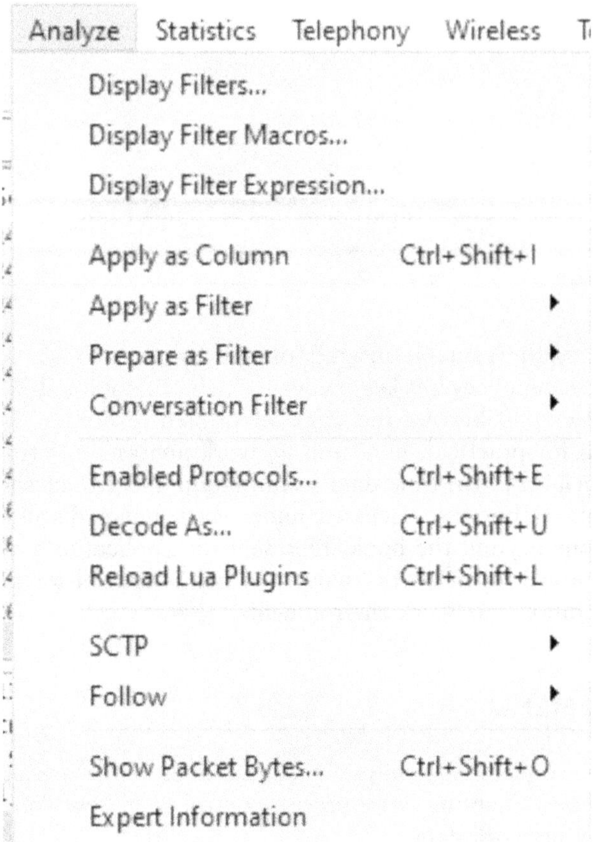

Figure A.1 A network analysis tool menu, showing options like "Display Filters", "Apply as a Column", "SCTP", "Follow", and various filter and protocol-related actions.

1. Display Filters
   Explanation: This option opens the Display Filters dialog box, where you can manage and create new display filters. Display filters allow you to specify criteria for displaying only certain packets that meet these criteria, making it easier to focus on relevant data in your packet capture.

   Example: You could use this to create a filter that only shows packets from a specific IP address or only TCP packets.

2. Apply as Column
   Explanation: This allows you to add a new column to the packet list pane based on the field you currently select in the packet details pane.

It helps customize the display to show specific protocol fields directly in the main packet list.

Example: If you frequently need to see the destination port in your captures, you can right-click that field in a packet detail and select "Apply as Column" to make this a permanent column in your overview.

3. Prepare as Filter
   Explanation: Provides options to create and add complex filters based on the selected packet or field. This is useful for quickly building filter expressions without manually entering the syntax.

   Example: By selecting a specific field like an IP address, you can use "Prepare as Filter" to automatically create a filter expression that you can then apply or edit.

4. Conversation Filter
   Explanation: This option allows you to create a display filter that only includes packets from a particular conversation. It helps isolate traffic between two specific endpoints.

   Example: If you're analyzing traffic between a client and server, this feature helps you focus only on packets exchanged between these two.

5. Enabled Protocols
   Explanation: Opens a dialog box where you can turn on or off protocols that Wireshark will recognize and parse. This helps declutter the protocol analysis or focus on specific protocols.

   Example: If you work primarily with IPv4 and TCP, you can turn off other protocols to simplify the view and processing.

6. Decode As
   Explanation: It allows you to change how packet data is interpreted and displayed by choosing a specific protocol that Wireshark should use to decode the selected traffic. This is crucial when protocols use non-standard ports or when you need to decode encapsulated protocol data.

   Example: You can use "Decode As" to interpret traffic on an unusual port as HTTP, which might be necessary if a service runs on a non-standard port.

7. Reload Lua Plugins
   Explanation: Reloads all Lua-based plugins without needing to restart Wireshark. This is especially useful for developers creating custom dissector scripts in Lua.

Example: If you're developing a Lua script for custom protocol analysis, you can make changes to the script and use this option to reload it instantly to test modifications.

8. Follow
   Explanation: Provides tools to visually trace and display the contents of a particular data stream within the captured traffic, such as TCP, UDP, or SSL streams.

   Example: To examine the contents of an HTTP session or follow a TCP connection from start to finish, you can use "Follow TCP Stream".

9. Show Packet Bytes
   Explanation: Opens a new window that displays the raw data bytes of the selected packet. Useful for in-depth analysis or when investigating malformed packets.

   Example: When checking for packet corruption or analyzing a payload that might contain hidden data, viewing the packet bytes can be invaluable.

10. Expert Information
    Explanation: This feature compiles and presents detailed notes, warnings, and errors identified by Wireshark during the capture analysis. It helps identify potential issues or anomalies in traffic.

    Example: To quickly identify network problems like repeated retransmissions or malformed packets, checking the Expert Information can give you insights based on accumulated analysis.

STATISTICS MENU

Each option in Wireshark's Statistics menu provides different lenses for viewing network data, aiding in everything from routine monitoring to deep dive troubleshooting and forensic analysis (Figure A.2).

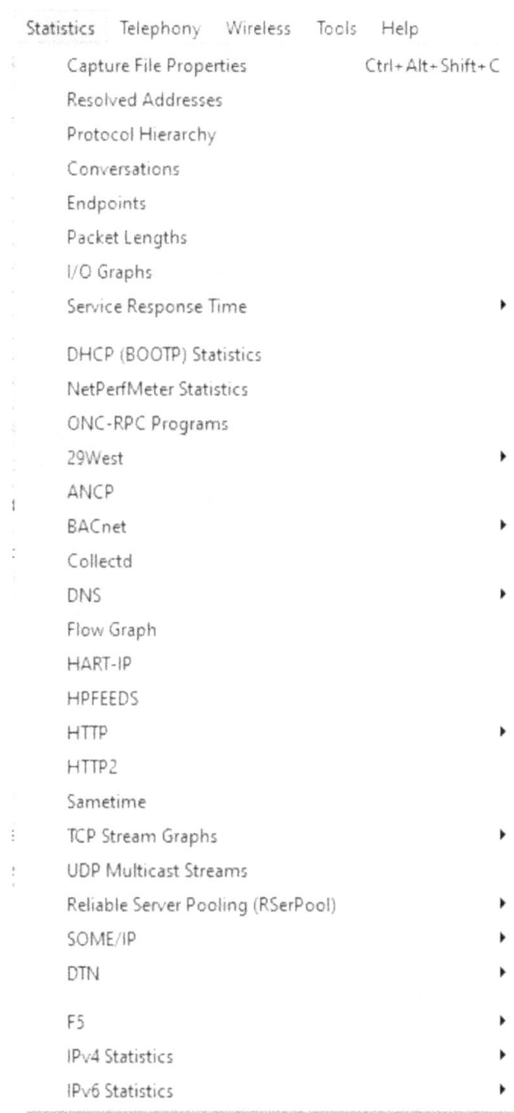

Figure A.2 A statistics menu in a network analysis tool, listing options such as "Capture File Properties", "Protocol Hierarchy", "Conversations", and various protocol-specific statistics.

Here are statistics options in Wireshark, each explained first, followed by an example:

1. Capture File Properties
   Explanation: This option provides basic information about the capture file, including metrics like the number of packets, capture duration, and file size. It gives a quick overview of the scope and scale of the data captured.

   Example: When determining if a capture file is comprehensive enough for analysis after a network incident, checking the capture file properties will show if the capture spanned the entire incident period.

2. Protocol Hierarchy
   Explanation: This view breaks down the communication captured by protocol, allowing you to see which protocols dominate your network traffic. This is crucial for identifying unexpected traffic or prioritizing analysis efforts.

   Example: Analyzing a capture from a corporate network might reveal an unusually high amount of P2P traffic, prompting further investigation into unauthorized file sharing.

3. Conversations
   Explanation: This feature lists all communication sessions grouped by protocol (like TCP, UDP, IPv4), showing data exchanged and endpoints involved. It helps identify the main data flows and pinpoint potential sources of issues.

   Example: In a troubleshooting scenario, identifying the top TCP conversations by bandwidth can help quickly locate a server overloading the network.

4. Endpoints
   Explanation: Endpoint statistics summarize the source and destination nodes in the traffic, showing data volumes and packet counts per endpoint. This helps identify the most active nodes in the network.

   Example: During an analysis of network anomalies, you might find an internal IP address sending or receiving significantly more data than typical, indicating a compromised or malfunctioning device.

5. IO Graphs
   Explanation: IO Graphs visualize data transmission over time, allowing you to measure throughput and identify peaks or lulls in traffic. This visual tool is key for analyzing traffic patterns and performance issues.

Example: After a network upgrade, using an IO Graph to compare throughput before and after the change can visually confirm the effectiveness of the upgrade.

6. Flow Graph
   Explanation: The Flow Graph visually represents the interaction between nodes, showing the packet flow and timing in a sequence diagram format. It's beneficial for understanding complex interactions in protocols.

   Example: In VoIP troubleshooting, a Flow Graph can show the sequence of SIP messages and RTP streams, helping identify delays or lost messages affecting call quality.

7. Packet Lengths
   Explanation: This statistic displays a histogram of packet sizes, which helps understand the distribution of traffic by packet size, which can impact network performance and infrastructure decisions.

   Example: If you optimize network performance, understanding packet size distribution can help configure network equipment buffers more efficiently.

8. Throughput
   Explanation: The Throughput graph measures data rates over time, providing insights into network load and capacity utilization. This is crucial for network performance monitoring and planning.

   Example: Monitoring network throughput during peak business hours can help plan bandwidth upgrades to meet growing demand.

9. TCP Stream Graphs
   Explanation: These graphs offer a detailed visual analysis of TCP streams, such as sequence numbers, window sizes, and round-trip times, which are crucial for diagnosing TCP performance issues.

   Example: Diagnosing a slow file transfer might involve using the Time-Sequence graph to spot retransmissions indicating packet loss on the network.

10. Expert Info
    Explanation: Expert Info compiles notices, warnings, and errors detected by Wireshark's analysis engine, offering quick insights into potential problems in traffic. This tool is invaluable for initial diagnostics.

Example: After deploying a new application, Expert Info might highlight numerous TCP reset errors, prompting a review of firewall or server configurations that could be improperly set up.

WIRELESS MENU

These options are designed to assist with detailed analysis and troubleshooting of Bluetooth devices and protocols, adding significant value for developers, network analysts, and security professionals dealing with Bluetooth technology in their networks or products (Figure A.3).

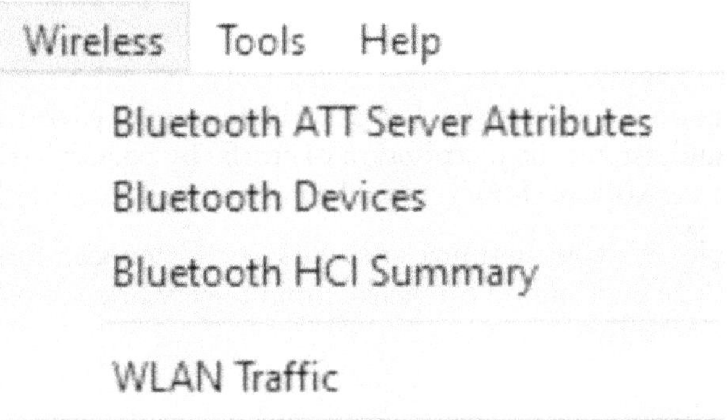

Figure A.3 A wireless analysis menu, displaying options like "Bluetooth ATT Server Attributes", "Bluetooth Devices", "Bluetooth HCI Summary", and "WLAN Traffic".

Here's an explanation of the visible options under the "Wireless" menu in Wireshark:

1. Bluetooth ATT Server Attributes
   Explanation: This tool lets you view and analyze Bluetooth Attribute Protocol (ATT) server attributes. ATT is used in Bluetooth Low Energy (BLE) for data exchange between devices, and this option helps analyze the structure and characteristics of the Bluetooth services and their attributes.

   Example: If you are debugging a BLE device that's not communicating correctly, using this option can help you inspect the ATT exchanges to ensure the correct attributes are being used and identify any anomalies.

2. Bluetooth Devices
   Explanation: Provides a list and details of all Bluetooth devices detected in the packet capture. This includes information like device

addresses, names, and other specifics that can help in analyzing Bluetooth traffic and device interactions.

Example: In a scenario where multiple Bluetooth devices are interfering with each other, this option can help identify all active devices and their properties to manage the wireless environment better.

3. Bluetooth HCI Summary
Explanation: Offers a summary of the Bluetooth Host Controller Interface (HCI) data, which is used for sending commands, receiving events, and data exchange between a host and a Bluetooth module. This summary helps in debugging Bluetooth connectivity and protocol issues.

   Example: When developing a new Bluetooth-enabled application, checking the HCI Summary can help ensure that the commands sent to the Bluetooth module are correctly formatted and executed.

TOOLS MENU

Each of these tools in Wireshark's "Tools" menu enhances the software's functionality, catering to advanced analysis needs, troubleshooting, and custom configuration, making Wireshark a versatile tool for network administrators, security experts, and protocol developers (Figure A.4).

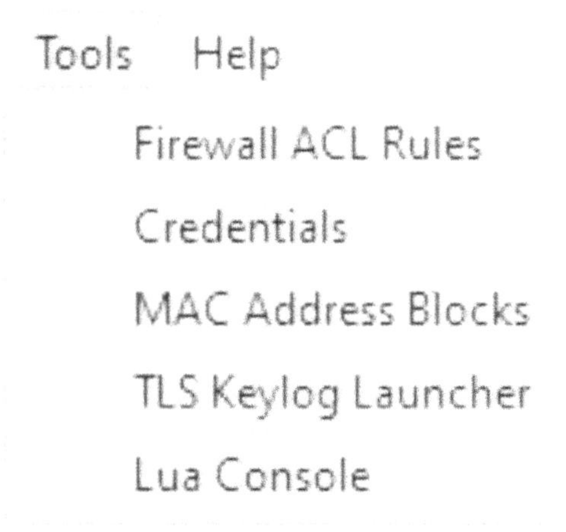

Figure A.4 A tools menu, showing options like "Firewall ACL Rules", "Credentials", "MAC Address Blocks", "TLS Keylog Launcher", and "Lua Console".

Here's an explanation of the key options available under the "Tools" menu in Wireshark, each followed by a practical example:

1. Firewall ACL Rules
Explanation: This tool helps generate firewall access control list (ACL) rules based on the captured packets. It supports several firewall platforms and can be customized according to the specific traffic observed in the capture.

   Example: After identifying malicious traffic originating from specific IP addresses during a capture session, you can use this tool to generate rules for a Cisco ASA firewall to block future traffic from those IPs.

2. Resolve Names
Explanation: This option toggles the resolution of names for addresses, protocols, and ports. It converts numeric address data into human-readable names, making the packet traces more manageable to read and understand.

   Example: When analyzing traffic for a network audit, enabling name resolution can help quickly identify services and endpoints by displaying domain names instead of IP addresses.

3. Compare Two Capture Files
Explanation: This tool allows you to compare two packet captures to identify differences in traffic patterns, packet sequences, or other metrics. It is helpful for before and after analyses of network configurations or security measures.

   Example: Before and after applying network optimization strategies, you can use this tool to compare captures and assess the effectiveness of those strategies in reducing traffic congestion or improving data flows.

4. Reload as File Format/Capture
Explanation: This feature lets you reload the current capture file as if it were in a different format or as if it were being captured live. This is particularly useful when dealing with corrupt or unusual file formats that Wireshark can still process.

   Example: If a capture file is not displaying correctly due to a suspected format issue, using this tool to reload it as a different file format can help troubleshoot and recover the data.

5. Export Packet Dissections
Explanation: This option allows you to export the detailed dissection of packets into various formats such as CSV, XML, or plain text. This

is beneficial for detailed analysis outside of Wireshark or for documentation purposes.

Example: For compliance reporting, you can export the dissections of specific packets that demonstrate adherence to data handling protocols within your network.

6. Manage Color Rules
   Explanation: Colors in Wireshark can differentiate packet types or highlight specific traffic, based on rules you can customize in this menu. This visual differentiation aids in quicker analysis and identification of patterns or issues.

   Example: To highlight all HTTP 400 error responses in red, you can manage and customize color rules, making these packets instantly recognizable during analysis.

7. **Lua**
   Explanation: Manage Lua plugins or scripts that extend Wireshark's capabilities. Lua can be used for custom dissectors or automating specific tasks within Wireshark.

   Example: If you frequently need to analyze a proprietary protocol, you could use Lua to write a custom dissector that automatically interprets and presents this protocol in an easily understandable format.

8. Internals
   Explanation: This provides insights into Wireshark's operation, including memory usage, plugin details, and supported protocols. It helps debug Wireshark itself or optimize its performance.

   Example: When Wireshark begins to perform slowly or consume excessive resources, checking the "Internals" for memory usage can help diagnose and resolve the issue.

CONCLUSION

In concluding this chapter on the additional capabilities of Wireshark beyond the core content covered in typical manuals and books, it's clear that the application is a powerful tool for capturing and analyzing network data and an extensive platform equipped with specialized functionalities for diverse network environments. The **Analyze**, **Statistics**, **Wireless**, and **Tools** menus enrich the user experience by providing detailed mechanisms for deep dive analyses, real-time troubleshooting, and customization to meet specific user needs.

The **Analyze** menu, for example, offers dynamic tools for packet inspection and stream following, enhancing the user's ability to decode and understand complex network exchanges. Meanwhile, the **Statistics** menu aggregates comprehensive network data, presenting it in an accessible format that aids in pinpointing issues and identifying traffic trends crucial for network management and security assessments. For scenarios involving wireless technologies, the **Wireless** menu offers specialized tools essential for analyzing protocols such as Bluetooth, making it indispensable for professionals working with IoT devices and modern wireless systems.

Furthermore, the **Tools** menu extends Wireshark's functionality beyond traditional packet analysis, supporting various activities from network forensic analysis to developing custom solutions via Lua scripting. These features underscore Wireshark's adaptability and depth, which are critical for tackling the challenges of modern network environments. Each of these tools complements the foundational knowledge found in Wireshark literature and expands its practical applications, ensuring that users are equipped to handle increasingly complex and diverse network scenarios.

MULTIPLE CHOICE QUESTIONS (MCQs)

1. What can the "Display Filters" option in Wireshark be used to do?
   A. Save filtered packets to a new file
   B. Specify criteria for displaying only certain packets
   C. Automatically decode selected protocols
   D. Increase the speed of packet capture

Answer: B)

2. How does the "Apply as Column" option benefit Wireshark users?
   A) It allows users to decode packets faster.
   B) It provides a method to add a new column to the packet list pane based on a selected field.
   C) It helps in exporting data to CSV format.
   D) It changes the color scheme of the interface.

Answer: B)

3. What is the purpose of the "Prepare as Filter" option in Wireshark?
   A) To reset all filters to default settings.
   B) To help quickly build filter expressions based on selected packet or field.
   C) To delete all existing filters.
   D) To prepare a report of all applied filters.

Answer: B)

4. What does the "Conversation Filter" option do in Wireshark?
   A) Filters out all conversations except for the selected one.
   B) Creates a display filter that includes only packets from a particular conversation.
   C) Highlights conversations in the user interface.
   D) Deletes conversations from the capture.

Answer: B)

5. Which option allows you to toggle protocols on or off in Wireshark?
   A) Protocol Hierarchy
   B) Enabled Protocols
   C) Protocol Preferences
   D) Protocol Analyzer

Answer: B)

6. What is the functionality of the "Decode As" option?
   A) To apply color coding to packet lists.
   B) To reload Lua plugins.
   C) To change how packet data is interpreted by selecting a specific protocol.
   D) To save packet data in a different format.

Answer: C)

7. Why would someone use "Reload Lua Plugins" option in Wireshark?
   A) To update the Wireshark version.
   B) Reload all Lua-based plugins without restarting the application.
   C) To check for errors in the Lua scripts.
   D) To uninstall Lua plugins.

Answer: B)

8. What does the "Follow" option provide in Wireshark?
   A) Navigation to different sections of the interface.
   B) Tools to trace and display the contents of a particular data stream.
   C) A method to follow updates in Wireshark development.
   D) Real-time alerts on network issues.

Answer: B)

9. What information does the "Show Packet Bytes" option provide in Wireshark?
   A) A graph of throughput over time.
   B) The raw data bytes of the selected packet for in-depth analysis.
   C) Summarized data about packet sizes.
   D) The encryption status of packets.

Answer: B)

10. What is the purpose of the "Expert Information" option in Wireshark?
    A) To offer advice on career development in IT.
    B) To provide a summary of packets.
    C) To display detailed notes, warnings, and errors identified during capture analysis.
    D) To connect users to a network of Wireshark experts.

Answer: C)

Index

D

E

F

G

H

I

U

V

W

X

Z

For Product Safety Concerns and Information please contact our EU
representative GPSR@taylorandfrancis.com
Taylor & Francis Verlag GmbH, Kaufingerstraße 24, 80331 München, Germany

www.ingramcontent.com/pod-product-compliance
Lightning Source LLC
Chambersburg PA
CBHW060333220326
41598CB00023B/2699

* 9 7 8 1 0 3 2 8 8 7 0 9 8 *